The Intuitive Edge

THE INTUITIVE EDGE

Understanding Intuition and
Applying it in Everyday Life

Philip Goldberg

AN AUTHORS GUILD BACKINPRINT.COM EDITION

The Intuitive Edge
Understanding Intuition and Applying it in Everyday Life

AN AUTHORS GUILD BACKINPRINT.COM EDITION
Published by iUniverse, Inc.

For information address:
iUniverse, Inc.
2021 Pine Lake Road, Suite 100
Lincoln, NE 68512
www.iuniverse.com

Originally published by Tarcher/ Perigree for Putnam

Illustration by Thom Dower

ISBN-13: 978-0-595-41665-3
ISBN-10: 0-595-41665-9

Printed in the United States of America

Contents

Acknowledgments

I am deeply grateful to all those who generously lent me their time in the preparation of this book. The following people shared their professional expertise, reviewed portions of the manuscript, sent me clippings and articles, related personal anecdotes, listened to and commented on my ideas as they developed, and helped me think. In many cases, their emotional support, encouragement, and enthusiasm was much-needed tonic. For simplicity's sake, I list them all, friends and virtual strangers alike, alphabetically, without mentioning their titles or affiliations. Quite possibly, many of the people who influenced my thinking and shared their experiences and insights with me are not remembered here, since their contributions were made informally, before I knew I would write this book. I regret those oversights and hope that they will be forgiven.

Thank you to: Betsy and Elliot Abravanel, Weston Agor, Charles Alexander, Terese Amabile, Alarick Aranander, Art and Elaine Aron, Bernard Baars, Ted Bartek, Steve R. Baumgardner, Marshall Berkowitz, Erick Bienstock, Diane Blumenson, Libby Bradshaw, Elizabeth Brenner, Jerome Bruner, Merry Bullock, Blythe Clinchy, Allan Collins, Peter Conrad, Bob Cushing, Ana Daniel, Eugene d'Aquili, Richard Davidson, Jack DeWitt, Ed DiEsso, Michael Dilbeck, Susan Dowe, Tom Drucker, Tom Duffy, David Dunlap, Peter Erskine, Earl Ettienne, Juliet Faithfull, Marilyn Ferguson, Linda Flower, Bob Forman, Diane Frank, Lisbeth Fried, Elliot Friedland, Jonathan Friedlander, Bob Fritz, Eugene Gendlin, Richard Germann, James A. Giannini, Rashi Glazer, Bob Goldberg, Bernard Goldhirsh, Bennett Goodspeed, Ruth Green, Bob Greenfield, Bob Hanson, Bo and Nancy Hathaway, John Hayes, John R. Hayes, Barbara Holland, Keith Holyoak, Jerry Jarvis, Alfred Jenkins, Paul E. Johnson, Paul Jones, Daniel Kaufman, Bill Kautz, Ralph Keyes, Julia Klein, Ellisa Koff, Barbara Landau, Lanny Lester, Jerre Levy, Marilyn Machlowitz, Tom Maeder, Rosanne Malinowski, Ellen Michaud, John Mihalasky, Jonathan Miller, Henry Mintzberg, Bevan Morris, Rick and Amy Moss, George Naddaff, Don Noble, Meredith B. Olson, Dean Portinga, Mitchell Posner, Robin Raphaelian, Dennis Raimondi, Margaret Robinson, Joan Rothberg, Robin and Dennis Rowe, Peter Russell, Art Sabatini, Ed Scher, Deanna Scott, Mike Schwartz, Elliot Seif, Peter Senge, Jonathan Shear, Dean Simonton, Dean Sluyter, Lyn Sonberg, Robert Sternberg, Bobbi Stevens, E. C. G. Sudarshan, Peggy Van Pelt, Gary Venter, Keith Wallace, Larry and Linea Wardwell, Robin Warshaw, Malcolm Westcott, Ken Wilber, Gretchen Woelfle, Roy Wyand, Bob Wynne, Arthur Young, Ron Zigler, and Connie Zweig.

In addition, I am grateful to my publisher, Jeremy Tarcher, who was intuitive enough to see the promise in what was essentially a half-formed idea. And I am deeply indebted to Janice Gallagher, who did an exceptional job of old-fashioned participatory editing; she often knew better than I what I was trying to say.

Finally, eternal appreciation to my beloved Jane, whose intuition is always—well, *almost* always—right, and who endures with dignity and strength the impossible role of Writer's Wife.

To my mother, who taught me to question.

Foreword

Intuition is an essential topic whose time has come. And *The Intuitive Edge* is must reading for anyone who wants to live on that most delightful edge of more creativity, joy, wisdom, and inner peace.

The creative function of intuition, as Philip Goldberg defines it in this informative and useful book, stretches our capacities by introducing options, alternatives, and possibilities. Accurate intuition also enables us to gain vital insight into ourselves and our environments, to evaluate choices, and to predict the future. It is, as Goldberg says, "a subtle guide to daily living." In short, intuition brings with it happiness, wonder, and harmony. *The Intuitive Edge* can help us discover the greatest therapist of all—the one that resides within.

Having worked with many thousands of clients, I no longer see my role as that of "shrink," but that of "stretch." Rather than endlessly trying to shrink problems with tranquilizers or a psychotherapeutic panacea, I am interested in stretching a person's capacities—physically, emotionally, socially, and spiritually. Through self-expansion and meaningful challenges, problems can be turned into opportunities for growth.

The word psychiatry comes from *psyche*, which refers to the spirit of a person, and *iatros*, which means to heal or make whole. Hence, psychiatry involves making the spirit whole. An essential tool in achieving that goal is to develop each individual's "intuitive edge." Trusting oneself—the ability to hear and utilize one's inner intuitive voice—is a key to self-improvement and a richer life, enabling one to convert problems into challenges and opportunities.

I sometimes humorously tell clients that the mind is the source of all mental illness. In a sense, we need to get "out of our minds" to overcome our preoccupation with problems and limitations. Trusting our intuition can cure us of "psychosclerosis," a hardening of the mind and spirit that stems from overdependence on rationality and analysis. With good intuition we can transcend our ordinary state of mind and become more deeply and completely ourselves. For this reason, *The Intuitive Edge* serves as a guide to becoming more spontaneous, independent, unconventional, and free.

Philip Goldberg provides acute insight into the nature of intuition, a valuable guide to the varieties of intuitive experience, and practical exercises to create favorable conditions for intuition to occur. An agitated, tense mind is too "noisy" for intuition to operate effectively. Techniques of meditation, yoga, breathing, muscle relaxation, and guided visualization are described to help create a more receptive and fertile mind. The book also provides other useful tips for improving your intuitive powers: for example, how to suspend judgment and listen to the inner voice, how to be flexible and playful in your thinking, how to brainstorm with free-style writing. I have found these and other techniques essential in my roles of psychiatrist, author, husband, and father.

The Intuitive Edge is the very best book on the subject I've ever read. It is must reading for anyone interested in being more innovative and enterprising—the scientist, artist, student, administrator, or entrepreneur. More, it is for any reader seeking improvement in his or her personal or professional life. Intuition plays a central role, for example, in choosing the right mate. Goldberg has integrated theory and practice in a well-written, clear, and imaginative way. I recommend this book highly to anyone interested in personal growth.

Harold H. Bloomfield, M.D.
Author of *Making Peace with Your Parents*

Preface

My interest in intuition and in the broader question of "How do we know what we know?" began in the 1960s, when I was a student questioning everything in sight. I had informally accumulated a great deal of information from a wide variety of sources when, in 1977, the idea to write a book on the subject came to me unbidden while I was riding a bicycle and trying to decide which of two apartments to move into that fall. Thus this book is an example of its own subject matter. The justification for following through on the intuitive idea was my conviction that the subject was not only interesting but of vital practical importance: what we know determines how we think, decide, and act. It does not seem unreasonable to assert that the quality of life is directly proportional to how well we go about knowing.

In writing this book I was always conscious of its two threads, the theoretical and the practical, and very much aware that many readers are interested primarily in one or the other. The two themes are actually closely intertwined, both in this book and in reality. The more we know about intuition, the better equipped we are to use our own; the better our intuition, the more we are in a position to understand it. Those readers who want specifically to improve their own intuition will find that Chapters 8, 9, and 10 have a how-to orientation built on the more theoretical information in earlier chapters. The descriptive and theoretical material is also useful if applied to oneself.

A stylistic explanation is in order. Like all contemporary writers, I had to decide what to do about the pronouns *him*, *his*, and *he*, which, when used to refer to both men and women, are considered offensive by many. With apologies, and assurances that no sexism is implied, I opted for standard usage. In a work of this length, the alternatives become so awkward as to detract from the reader's comprehension and enjoyment.

In his 1968 book, *Toward a Contemporary Psychology of Intuition*, Malcolm Westcott ended his introduction by writing, "The last word on intuition is as far in the future as the first word on intuition is in the past." Fifteen years later, I must echo the same sentiment. We are dealing with a complex and elusive subject, one that many great minds have wrestled to a draw and on which there is much disagreement. Intuition has been a peripheral subject in science, a difficult one to study even when interest is high. Hence there is not much by way of a research tradition or accepted body of knowledge. For this book I drew on philosophers both Eastern and Western, tangentially related science and scholarship, writers and artists, my own experience, and the reports of people in all walks of life. Many of the ideas found here, therefore, must be regarded as conjectural, speculative, and inferential. I hope they will stimulate others to expand and develop our knowledge of intuition, and that the book will help others obtain more time and resources for research than I was able to devote.

Truth is within ourselves, it takes no rise
From outward things, whate'er you may believe
. . . and to *know*
Rather consists in opening out a way
Whence the imprisoned splendour may escape,
Than in effecting entry for a light
Supposed to be without.

—Robert Browning

The soul of every man does possess the power of learning the truth, and the organ to see it with. . . . Just as one might have to turn the whole body round in order that the eyes should see the light instead of darkness, so the entire soul must be turned away from this changing world until its eye can bear to contemplate reality.

—Plato

1

The Emergence of Intuition

The really valuable thing is intuition.

—Albert Einstein

Until recently intuition has been treated like an employee who, forced to retire, keeps going to work because he is indispensable. Attitudes about him vary: some people don't know he exists, some downgrade his contributions as trivial, some revere him privately while trying to keep his presence a secret. A growing minority are exuberant supporters who feel that credit is long overdue and that such a valuable asset can function even better when recognized and encouraged. This book is in the latter category, part of the corrective effort to bring intuition out into the open, to demystify it, to see what it is, how it works, and what can be done to cultivate its full potential.

In recent years, the subject has emerged from obscurity. Intuition is increasingly recognized as a natural mental faculty, a key element in discovery, problem solving, and decision making, a generator of creative ideas, a forecaster, a revealer of truth. An important ingredient in what we call genius, it is also a subtle guide to daily living. Those people who always seem to be in the right place at the right time, and for whom good things happen with uncanny frequency, are not just lucky; they have an intuitive sense of what to choose and how to act. We are also coming to realize that intuition is not just a chance phenomenon or a mysterious gift, like jumping ability or perfect pitch. While individual capacities vary, we are all intuitive, and we can all be *more* intuitive, just as we can all learn to jump higher and sing on key.

The emergence of intuition is part of a more global shift in values that has been chronicled by numerous sharp-eyed observers. The passionate pursuit of both individual growth and a better world, begun in earnest in the 1960s, has led to a reevaluation of conventional beliefs, among them the way we use our minds and the way we approach knowledge. Our decisions and actions spring from what we know. Therefore, if collective problems remain intractable and the gap between individual desires and fulfillment remains vast, it is only natural that we start to wonder if there isn't a better way to go about knowing.

Contributing to the new attitude is a resurgence of respect for the world within. The behaviorist school of psychology, which dominated the field during most of this century, had declared irrelevant the deeper realms of mind and spirit. To believers in orthodox religions and Freudian psychotherapy, those areas seethed with dark urges and repressed instincts that, depending on the point of view, should either be kept under cover, liberated, or therapeutically neutralized. These assumptions are giving way to a more positive, often sublime vision. The growth of cognitive research, theoretical advances in humanistic and transpersonal psychologies, provocative brain studies, the remarkable acceptance of Eastern philosophies and disciplines—such developments have led large numbers of people to believe that there is untapped power and wisdom within us. They sense there is a part of ourselves that—although obscured by bad habits and ignorance—understands who we are and what we need and is programmed to move us toward the realization of our highest potential. There is a growing conviction that perhaps we ought to trust the hunches, vague feelings, premonitions, and inarticulate signals we usually ignore.

These trends are characteristic of a basic contemporary pattern: the desire to eliminate obstacles that keep us from being what we really are. Where intuition is concerned, the obstacles are rooted in long-standing epistemological assumptions, which are perpetuated in the institutions that teach us how to use our minds. A brief look at those premises will help us understand why we have not been encouraged to use and develop our intuitive capacities.

THE LEGACY OF SCIENTISM

For over three centuries the prevailing model for gaining knowledge in the Western world has been what we loosely call science, that robust and precocious offspring of such giants as Galileo, Descartes, and Newton. Let's use the word *scientism* to refer to the ideology, as opposed to the practice, of science, since the two are rather different. According to scientism, the right way to approach knowledge is with a rigorous interchange of reason and systematically acquired experience.

This philosophy developed as a hybrid of rationalism and empiricism. Empiricism holds, essentially, that the experience of the senses is the only reliable basis for knowing; rationalism contends that reasoning is the prime avenue to truth. In science, empirical information and reason are supposed to work in tandem, each acting as a check on the other's shortcomings. Since experience can be deceptive, information is scrutinized with rigorous logic; since reason is not entirely flawless, tentative conclusions—hypotheses—are put to the empirical test with controlled experiments subject to repeated verification. For this game plan to work, the data should be quantifiable and the players should be objective, thus keeping biases, emotions, and opinions from contaminating the findings.

Ancients such as Plato and modern philosophers such as Spinoza, Nietzsche, and, at the turn of the century, Henri Bergson pointed beyond reason and sense data to higher, intuitive forms of knowing. So, too, have mystics, romantics, poets, and visionaries in all cultures. There have been "intuitionist" schools in mathematics and ethics, and psychologists such as Gordon Allport, Abraham Maslow, Carl Jung, and Jerome Bruner have all acknowledged the importance of intuition. For the most part, however, intuition has been only a peripheral concern in the West, where the revered mode of knowing has been rational empiricism, thanks largely to the astonishing success of science.

Nothing said on behalf of intuition in this book should be taken as a deprecation of either science or rational thought. In wresting authority from faltering religious institutions, they freed us from the tyranny of dogma and arbitrary ideas. Insistence on evidence and rigorous verification, the heart and soul of scientism, enables us—collectively and over time—to sort out the true from the false. In a secular, pluralistic society, such standards are imperative. And science has given us a way to precisely analyze and shape the material world, providing us with unprecedented affluence, comfort, and health.

Like most rebellions, however, the scientific revolution created some new problems. Flushed with success, the juggernaut of science gobbled up terrain formerly held by philosophy, metaphysics, theology, and cultural tradition. We sought to apply the methods that worked so well in the material realm to answer questions about the psyche, the spirit, and society. Through experimentation and the application of reason—which was elevated to the pinnacle of the mind—it was assumed we would come to know the secrets of the universe and learn how to live. To accomplish this, we set out to perfect the objective tools of knowing; we invented devices and procedures that extended the range of our senses and made more rigorous our logic and our calculations. Over time, our organizations and educational institutions made scientism the sine qua non of knowing, the model for how to think.

This ideological bias is reflected in our vocabulary; words that suggest truthfulness stem from the rational-empirical tradition. We use the word *logical*, even when the rules of logic have not been applied, to indicate that a statement seems correct. So highly regarded is reason that we use the word *reasonable* to refer to anything we consider appropriate—for example, "Twenty dollars is a reasonable price to pay for a theater ticket." We also have the noun form of reason, which is what you are asked to provide in order to justify a proposition. People demand *reasons*; they seldom say, "Give me one good feeling why you think John is wrong" or "What are your intuitions for claiming that jogging will cure insomnia?"

The word *rational*—which, strictly speaking, suggests the use of reason and logic—has come to be synonymous with sanity, while *irrational* connotes madness. *Sensible* and *making sense*, along with their antonym *nonsense*, link soundness and truth with the sense organs, as if adequate meaning came through those channels alone—the classic conviction of empiricism. *Objective* has come to imply fairness, honesty, and precision, suggesting that the only way to gain untainted knowledge is to remain detached and treat whatever you study as if it were a material object. As for the word *scientific*, that is the ultimate pedigree for any claim whatsoever.

Fortunately, the language also contains some reservations about the rational-empirical ideal. Thanks to Freud, we have the word *rationalize*, a pejorative term referring to the way we justify bad guesses, mistakes, and neurotic behavior with faulty reasoning. We also use the term *sense* in an effort to legitimize knowledge that can't be attributed to the customary five senses, as when we say "I sense danger in this room" or "I have a sense of what that poem is about." But, despite these few colloquial exceptions, we generally act as if sense perceptions and rational thought are the only ways to know anything. This strikes many people as illogical, unreasonable, and maybe even nonsensical.

The unfortunate aspect of this tendency is not the veneration of rationality or the insistence on experimental evidence, but the discrediting of intuition. The whole thrust of scientism has been to minimize the influence of the knower. It protects knowledge from the vagaries of subjectivity with a system of checks and balances that are as essential as their equivalent in democracies. But if the system becomes imbalanced, the power of a particular branch can become so diluted as to lose its real effectiveness.

The institutions that teach us how to use our minds, as well as the organizations in which we use them, are so skewed toward the rational-empirical ideal that intuition is seldom discussed, much less honored or encouraged. From grade school to graduate school, and in most of our work settings, we are taught to emulate the idealized model of scientism in our thinking, problem solving, and decision making. As a result, intuition is subject to various forms of censure and constraint. What psychologist Blythe Clinchy said of early education applies throughout our culture: "We may convince our students that this mode of thought is an irrelevant or indecent way of approaching formal subject matter. We do not actually stamp out intuition; rather, I think, we drive it underground."

There are twin ironies in this situation. First, the model we seek to emulate is something of a fiction, erroneous in some of its assumptions and inappropriate in many of its applications. Second, like the employee in our opening metaphor, intuition is a vital—although restricted—contributor to the very institutions that tried to retire it.

DO AS IT DOES, NOT AS IT SAYS

Real day-to-day science and real day-to-day problem solving are to their formal descriptions what a jam session is to sheet music. For one thing, the detached objectivity that scientism prizes is an impossible ideal. Psychological research tells us that even ordinary sense perception is an interpretive act, influenced by expectations, beliefs, and values. For example, the same coin is perceived as larger in size by poor children than by their more affluent counterparts.

We also know from science itself that the long-standing theoretical separation of observer and observed, object and subject, can no longer be assumed. As Werner Heisenberg noted when he formulated the uncertainty principle, which proved that on the subatomic level the act of observation influences what is being observed: "Even in science, the object of research is no longer nature itself but man's investigation of nature." Furthermore, every discipline is rooted in a set of assumptions and beliefs—what philosopher Thomas Kuhn called a *paradigm*—and, like all of us, individual scientists have convictions, attachments, and passions that influence their work. Indeed, without them scientists could never muster the courage and tenacity to discover anything worthwhile.

The real objectivity of science pertains to the macrocosm, the collective enterprise where hunches, beliefs, and intuitive convictions confront one another in the public arena and are rigorously evaluated. What survives we call objective, scientific knowledge. The knower will always be subjective and will always use his intuition. We have tried to minimize the imperfections of subjectivity; what we have not done is try to elevate the knower's subjective ability to know.

When given the opportunity, intuition has done wonders. If reason and empirical observation steer the course of discovery and the passion for truth supplies the fuel, it is intuition that provides the spark. (Although we are discussing science, the same comments apply to creative decision making and problem solving in any field.) Abraham Maslow distinguished two types of scientists, each essential to the overall endeavor. One type he compared to tiny marine animals who build up a coral reef; they patiently pile up fact after fact, repeat experiments, and cautiously modify theories. The other breed, whom Maslow called the "eagles of science," make the soaring leaps and imaginative flights that lead to revolutions in thought. Intuition is what gives wing to the eagles.

Many of the anecdotes throughout the book will demonstrate this point, and an army of quotations could be culled from the pantheon of science and mathematics to support it. Here are just two.

First, Einstein on the discovery of natural laws: "There are no logical paths to these laws, only intuition resting on sympathetic understanding of experience can reach them." Second, John Maynard Keynes on Isaac Newton: "It was his intuition which was preeminently extraordinary. So happy in his conjectures that he seemed to know more than he could have possibly any hope of proving. The proofs were . . . dressed up afterwards; they were not the instrument of discovery."

Keynes's point is an essential one: formal proofs are instruments of verification and communication. The final descriptions of research are what the public sees and what we learn about in school. But they are the end products, the logical, orderly presentations compiled after all the sloppy work has been done, all the false starts and dead ends corrected, all the vague hunches and gut feelings sorted out. What we see is an idealized road map, constructed retrospectively, like a traveler's outline of a cross-country journey that excludes the side trips, the backtracking, the mistakes, and the spontaneous changes of direction.

We are led to believe that the finished product depicts the actual process. Then we are advised to emulate it in our thinking. Hence our schooling centers on recalling facts and following standardized methods for solving problems whose beginning and end points are clearly defined. Imagination and the vague intuitive notions that prefigure discovery are devalued or ignored. In classrooms they are even considered to be mere guessing, particularly when the student is unable immediately to produce a logical defense. We are asked to do what science says, not what it does, which is both unfortunate and ironic. As psychologist Jerome Bruner wrote in *The Process of Education*: "The warm praise that scientists lavish on those of their colleagues who earn the label 'intuitive' is major evidence that intuition is a valuable commodity in science and one we should endeavor to foster in our students."

If great ideas actually did follow inexorably from piling up facts through reason and experimentation, as the orthodox model suggests, then all it would take to walk away with history's prizes would be to show up in the right place at the right time, like the millionth customer to enter a supermarket. Nothing but chance would distinguish the geniuses we venerate, the ones who looked at the same facts everyone else had looked at and thought what no one else had ever thought. But, as the philosopher of science Karl Popper says, "There is no such thing as a logical method of having new ideas, or a logical reconstruction of this process. . . . Every discovery contains an 'irrational element' or a creative intuition."

The very essence of breakthroughs is that they defy conventional assumptions. They go beyond anything we have any logical or factual reason to accept. The general relativity theory, for example, was born when Einstein had what he called "the happiest thought of my life." He realized that a person falling from a roof was both at rest and in motion at the same time. What could be more illogical? Years later, when the theory was proven, it started to seem logical because our assumptions about space and time had been transformed, thanks to Einstein's intuition.

Most people associate the flash of discovery—the "Aha!" or "Eureka!"—with intuition, but that is not its only function, as we shall see in Chapter 3. Scientists, and problem solvers in general, make advances by spotting difficulties and knowing which questions to ask and how to frame problems, a step that Einstein said was "often more essential than its solution." Those acts are guided, at least in part, by intuition. This is particularly so when deeply ingrained assumptions are called into question by anomolous findings—the first step in scientific revolutions, Thomas Kuhn tells us. When hypotheses are proposed, individuals intuitively decide whether they are worth trying to prove or refute. Intuition also helps them decide where to look for facts, how to design experiments, and how to interpret data and recognize what is relevant.

If all this could be accomplished through formal, mechanical procedures, experts, like computers, would never disagree. Yet in all disciplines they are frequently on the warpath. Individuals become intense advocates of ideas, even those that are ridiculed and contradicted by evidence. When their intuitive convictions prove incorrect we call them madmen; when they are right they secure a place in history, as Marconi did when he insisted that wireless signals could traverse the ocean even though the laws of physics at the time proved otherwise, or as Ray Kroc did when he followed a feeling in his "funny bone" instead of the advice of his experts and purchased McDonald's.

The same analysis also applies to mathematics, that exacting and meticulous language which imparts precision to science. All attempts to establish a formalized, logically sound foundation for mathematics have failed. The effort culminated in Kurt Gödel's incompleteness theorem, which demonstrated that no formal system can ever be both consistent and complete. "What then is mathematics if it is not a unique, rigorous, logical structure?" asks Morris Kline in *Mathematics: The End of Certainty*. "It is a series of great intuitions carefully sifted, refined, and organized by the logic men are willing and able to apply at any time."

That which holds true in the abstract realms of science and mathematics also holds true in the practical world, where we have tried to apply the rigors of scientism to decisions and problems. Business schools and other arenas of professional training emphasize sophisticated quantitative analysis. But many executives feel that modern techniques, while potent and important, are not enough in an uncertain and changeable environment. For that reason, ivory-tower management scientists have had trouble getting working managers to apply their methods.

It seems that successful decision making requires the same uncanny sense of direction and the same creative fertility that characterize great science. Executive suites and laboratories have more in common with artists' studios than we have realized. In a widely quoted article in the *Harvard Business Review*, Henry Mintzberg of the McGill University Faculty of Management reported the results of an extensive study of corporate executives. He found that the high-ranking manager operating under chaotic and unpredictable conditions is a "holistic thinker . . . constantly relying on hunches to cope with problems far too complex for rational analysis." Mintzberg concludes that "organizational effectiveness does not lie in that narrow-minded concept called 'rationality'; it lies in a blend of clearheaded logic *and* powerful intuition."

Despite the evidence, there are many in academic and scientific circles—those arbiters of knowledge who tell us what is true and real—who insist that intuition has no significant role in discovery or decision making. To them, the process of knowing is as mechanical as putting together a model airplane from an instruction manual. They seem to feel that scientists and executives who praise intuition are indulging in a bit of romantic poetic license, perhaps to counteract their dull public image.

There have always been those who embraced and celebrated their intuition. Jonas Salk, for example, has said, "It is always with excitement that I wake up in the morning wondering what my intuition will toss up to me, like gifts from the sea. I work with it and rely on it. It's my partner." Most scholars and scientists acknowledge the value of their intuition but are more circumspect, partly because they fear the ridicule of their peers. There may be another reason, too; E. C. G. Sudarshan, a theoretical physicist at the University of Texas, maintains that some of his colleagues don't talk about their intuition because "they fear the wellspring will dry up. Very few will admit to being superstitious, but when inspiration doesn't come they get alarmed."

Another reason people are quiet about intuition is that it is hard to pin down. Researchers prefer phenomena that can be directly observed and measured, so we have only a small body of knowledge, mostly anecdotal, about ephemeral intuition, with a few brave attempts at experimentation. It has also been considered—when it is considered at all—a chance phenomenon, something that either happens or doesn't. There does not seem to be any way to arrange it into a set of rules that can be taught the way logic and quantitative procedures can be taught. These skills are transmitted in schools while intuition is neglected, for the same reasons that we have courses dealing with sex education but not with love.

All that is changing, however, despite the ideological obstacles. New discoveries about the brain, growing awareness of the limits of scientism, and insights from ancient teachings and progressive psychologists are creating an intellectual atmosphere more receptive to understanding intuition. And progress is being made on the applied level as well. Intuition is a spontaneous phenomenon in that it can't be contrived or forced. But, as we shall see, a good deal can be done to develop intuitive capacity and to create conditions that are conducive to it.

Perhaps the biggest single reason for the emergence of intuition, however, is necessity. It may be underdeveloped and underemployed, but intuition still works, and one of the truths it is whispering to large numbers of people is that we need more of it.

THE GROOMING OF INTUITION

So far we have examined the ideology of scientism to understand why we have heard so little about intuition and done so little to cultivate it. It is important to understand these attitudes since they cause us to mistrust our own intuition; we encounter resistance not only from outside sources but from ourselves, for we have internalized the same belief patterns. We often force ourselves to think in a rigidly rational-empirical manner when it is inappropriate or futile. This can restrain our intuition, causing us to stagger mentally, just as we might stagger physically if we had learned to walk on our heel instead of using the entire foot.

The rational-empirical mode works best under three conditions: when we can control or predict all the variables that affect the subject matter under consideration; when we can measure, quantify, and define with precision; and when we have complete and adequate information. Needless to say, those conditions are not always met in a complex world, especially when human beings are involved or when emotions or metaphysical questions concern us. It is often forgotten that science was designed to deal with the material world; extending it to the nonmaterial without the added dimension of an acute intuitive sense is like promoting a crack salesman or engineer to a managerial position for which his skills are inadequate.

"If your only tool is a hammer," said Abraham Maslow, "you begin to see everything in terms of nails." If your only cognitive tools are rational-empirical, your vision will be restricted to what can be analyzed and measured. Ask the grand metaphysical questions about human identity and the nature of reality, and materialistic answers will come back. The self comes to be seen as a catalog of analyzable personality traits, and the cosmos becomes a collection of objects separated from the self, an incomplete vision with consequences that range from short-changing human potential to pillaging nature. As we will see, deep intuition alone can penetrate the transcendent and illuminate the sublime.

An exclusively rational-empirical approach to problem solving and decision making will not enable us to deal adequately with essential but nonmeasurable considerations such as values, morals, and human will. It also encourages a bottom-line mentality that can't see beyond narrow, measurable benefits. To accommodate the requirements of scientism, we break into parts things that should be viewed as wholes and we separate items that might better be understood as complementary. We might look for single, identifiable causes when multilevel causation, or *no* causation, might be more accurate. We reduce uncertainty by disregarding the unpredictable and by squeezing variables with multiple meanings and subtle nuances into neat but artificial compartments. And we often lean too heavily on analyzing the past because the past is easy to quantify.

What often happens is that, in practical situations, we sacrifice innovation for control, and in the quest for knowledge we sacrifice wisdom and depth for predictability. This might be why, in the study of human beings, increased quantification seems to produce banality, while the truly significant contributions come from the intuitive insights of gifted thinkers and healers.

Our economy is a good example of the limits of applied scientism, and also of how its requirements determine the way we define reality. Sacrosanct formulas and sophisticated mathematical models have for years consistently gone awry. This failure has baffled economists, but they never seem to question certain premises on which economic theories are based: that people are well-informed, rational thinkers who calculate the costs and benefits of their alternatives and arrive inexorably at the right choices. No intuitive shopkeeper or advertising copywriter would swallow that, but scientists need this assumption in order to design and use formal methodologies.

This is not to disparage rational thinking or empirical procedures for processing information; we would be in sad shape without them. It is simply to point out that we have trouble making our way through a complex, incessantly changing world by relying on rational-empirical thinking alone. "In a human situation," wrote philosopher William Barrett, "the waters are usually muddy and the air a little foggy; and whatever the intuitive person—whether he be a politician, courtier, or lover—can perceive in that situation is not by virtue of well-defined logical ideas. Quite to the contrary; such ideas are more likely to impede his vision."

As individuals, we can't expect to approach real-life decisions—particularly in relationships and other areas where emotions and ambiguities are involved—as if they were problems in an algebra class. There are usually too many unknowns to fit the equations. For example, psychologist Steve Baumgardner of the University of Wisconsin at Eau Claire studied vocational decision making among college students and concluded that "the uncertainties surrounding career opportunities and the involvement of emotions and broad life goals in career choice may make fully rational career planning impossible and undesirable."

Baumgardner discovered that when students think about careers, they tend to shift from an analytic approach in their freshman years to a more intuitive attitude as sophomores. This trend is lamented by most counselors, who urge students to analyze job-availability data and make objective, even quantitative assessments of their abilities. Baumgardner suggests that the shift to intuition is actually an adaptive response to uncertainty and complexity. He argues that "we ought to give up systematic career planning, both as a description of how careers *are* chosen and as a prescriptive ideal of how careers *ought* to be chosen."

Like scientists and executives, humans in general don't always follow the formalized thought patterns that are customarily prescribed. We are not by nature the logical creatures of recent Western mythology. As Morton Hunt points out in *The Universe Within*, a survey of cognitive psychology, logic is a tool invented for certain uses; it is not the way we deal with reality most of the time, despite our conditioning. That is not a flaw, but a useful strategy. Hunt quotes psychologist Donald Norman: "We leap to correct answers before there are sufficient data, we intuit, we grasp, we jump to conclusions despite the lack of convincing evidence. That we are right more often than wrong is the miracle of human intellect."

Most of that miracle is what we call intuition. When we mistrust it or let it atrophy by persisting with exclusively rational-empirical thought patterns, we end up tuning in with mono to a stereo world. It is time to acknowledge the importance of intuition in our lives, to understand it, and to find ways to nurture it. For individuals, the intuitive edge means better decisions, more creative ideas, deeper insight, and a smoother, more direct route from desire to fulfillment. But the effort promises more than personal advantage. It will help society at large meet the demands of a turbulent, unpredictable world. A lack of intuition among our thinkers, decision makers, and citizens can be fatal.

This entreaty does not constitute a threat to rationality or empirical science. It is often feared that endorsing intuition might be the first step toward intellectual anarchy, dogmatism, or authoritarianism. But what people actually fear is not so much intuition as the sacrifice of verifiable proof to antireason, arbitrariness, and claims of infallibility. There is some justification for this, and it is worthy of more than passing mention.

There have always been those who disdain science and rigorous analytic thought, which they perceive as cold and impersonal. Sometimes their embrace of the nonrational becomes *irrational* in the worst sense, degenerating into uncritical thinking, emotionalism, and an impulsiveness that is mistaken for intuitive spontaneity. Some people assume that the way to be more intuitive is to be less rational. However, it is not as simple as "getting in touch with your feelings" or "trusting your intuition," as some self-help magazine articles have suggested. The theory in some circles seems to be "If it feels good, believe it," an admonition that threatens to do for thinking what "If it feels good, do it" did for manners.

A related problem is to assume that if something seems like intuition it is necessarily right. Just as there are people who won't accept anything that doesn't meet rigorous standards of proof, there are others who want so badly to believe in their inner voices that they may mistake fear or wishful thinking for intuition. Those with a spiritual orientation often act as if every feeling, every dream, every bodily sensation is a message from the Higher Mind. They elevate all nonrational events to the level of divine inspiration, which is as incorrect as the tendency among super-rationalists to reduce genuine mystical vision to hallucination or neurosis.

I have seen polemics on intuition that cite a study, first noted by Arthur Koestler in *The Act of Creation*, in which 83 percent of the scientists surveyed admitted to having had frequent or occasional assistance from their intuition. Often ignored is the fact that only 7 percent said their intuition was always correct; the other estimates ranged from 90 percent accuracy to 10 percent. The underdeveloped intuitive mind can be fickle and enigmatic: what it delivers is sometimes right, sometimes wrong; sometimes clear, sometimes hazy; sometimes certain, sometimes ambivalent; sometimes meaningful, sometimes impertinent babble.

There is a need for balance and a recognition of the intricate, mutually enhancing relationship between intuition and rationality. We need not just more intuition but *better* intuition. We need not only to trust it but to make it more trustworthy. And at the same time we need sharp, discriminating rationality. In a healthy mind and a healthy society, all faculties should develop harmoniously, each supplementing the other's strengths and shoring up its weaknesses.

In this chapter we have started toward this goal, because developing intuition is largely a matter of being aware of the obstacles that inhibit its effectiveness. It also helps to appreciate what intuition is, its functions, and its various nuances and forms. These are among the areas we will explore in the next few chapters. We will then address such questions as "Who is intuitive?" and "How can intuition be explained?" before turning exclusively to practical considerations. The theoretical and applied components are meant to reinforce one another: understanding intuition helps us get the most out of it; experiencing intuition helps us understand it.

2

What It Is: Definitions and Distinctions

Intuition is when you know something, but, like, where did it come from?

Like the fifteen-year-old girl quoted above, most people have their own idea of what intuition is. It is one of those words—like love, beauty, intelligence, value, happiness, quality—that is applied and defined in various ways but that has an agreed-upon essence that enables everyone to use it in conversation. I went through Chapter 1 without stopping to define it in order to demonstrate just that point.

Derived from the Latin *intueri*—which has been translated "to look upon," "to see within," and "to consider or contemplate"—the word *intuition* means various things to different philosophers, psychologists, and laypersons, but the basic sense of the term is captured in the dictionary definition: "the act or faculty of knowing directly, without the use of rational processes."

This definition is so broad that it can be applied to a vast range of cognitive experiences. Immanuel Kant, for example, used it to refer to ordinary sensory perception, which is, strictly speaking, justifiable. Other applications have limited it to a single realm, such as problem solving, creativity, or mysticism. For our purposes, we will not use Kant's perception-oriented meaning, since that would trivialize the term, but we will not otherwise limit its use. Intuition applies to anything knowable, including vague hunches and feelings about mundane matters, significant discoveries of concepts and facts, and divine revelation.

In ordinary usage, intuition might signify an event or occurrence ("I had an intuition") or a faculty of the mind ("I used my intuition"). There is also a verb form: "I intuited the answer." It can also apply to a personality attribute ("That guy is really intuitive") or a style of functioning, a relatively loose, unstructured, and informal approach to problems that contrasts with the more deliberate, systematic style commonly referred to as "analytic" or "rational." The basic sense of the word, though, suggests spontaneity and immediacy; intuitive knowing is not *mediated* by a conscious or deliberate rational process. We use the word when we know something but don't know how we know it.

That seems clear enough, but in this chapter we will discuss two areas in which the basic definition runs into complications. These are both interesting and of practical value for developing intuition; it is important to become aware of intuition's presence in our lives and to have a reasonably clear personal idea of what it means. These are the two main points to remember: first, the real relationship between intuition and rationality is richer and more complex than is generally realized; and, second, applying the label "intuitive" to specific experiences is frequently difficult and sometimes arbitrary.

RELAXING THE DICHOTOMY

As we have seen, intuition is defined mainly in terms of what it is not: rationality, which entails the use of reason, logic, and analysis. It is also not mere observation; when you see a shiny red object with a siren and conclude "That is a fire engine," you would not be called intuitive. In many ways the rationality/intuition dichotomy is a valid one. Rational thought is drawn out over time; it takes place in a definable sequence of steps with a beginning, middle, and end. It is linear. It requires effort and deliberate intention.

By contrast, intuition is experienced as nonsequential. It is a single event as opposed to a series, a snapshot as opposed to a motion picture. And it just seems to happen, often when least expected, without the application of specific rules. When you arrive at a conclusion through rational thought you can usually trace the mental process backward and identify the antecedent steps. Intuition is inexplicable. The intuiter might be able to provide a plausible explanation for what led to his knowledge, but he would be reasoning retroactively and couldn't be sure that the explanation matched the actual process.

Although some writers make the two functions sound like rivals, they are complementary. Typically, rationality is said to precede and follow intuition. We reason, analyze, gather facts; then there is an intuitive breakthrough; then we reason and analyze again in order to verify, elaborate, and apply the product of intuition. This is a useful division of labor, and it is a more or less accurate picture of how things generally go in protracted decision making, problem solving, and creative work of all kinds. However, it limits intuition to the Eureka! experience associated with breakthroughs, whereas it has other functions, too, as we will see in the next chapter. Sometimes, in fact, the roles are reversed: intuition feeds and stimulates rational thought and evaluates its products.

Also, rationality and intuition are much more symbiotic than the model suggests. They work not only in tandem but together, like two separate pipes feeding into the same faucet. *Intuition is part of rational thinking.* This is readily apparent in the informal reasoning of everyday thought. Generally speaking, we rarely follow the formal rules of logic. When we are thinking through a decision or problem, we tend to hop back and forth between conscientiously applied analysis and intuition. Because we usually have insufficient information and too little time to gather it when we reason, we skip many of the intermediary steps required by strict logic and leap to conclusions that are not strictly defensible.

Many of these leaps are, in fact, intuitive connections that aid the reasoning process. We might start to analyze something, then have a spontaneous hunch and leap to another track entirely, reason further or calculate, and then find that a new hypothesis or an alternative pops suddenly to mind, conjuring up a whole new set of data or stimulating a different analysis. Then maybe something doesn't *feel* quite right, so we shift over to another track or another theory, or decide for no apparent reason to redefine the problem entirely. At any given point it might be difficult to stop and say, "Now I am being intuitive" or "Just then I was being rational."

Intuition even participates in formal rational thought. Deductive logic is a set of rules enabling us to go from a general proposition to a specific application, as in the classic syllogism: All men are mortal; Socrates is a man; therefore, Socrates is mortal. The rationalist philosophers understood that logic has to begin with self-evident, or axiomatic, premises. It could be argued that intuition provides the apprehension of self-evidence. Descartes used the term that way. "By intuition," he wrote, "I understand not the fluctuating testimony of the sense, but the conception which an unclouded and attentive mind gives us so readily and distinctly that we are wholly freed from doubt about that which we understand."

Sometimes, of course, we make deductions on the basis of commonly accepted facts or simple observations, and it would be stretching the point to call such a process intuitive. But often we will have a hunch about something and use it as the basis for a deductive sequence. For example, an art collector has a feeling that a particular artist is going to become popular; from that he deduces that he ought to buy the artist's work, and reasons through a strategy. A scientist has a hunch about the relationship between two chemicals; from that he deduces what would happen when the chemicals interact under certain conditions. You meet a gregarious man and something tells you he is actually shy and insecure underneath his pose; from that you deduce how he will respond if you introduce him to your sister.

When we attempt to be logical in complex situations, when we are forced to deal with incomplete information, unfamiliar subject matter, or ambiguous premises, we are dependent on intuition to tell us whether we are on the right track. Sherlock Holmes, that quintessential deducer, was more intuitive than Conan Doyle would probably have admitted. Take, for example, the case in which Holmes quickly concluded that the murderer was someone very familiar to the victim. Pure deduction, my dear Watson: hounds don't bark at trusted visitors; the victim's hounds had not barked; therefore, the intruder was familiar and trusted.

But was it really pure deduction? Because a dog's bark was generally used to pinpoint the time of an intrusion, Watson and the others were disappointed at the absence of barking and directed their attention elsewhere. Holmes made a connection that no one else made, not because he was a superior logician—anyone could have made the same deduction had he thought to do so—but because something told Holmes that the nonbarking dog was significant. I suggest that intuition turns us in the right direction, toward meaningful information, and to the starting point for reasoning.

Intuition also helps us evaluate conclusions that are derived logically. In the mélange of thoughts that constitutes ordinary reasoning, we don't often run into formal syllogisms that can be judged according to Aristotle's rules. In ambiguous or overly complex situations, intuition helps us recognize false premises or invalid inferences, either of which can make logical thinking go awry. This is especially true, of course, if there is not enough time or information available to submit propositions to a rigorous test. Indeed, we could go a step further and say that the feeling of comfort and "rightness" that allows us to accept any proposition is a function of intuition. Aristotle—who must have been intuitive himself to set down the rules of logic without the rules of logic to help him—said that the syllogism was a perfect configuration because the inferences it depicts are intuitively valid.

What is true of deduction applies even more to *induction*, the process of reasoning from specific instances to general principles. Intuitive insights can spark an inductive process, guide the search for appropriate information and associations, and help us evaluate inductive inferences. There are no formal rules for making inductive statements or for determining their validity. They are always probabilistic, since induction entails drawing conclusions from a limited set of observations. In some instances, conclusions are inarguable (few would dispute "All men are mortal," even though we haven't yet seen the death of every human being) or obviously absurd, as is the case with flagrant stereotyping or this story: A psychologist trains a flea to jump when it hears "Jump!" The researcher pulls off one of the flea's legs, and the flea still obeys the command. This continues with the scientist removing one leg after the other and the flea following orders, until one day the insect, legless, doesn't jump. Then the scientist induces: "When a flea loses its legs it can no longer hear."

We don't need much intuition to recognize that as a ludicrous inference, but in many ordinary situations we do. Often we hear someone make a general statement and can't evaluate it logically. In many cases, logic can lead to contradictory conclusions, as the violent clashes among factions in politics or any other field attest. We are aided by a certain inner response; it somehow feels either right or wrong, and we can't explain why. I suggest that intuition is guiding that process.

IS INTUITION MERELY FAST REASONING?

Many people contend that intuition is nothing but a romantic word for a process of reasoning that takes place so quickly we are unaware of the steps involved. In this model, the mind is like a computer that is programmed to perform in strict, logical sequences and can do so with such incredible speed we perceive it as a flash. Many psychologists hold to this intuition-as-inference model, largely because it enables them to do experiments. Malcolm Westcott, whose research we will discuss in Chapter 5, used problems in which a series of clues led logically to a single correct answer. One at a time, clues were revealed, such as A, then C, then E, then G, then I. The answer, of course, is K. Those who responded correctly with few clues were considered intuitive.

The problem with definitions geared to experimentation is that they are so tightly focused that the richness of the subject matter can be lost. Intuition becomes that which is measured by a particular test, just as intelligence has come to mean that which is measured by IQ tests. Although it is debatable, one can concede that solving a linear problem with less information than most people require qualifies as one type of intuition. But it is mistaken to conclude that intuition *is* inference or that *all* intuitive experiences can somehow fit this model. The "nothing but" argument overlooks several important points.

For one thing, much of what intuition does can't be done by reasoning. Logic requires indubitable facts, and each step has to be correct before we can proceed. In complex situations, the information isn't always available. Also, creative discoveries and innovations can't be acquired by following the narrow linear path of logic; we have to make unusual connections, imaginative associations that are not obvious and would not show up in a logical sequence. It is intuition that leaps across chasms of missing information, makes sideways detours, and brings together unusual, even illogical combinations.

This is not to say that intuition pulls answers from nothing; it is not magic. It works with the raw materials of information, but it can work with information that is not consciously available, that may have been stored in the past or acquired through subliminal and other non-sensory means. Rational thinking has to work with whatever the mind is aware of at that time, one of the limitations that inspired the mathematician and philosopher Blaise Pascal to say, "Reason is the slow and tortuous method by which those who do not know the truth discover it." Intuition has no such restrictions; it is the product of the mind's capacity to do many things at once without our being aware of them.

Even in situations where the information is available and a conclusion could be reached with straight reasoning, the fact that it is done intuitively represents a distinct improvement in efficiency. Let's look at an example from science.

Charles Nicolle, a physician working in Tunis during a typhus epidemic, was bewildered by the fact that, although the disease was spreading rapidly throughout the city, in the hospital it did not seem contagious. One day as he entered the hospital, he stepped over a typhus victim who had collapsed. In an instantaneous flash, he realized that typhus was transmitted by lice. It is easy to trace a sequence of logical steps touched off by the sight of the new patient: typhus victims don't spread the disease in the hospital; when patients are admitted to the hospital, they are shaved and bathed; the cleansing process eliminates lice; therefore, lice are carriers of typhus.

To argue that Nicolle actually took each of those steps en route to his discovery, or that he *could* have, is not entirely justified. In fact, he reported it as a Eureka! experience, and we cannot undervalue the advantages of its happening that way. A computer could, perhaps, be programmed in such a way as to come up with the same hypothesis, but first it would have to follow and evaluate a huge number of logical sequences. Patients have scores of characteristics other than being shaved and bathed; shaving and bathing have many effects besides eliminating lice. What a waste of time and mental energy if Nicolle had had to go through all the possible permutations!

Following a straightforward rational procedure not only would have been tedious, but it would likely have resulted in many equally plausible hypotheses, each of which would have had to be evaluated. Somehow, the intuitive mind made the right choices and put together the appropriate information in an instant; or perhaps Nicolle apprehended in an instant the product of nonconscious work that had a more protracted history. His intuition also convinced him of the theory's veracity through some inner feeling, for he was certain of it from the start, even though it took some time to prove in a series of experiments on monkeys.

In this light, calling intuition "nothing but rapid inference" is ludicrous. Even when it can be explained as quick inference and its products can be readily duplicated by reason, the advantages of doing the job intuitively are enormous. Perhaps it would be more appropriate to say that reason is nothing but slow intuition. Writing of philosophy, the romantic Friedrich Nietzsche expressed it this way:

> Hope and intuition lend wings to its feet. Calculating reason lumbers heavily behind, looking for better footholds, for reason too wants to reach that alluring goal which its divine comrade has long since reached. It is like seeing two

mountain climbers standing before a wild mountain stream that is tossing boulders along its course: one of them light-footedly leaps over it, using the rocks to cross, even though behind and beneath him they hurtle into the depths. The other stands helpless; he must first build himself a fundament which will carry his heavy cautious steps. Occasionally this is not possible, and then there exists no god who can help him across.

One more point should be made about what intuition can add to rationality. Pure reason might lead to a conclusion, but our understanding and conviction might be shallow unless the knowledge is also intuitively absorbed. The physicist Sir Arthur Eddington wrote: "We have two kinds of knowledge which I shall call symbolic knowledge and intimate knowledge. . . . Customary forms of reasoning have been developed for symbolic knowledge only. The intimate knowledge will not submit to codification and analysis; or, rather, when we attempt to analyze, the intimacies are lost and it is replaced by symbolism."

Eddington's distinction might be made colloquially by any of us—for example, as the difference between mere understanding and *really knowing*. It is the difference between reading a travel brochure and making the actual journey; something like an experiential element is added that draws the knowledge to the level of feeling as well as thinking. We might, for example, use logic or personality tests to understand someone, but *knowing* that person is a different matter, requiring what psychologists call empathy. I suggest that, at least in part, the factor that turns analytic or symbolic knowledge into intimate knowledge is intuition.

We might study quantum mechanics or relativity theory well enough to memorize facts and pass exams, but physicists say that at some point the fortunate ones come to *feel* something for certain abstractions—the unity of space and time, perhaps, or the wave-particle nature of electrons—that lifts the knowledge to another level. Similarly, we might, through ecological analysis, come to understand that all organisms are connected, but a true sense of the wholeness and unity of nature involves the higher comprehension of intuitive feeling, an experienced union of the knower and the known. This added dimension is particularly significant when relationships, patterns, and paradoxes are involved; logic bogs down in their presence because it requires neatly drawn categories and depends on rules that force us to think in either/or terms.

Intuition can elevate rational knowledge to a higher level of both appreciation and conviction through some ineffable combination of feeling and experience. Henri Bergson described it as "entering into" the object of knowledge and knowing its "essence." Intuition, then, can provide the kind of knowing implied by the biblical use of "know"—intimate, felt, unifying, and fecund.

WHAT QUALIFIES AS INTUITION?

Since I began my research, I have been involved in countless debates over whether particular events are actually intuitive. Just as a group of people can concur on a basic definition of the word *love* and then vehemently disagree when applying it to specific situations— one person calling it love while others call it lust, attraction, affection, need, or whatever—so will one person call a cognitive experience intuition while others might call it a guess, speculation, inference, conjecture, extrasensory perception, or a number of other things, both flattering and disparaging. For that reason, two points have to be kept in mind when classifying any experience: first, the basic definition of intuition has to be enriched, and, second, in many cases the ultimate verdict will be somewhat arbitrary, depending on the intuiter's own interpretation.

To be called an intuition the idea or feeling must be accurate. I agree with Frances Vaughan, author of *Awakening Intuition*, who feels that when something turns out *not* to be correct it should be labeled a bad guess. It must be kept in mind, however, that intuition will often lack the sort of precision of detail we expect from something that is either true or false. Frequently it is a vague, hazy sensation, providing little more than an inkling or a sense of direction. This makes it no less valuable, only more difficult to evaluate.

Also, intuition might be only partly correct. A woman named Diane related this typical experience: "I was thinking about an old boyfriend, Roy, whom I hadn't been able to track down, when I had a sudden flash that he would show up that weekend. He didn't, but less than a week later he rang my doorbell." Perhaps Diane's experience was half intuition, half bad guess.

An intuition might also require some interpetation, and if it turns out to be incorrect the fault may lie in what has been read into it. For example, a novelist friend of mind had a strong, persistent feeling that he should go to London. As he saw it, his intuition was telling him that British publishers were going to bestow on him the fame and fortune their American counterparts had foolishly denied him. He sold everything and moved to London, with disastrous results, personal and financial. He bitterly concluded that what he thought was intuition was really a farce and returned to the United States. But his intuition had said nothing about *moving* to London, or *when* to go, or what would happen there. Quite possibly, he had jumped the gun, gone too far, or was being guided to some experience he did not appreciate at the time. Five years later, in fact, he moved back to London and married someone he'd met on the first trip.

The relationship between intuition and psychic phenomena frequently comes up, and it is not an easy one to sort out. Some people use the terms almost interchangeably. What we call "psychic" comes in several varieties: mental telepathy or thought transfer; clairvoyance and clairaudience (seeing or hearing at a distance); precognition; and other categories that are not germane to our discussion, such as influencing material objects via thought. To my mind, only precognition qualifies as intuition; the other phenomena seem more closely linked to perception than to knowing.

Telepathy and clairvoyance are not intuition; they are ways of bringing in information that intuition may then work on. They extend the range of the five senses, as the term *extrasensory* suggests, and their existence, which I accept unequivocally, helps explain how we sometimes intuit things beyond what the information gathered by our senses could possibly justify. The intuitive mind might process data brought in subliminally or psychically as well as through ordinary sensory channels.

The distinction can be illustrated with an example. Suppose you looked out your window and saw a young man walking toward an old woman. The mere reporting of that would not, of course, qualify as intuition. But it would if you glanced at that scene and said, "That boy is going to snatch that woman's purse." Now, suppose you were sitting in your living room a mile away and saw this same scene in your mind's eye. That would be clairvoyance, but it would be intuitive only if, as in the initial situation, you went beyond the information provided by ESP.

Similarly, if you could read someone's mind and state what he was thinking, it would be telepathy; but if you then had an insight into the person's character, that would be intuition. You would have gone beyond the information to unobvious but accurate knowledge. Admittedly, this distinction may be debatable, but it seems appropriate in a book concerned more with reading our own minds than other people's.

Implied in the use of the word *intuition* is something unexpected, out of the ordinary, nonautomatic. The knowledge revealed can't be something that most people would come up with under the same circumstances. And the circumstances usually boil down to the amount of information the person has to draw on and the precision of the knowledge.

This is where context and individual interpretation enter. In many situations the line between intuition and other types of knowing is blurred. Let's use some examples to get a sense of the usual boundaries. In an example we used before, Diane intuited a forthcoming visit from her old boyfriend. Her intuition was diminished somewhat by her inaccurate forecast of the arrival time, but how close need she have been? Within a day? An hour? There are no set criteria, but obviously the more precise her prediction, the more people would grant her the appelation intuitive. Now consider this: what if Diane had recently received a letter in which Roy had indicated an intention to look her up? That would lessen her achievement a bit. And if the letter had also stated that Roy was on his way to town on a business trip, Diane would probably fall from the ranks of the intuitive.

Virtually every claim to intuition has to be evaluated in a similar way. In an earlier example, we called intuitive the person who, on meeting a gregarious man for the first time, sensed he was actually shy. Well, you might not call it intuitive if the knower was an intimate friend of the man's ex-wife. Similarly, the collector who anticipated success for a particular artist would not be called intuitive if, prior to making the judgment, he had been told that a half dozen other collectors had been purchasing the artist's work.

Along these lines, behavior that some people call inductive reasoning others will call intuitive. Induction is, in fact, a leap, going from a limited set of facts to a general principle. When it has an obvious, defensible basis, the act is likely to be labeled logic; when it does not, it might be called intuition. If, for example, you start a new job and see your boss have a temper tantrum every day for a week, you might induce that he is volatile. Most people would call that an undistinguished logical inference. If, on the other hand, you leap to the same conclusion—assuming it is correct—after a brief, pleasant encounter with the boss, you might call it intuitive.

Finally, let's go back to the intuition-or-inference argument, which seems to be the most nettlesome distinction. Here is an example from my own experience. I entered my office one day to find a message from an old friend named Jerry. The instant I saw the note, this thought popped into my head: "Jerry is married." Since I was researching this book at the time, I contemplated the event and concluded that if Jerry *was* married, my knowing so would clearly be intuitive. The note contained nothing but the name and phone number, and I hadn't heard from my friend in three years. The last time I had seen him he'd been living a happy single's life in New York City, not even dating anyone regularly.

Then I realized that the phone number might have been enough to tip me off. The area code was 914, which I knew to be located in Westchester County, a suburban area just north of New York. Hence, the line of reasoning could have been: Most people who move to Westchester are married and raising families; Jerry, who likes the city's night life, has moved to Westchester; therefore, Jerry must be married and raising a family. When I related the story to others, there was a split on whether to call it intuition or reason.

But to me the important point is this: I did not consciously think through those steps. The message just flew into my head like a bird through an open window. I hadn't even opened the window by wondering about Jerry's marital status. One could argue that I zipped through the logical sequence like a mercurial computer, or that I just did not remember having taken the steps. And for all I know such an analysis is correct. But I would argue that the insight deserves the appellation intuitive, simply because the steps—if they had, in fact, been taken—were neither conscious nor deliberate. That is a crucial distinction. The fact that a logical sequence can be constructed afterward does not mean the sequence was actually employed.

Hence, in many situations, the subjective account of the knower has to be weighed along with the other criteria. And even then there will be disagreement, since individuals will have different standards depending on what intuition means to them. You might want to think about your own experiences and the examples used here and determine your own criteria. Doing so will help you recognize and understand your own intuition. But before you settle on your position, I urge you to consider what happened when I returned Jerry's phone call.

"You're married, aren't you?" I said after we had exchanged greetings.

Jerry confirmed this and asked how I'd found out. To keep things simple, I said I'd deduced it from his area code.

"That's pretty clever," said Jerry, "except for one thing. I moved up here two years ago because my company relocated. I didn't meet my wife until a year later."

3

The Many Faces of Intuition

Following is one of a series of related incidents in a frequently quoted memoir by the French mathematician Henri Poincaré, a story that exemplifies the intuition of discovery: the sudden leap to understanding, the spark of insight, the precipitous penetration to the truth.

> The changes of travel made me forget my mathematical work. Having reached Coutances, we entered an omnibus to go some place or other. At the moment when I put my foot on the step the idea came to me, without anything in my former thoughts seeming to have paved the way for it, that the transformations I had used to define the Fuchsian functions were identical with those of non-Euclidean geometry. I did not verify the idea; I should not have had time, as, upon taking my seat in the omnibus, I went on with a conversation already commenced, but I felt a perfect certainty. On my return to Caen, for conscience's sake I verified the result at my leisure.

This kind of experience is what most people mean when they think of intuition, and it is one of six functional types we will discuss in this chapter. The first five categories interact with each other and occur in various combinations to comprise the full range of ordinary intuitive experience. The sixth type pertains to what is generally known as mystical experience and has intriguing implications for the other five.

DISCOVERY

The history of thought contains innumerable examples of discovery intuition, or detection. Archimedes' fortuitous bath, in which he discovered the principle of water displacement and gave us the term *Eureka!* ("I have found it"), is probably the most famous. A contemporary example is that of Nobel laureate Melvin Calvin, who was sitting in car waiting for his wife to complete an errand when the answer to a perplexing inconsistency in his research on photosynthesis dawned. Calvin wrote of the discovery, "It occurred just like that—quite suddenly—and suddenly also, in a matter of seconds, the path of carbon became apparent to me."

While intuitive discovery often seems to occur when the mind is engaged in something other than the subject of the insight, that is not always the case. The key breakthrough in the search for the structure of the DNA molecule came when the discoverer was working on the problem itself. Like other researchers, James Watson and Francis Crick had labored arduously on the problem for some time. One day, after an interruption, Watson was shifting around components of a model molecule, trying different ways to fit them together. It had always been assumed that each segment had to be paired with its twin.

Then, in Watson's words, "Suddenly I became aware . . . that both pairs could be flip-flopped over and still have their . . . bonds facing in the same direction. It strongly suggested that the backbones of the two chains run in opposite directions." Thus the famous double helix was discovered.

Intuitive discovery applies to the full range of knowable subject matter, including mundane questions, matters of personal or social importance, and abstract conceptual puzzles. What separates it from the other functions of intuition is its detective quality. It reveals verifiable facts. It might tell a businessman that his competitor has tried to interfere with a customer; it might reveal to a physician the real cause of a patient's pain; it might tell a parent exactly what is troubling a child who won't even admit he is troubled; it might signal a stymied inventor to put the gizmo in the widget instead of in its present location.

In short, this aspect of intuition can supply answers to a specific problem or to a more general need. We program our intuitive minds with our questions and desires. Sometimes the answer is not so much a solution as an insight into the real nature of the problem, as in the case of one boutique owner: "Sales were down and I just assumed it was because of the recession. But I kept getting this suspicious feeling inside about one of the sales staff. I though I was nuts, but I investigated anyway, and sure enough she was ripping off the cash sales."

It should be noted that many students of scientific discovery object to assigning intuition a major role in the process. Howard Gruber, director of the Institute for Cognitive Studies at Rutgers University, says that, according to his research, breakthroughs emerge from a "lengthy complex pondering" and the growth of ideas over a long period of time, not a "magical moment." Similarly, Harvard's D. N. Perkins, author of *The Mind's Best Work*, contends that Poincaré-like experiences are rare and that discovery is the outcome of arduous, conscious, rational work. "I have never heard of a completely out-of-the-blue insight," writes Perkins.

This is true. Intuition doesn't come from nowhere. Dogged rational work in the preparation phase is of extreme importance, particularly in a specialized field. It supplies the intuitive mind with the incentive and raw material it needs. As already noted, intuition is not necessarily an all-at-once flash. The fireworks that are recorded for posterity are the dramatic prototypes. The key breakthrough may come either at once or in stages, as Perkins and Gruber point out, but part of that gradual process may be a series of incremental intuitions, perhaps with only candlelight intensity, that supply pieces of the total product.

Others who reject the notion of inspiration hold that the process of discovery is conscious and rational. Yale psychiatrist Albert Rothenberg, for example, contends that when James Watson made his DNA breakthrough he was "fully conscious, aware, and logical at that moment." But Rothenberg also calls Watson's discovery a "creative leap" that somehow was able to "transcend ordinary logic." I don't know how you can transcend logic and still be logical. It seems obvious that the leap was a function of intuition. Perhaps what Rothenberg meant is that such leaps would not ordinarily be made by formal logical thought, but they have a logic of their own that becomes obvious afterward. It is like one of those drawings in which you have to find the concealed face; once you find the face it is almost impossible *not* to see it. So it is with the illogical logic of many intuitions.

Rothenberg uses the term *Janusian thinking* to characterize a central element in creative breakthroughs—when seemingly opposite components are seen to be equally valid or complementary. He claims that Janusian thinking is fully intentional and fully conscious, thus disagreeing with Arthur Koestler, who, in *The Act of Creation*, used the term *bisociation* for essentially the same phenomenon and said the connections were made outside awareness. I think that the merging of opposites is characteristic of intuition, not the sort of thing that rational thought would readily accomplish. Rothenberg himself supports that conclusion by using the word *surprising* to describe the products of Janusian thinking. Watson used the term *suddenly*. To my mind, such terminology indicates that the event was spontaneous, unforeseen, and swift. The discoverer may have been conscious in the sense of being awake, but if he had been aware of the steps by which the crucial connection was made it would have been neither sudden nor surprising.

As for the word *intentional*, I don't doubt that some thinkers intend to find unusual connections. They certainly intend to find answers. Purposefulness and intensity of desire may well be important prerequisites for intuition, as is a certain open-minded attitude that expects the unexpected. But, again, the discoverers could not have *intended* to make the particular connections they did and then have been surprised when they did so. If you set out to pull a rabbit out of a hat, you will hardly be surprised when you perform the trick. For all these reasons, it seems safe to say that the sudden logic-transcending connections that typically accompany discoveries are a function of intuition.

Perhaps those who deny the importance of sudden intuition fear, with some justification, that accepting such a theory might downgrade the value of the conscious, rational preparation that precedes breakthroughs in formal work. Maybe they want to conteract the overly romantic view that discoveries are always flashy. But the danger is that by going too far in the other direction they erroneously negate the intuitive component.

CREATIVITY

The poet A. E. Housman has given us a description of another function of intuition: "As I went along, thinking nothing in particular, only looking at things around me and following the progress of the seasons, there would flow into my mind, with sudden and unaccountable emotion, sometimes a line or two of verse, sometimes a whole stanza at once."

As Housman's remarks suggest, creative, or generative, intuition is quite similar to discovery intuition. The dynamics are more or less identical, the experience itself perhaps indistinguishable. I separate them because of one salient distinction: instead of singular truths, facts, or verifiable information, the creative function of intuition deals with alternatives, options, or possibilities. This function generates ideas that may not be right or wrong in the factual sense but are more or less appropriate to a situation. It might deliver alternatives in quantity, some of which will be more suitable than others.

Creative intuition can be compared to imagination. The distinction has to do with appropriateness. A merely imaginative person might not be intuitive but, rather, a fecund generator of lunatic fantasies or inane outpourings that are not satisfying on either the practical or esthetic level. The creatively intuitive person, on the other hand, would be imaginative in a relevant and apt manner. If he were a problem solver, he would generate a lot of unusual solutions, a high percentage of which would achieve the desired results. If he were an artist, his conceptions would "work" on canvas, on paper, or on stage, and the products would have the ring of "truth" that enables some art to endure. If he were a scientist or mathematician, he would generate hypotheses and theories, or unusual ways to test them, and a good proportion would contribute to the body of knowledge in his field.

Creative intuition works hand in hand with discovery intuition. You might, for example, detect the answer to a problem and then intuit alternative ways to prove it or execute it. Or you might intuitively apprehend what the problem itself is and then generate possible solutions. Sometimes the two functions overlap. In response to a perplexing question your intuition might generate a lot of hypotheses, one of which subsequently turns out true. Strictly speaking, when it is verified it would be termed a discovery.

The distinction is situation-dependent. Discovery intuition would apply when there is a single answer to such questions as, "What is the structure of the DNA molecule?" or "Who killed the victim?" Creative intuition would apply where there are a number of possible solutions, some better than others. Works of art would be an obvious example, although many artists will tell you there is one and only one way to finish this novel or paint that sunflower. Giacometti, for example, might have used the term *discovery* for this process: "In 1949 I saw the sculpture before me as if it were finished, and in 1950 it became impossible for me not to make it."

With great art, the distinction between creativity and discovery is often irrelevant. Art, wrote novelist Shirley Hazzard, is "an endless access to revelatory states of mind." That state of mind is what gives rise to creative intuition and makes great art an epiphany, not just entertainment. It is why we learn things about jealousy from Shakespeare or crime from Dostoevski that we can't learn from scientific studies. What psychologist Morris Parloff wrote of Lewis Carroll could have been said of any number of artists: "His contributions to the field of psychology, were we to enumerate them all, would undoubtedly qualify him for immediate fellowship status in at least two dozen of the 41 divisions of the American Psychological Association." You might also say the same of historical, sociological, and even physical-science associations.

The intuition of creativity is also important in solving practical problems and making decisions. The ability to generate alternative ways of viewing situations, or a variety of potential solutions, is an important component of innovation. Creative intuition will also seize opportunities to satisfy objectives. Always on the alert for new ways to generate business, liquor company executive Marshall Berkowitz was at a bar one day when he noticed that brandy Alexanders were extremely popular. He wondered why no one ever served them at home, and the answer came to him: they were too difficult to prepare. On the heels of that came the then-revolutionary idea of packaged cocktails.

There are probably personality differences between intuitive discoverers and intuitive creators. Some might be detective types; they come up with a small number of ideas, most of which are right on the mark. They are attracted to single-answer problems. Others might generate ideas in the same way that flowers produce pollen, and have a small percentage of healthy offspring. They are attracted to ill-defined, open-ended problems. Personally, I would like to have both types on my team.

EVALUATION

"By the favour of the Gods, I have since my childhood been attended by a semi-divine being whose voice from time to time dissuades me from some undertaking, but never directs me what I am to do." Thus Socrates, in Plato's *Theagetes*, referred to a divine voice, and perhaps it was. In more secular terminology, I call it the evaluative function of intuition.

It is frequently said that intuition does not evaluate or decide; rational analysis does that, while intuition provides the possibilities. This division of labor short changes both intuition and rationality. Often the opposite of the customary description occurs. For example, financial planner Tom Duffy says, "I might make contingency plans on the basis of a formal analysis of technical data, but the actual decision—to commit or hold off or abandon—is a question of timing, and for that I look to my feelings."

What most people mean when they say that intuition does not evaluate is that it doesn't examine or investigate. Those functions are largely analytic, although intuition will help guide the process. But rational and quantitative evaluations often leave us with uncertainty or ambiguity, not with a single obvious decision. They might narrow down the alternatives and provide solid facts and figures to consider, but much of the time we turn to intuition for the ultimate choice.

Intuitive evaluation is a binary kind of function that tells us go or don't go, yes or no. Like other types of intuition, it can be clear or faint, resolute or hesitant, convincing or dubious. We have all had these promptings and urgings, although too often we ignore them. How many times have you run into trouble and afterward cursed yourself: "I *knew* I shouldn't have done that. Something told me not to. Next time I'll pay attention." Sometimes we feel strongly about something, but the inarticulate nature of intuition prevents us from convincing others. That happened to Socrates, as Plato's account suggests: "You know Charmides, the son of Glaucon. One day he told me that he intended to compete at the Nemean games. . . . I tried to turn Charmides from his design, telling him, 'While you were speaking, I heard the divine voice . . . "Go not to Nemea." ' He would not listen. Well, you know he has fallen."

Evaluative intuition might work directly on possibilities that present themselves from outside. Should you call that man you met on the train? Should you take that job offer? Much of the time we don't even have to ask the question; our intuition is programmed by our desires, needs, and goals. Here is an example from my own experience, when I was interviewing prospective literary agents. Usually I would leave such meetings feeling ambivalent, torn between rejecting and accepting the agent. In one case, however, I knew in the first minute that the person across the desk was not my future agent. I had not consciously evaluated her, and there were no remarkable traits that stood out as *the* reasons, but as she was describing one of her client's books, a strong but undeniable sensation came over me, wordlessly screaming "No!"

The evaluative function of intuition also works on the other products of intuition, adding the element of discrimination. Ideas feel more or less true; tentative solutions feel more or less right. Marshall Berkowitz, for example, had to decide whether or not his idea for packaging cocktails was worth pursuing, and later he had to decide whether to go ahead with production. Certainly, he gathered the facts and figures, consulted with colleagues, and thought it all through carefully. But at some point it was go or no-go, and he had to consult his inner barometer. Watson and Crick had to recognize that their Janusian connection was worth pursuing; something told them to go ahead and try to verify it.

Writers and artists have to evaluate intuitively all the time, for there is no objective, rational way they can evaluate their work beyond such technical considerations as syntax and grammar. Saul Bellow speaks of a commentator within that guides his work: "I think a writer is on track when the door of his native and deeper intuitions is open. You write a sentence that doesn't come from that source and you can't build around it—it makes the page seem somehow false. You have a gyroscope within that tells you whether what you're doing is right or wrong." And in his study of Beethoven's work, Roger Sessions writes that the composer's inspiration was an impulse that led him toward a goal: "When this perfect realization was attained, however, there could have been no hesitation—rather a flash of recognition that this was exactly what he wanted."

It is this discriminatory function of intuition that prompts a feeling of certitude or self-evidence about propositions, whether they come from within or from outside. It is important, however, and often difficult, not to confuse these feelings with ordinary emotions. We may like or dislike something, feel strongly attracted or repelled, but that may be hope or fear speaking, not intuition. There is a subtle distinction, and it can be discerned only by paying attention to our own experiences. The potential for confusion might be greater in some areas of life than others. As an advertising executive named Karen said, "When it comes to people, I often have urges to get involved with someone or stay away, whether it is a social or professional encounter. Those feelings often haunt me afterward; they get all tangled up in my own needs and desires. But when it comes to a slogan or a jingle or a storyboard, when I get a strong feeling it is almost always right."

Einstein must have had evaluative intuition working on his theory of general relativity, because he seemed to be unreasonably confident it would stand up to empirical testing. For two years the scientific world prepared for the solar eclipse of May 29, 1919, when conditions would allow them to see whether starlight would be affected by the sun's gravitational field as the theory predicted. According to Einstein's biographer, Jeremy Bernstein, the great man was in Princeton when the results were computed. A student reported that she was engaged in conversation with Einstein when he casually handed her a telegram that had been on a windowsill. It was from Sir Arthur Eddington, confirming the revolutionary theory. Overjoyed by the news, the student was somewhat surprised by the master's apparent indifference. "What if the theory had not been confirmed?" she asked. Einstein replied, "Then I would have been sorry for the dear Lord. The theory is correct."

I have never been able to determine whether Einstein was referring to Lord Eddington or the Almighty. Either way, he seemed awfully sure of his theory.

OPERATION

In the fall of 1941, when London was under siege, Winston Churchill regularly ventured out at night in a staff car to visit antiaircraft batteries. One evening as the prime minister prepared to leave a site, an aide opened the customary door, but Churchill walked around the car and let himself in the far door instead. Not long afterward, a bomb exploded, nearly turning the car over. "It must have been my beef on that side that pulled it down," laughed Churchill. When his wife, Lady Clementine, asked him why he had sat on the far side of the car, Churchill said, "Something said to me, 'Stop!' before I reached the car door held open for me. It then appeared to me that I was told I was meant to open the door on the other side and get in and sit there—and that's what I did."

Churchill had what I would call an operative intuition (he evidently had a lot of them). This most subtle, almost spooky form of intuition is what guides us this way and that, sometimes with declarative force, sometimes with gentle grace. It prompts us without telling us why, and sometimes without our knowing that we are being prompted at all. More like a sense of direction than a map, it can be ill defined or quite explicit. It might operate on minor, localized situations, nudging us toward this or tugging us away from that. Or it might manifest itself in larger issues, such as a sense of "calling," for example, that overpowering certainty that we are meant to follow a particular vocation or accept some mission. Such compelling attractions can often be justified logically, but they are never logically derived. Rather, we feel like an iron filing drawn quite irresistibly to a magnet.

In some ways operative intuition is similar to the evaluative function, since there might be a "do/don't do" or "go/don't go" quality to it. But with evaluative intuition there first has to be something to evaluate. For example, when Ray Kroc's consultants advised him not to buy McDonald's, he says, "I closed the office door, cussed up and down, threw things out of the window, called my lawyer back, and said, 'Take it!' I felt in my funny bone it was a sure thing." That was evaluative intuition working on a specific yes-or-no question. Not so with the toy manufacturer who, in June 1971, had an inexplicable urge to increase production of panda dolls. The next February Richard Nixon made his historic trip to China, where he was given two pandas, touching off a small fad.

Operative intuition might be responsible for what often seems like luck. Those persons who seem to be in the right place at the right time, to whom terrific accidents seem to happen, are perhaps gifted with a kind of radar system and the good sense to obey it. It might also account for the phenomenon that Carl Jung called "synchronicity," those uncanny coincidences of outer and inner events that have no apparent causal connection but have meaning or significant impact. One artist relates: "I had met someone at an opening who wanted to commission a painting. The next day, when I went to phone him, I could not find his business card. On a train ride to the suburbs to visit friends I thought I saw him, but it turned out to be a look-alike. When I arrived at the station, I felt irresistibly drawn to the flower shop, and I gave in to the urge despite the fact that I had brought a gift with me and had no intention of purchasing flowers. In the flower shop was the man I thought I'd lost forever."

The role of accidents in scientific discoveries has often been noted. Perhaps it is operative intuition that tells the seemingly lucky discoverers that there is something worth looking into. Bacteriologist Alexander Fleming, for example, noticed that some of the plates on which he was growing colonies of bacteria had been contaminated by dust and that the bacteria on them had died. Most researchers would have thrown the plates out, since they were just nuisances in the context of the research. Fleming, however, sensed something significant and asked, "Why did the bacteria die?" The eventual result of that question was the discovery of penicillin.

Discoveries and creative ideas are often preceded by what Graham Wallas, in *The Art of Thought*, termed "intimations," those vague, fuzzy feelings that indicate something is about to happen. Jung also noticed a kind of emotional aura that accompanies synchronistic events. Perhaps it is a form of operative intuition, guiding the attention in the right direction, either alerting the mind to an impending thought of its own or to something about to occur in the environment. Wallas recalls a major shift in his own political attitude that was preceded by "a vague, almost physical, recurrent feeling as if my clothes did not quite fit me." Perhaps those intimations are like the early, barely perceptible glow that turns our attention toward the sunrise.

Operative intuition can be puzzling, since it might urge us to move in what seems to be a strange direction. If we follow it, we find ourselves doing things for no apparent reason, perhaps feeling somewhat foolish, wondering what on earth has possessed us. At times these whispers are easy to resist, since they might seem to go against our best interests.

Let's go back to that agent I discussed in the previous section. When it was time to depart her office, something told me to leave behind my outline for this book, which at the time had no publisher. There was no reason to do this, since I knew the agent was not going to represent me. Furthermore, there was *every* reason *not* to do it. I would have to go across the street to make a copy of the outline, and I was already late for my next appointment, which was quite important. Yet I did it. On the elevator, in the copy shop, in the cab, and all during the rest of the day I told myself what an idiot I had been for following that impulse.

The next day I got a call from an editor friend. She suggested that I contact Jeremy Tarcher, whom she had met the night before and who happened to mention an outline for a book on intuition that he had seen that afternoon on an agent's desk.

Coincidence? Who knows? I can only say that what I felt in that agent's office was as powerful and impelling as a strong wind. I have, of course, experienced other nonrational shoves and tugs; some led nowhere, or even to trouble—or at least they *seemed* to. Who can say what would have happened if I hadn't followed them? And who can say what might have happened if I *had* followed the ones I battled against successfully? We usually resist those intuitive urges when they don't seem to make sense. Perhaps we ought not fight so stubbornly.

PREDICTION

"If you can look into the seeds of time," wrote Shakespeare in *Macbeth*, "And say which grain will grow and which will not, Speak then to me." In most intuitive experiences—indeed, in a large percentage of all mental activities—there is an element of prophecy. When a scientist intuits a hypothesis, he is, at least in part, predicting what will happen to certain phenomena under certain conditions. If your intuition tells you to accept a dinner invitation from a virtual stranger, you are predicting that the evening will be pleasurable. When you obey a feeling to hire someone, you are predicting that he or she will produce desirable results. When an artist is inspired to use a dab of red or an arpeggio suggests itself to a composer, they are predicting what the impact will be on the rest of the work and on the viewer or listener.

Decisions are by nature predictive—you are banking on a certain outcome. For this reason, the ability to forecast is a prized quality in executives and policy makers. Indeed, a study by John Mihalasky and Douglas Dean, authors of *Executive ESP*, found a significant correlation between the precognitive ability of company presidents and the profit ratings of their companies.

Certainly, predictions are routinely made by analyzing quantitative data, and specialized knowledge is often necessary. Without an understanding of probability theory, for example, an intuitive judgment might be be way off the mark. To use a rather trivial illustration, suppose in five consecutive coin tosses heads were to come up each time. Would heads or tails be more likely to turn up on the sixth try? Most people choose tails. However, the actual odds are the same old 50/50.

But rational-analytic methods can seldom be used exclusively; by its very nature, prediction deals with the unknown, and we can calculate or measure only what is known. We can analyze past trends and determine probabilities, but we can never be sure the future will be anything like the past, particularly in human situations in a turbulent era like ours. At the very least, a forecaster has to use intuition in gathering and interpreting data and in deciding which unusual future events might influence the outcome. Hence in virtually every prediction there is always some intuitive component.

The predictive function can be either explicit or implicit. When I followed my urge to photocopy that outline and leave it with the agent, I had no idea why. But the intuition to which I give the credit must have had some implicit prophetic quality mixed in. The intuition would have been more predictive than operative if I'd had a strong feeling that something good would come of the behavior or if I'd had a premonition of what would actually take place.

This story, related by Harvard student Juliet Faithfull, is an example of predictive intuition at work. As a young girl, Juliet was on vacation in Barcelona with her parents. For days she implored them to take her to a particular nightclub, and on their last night in the city the parents relented. Juliet eagerly primped for the occasion. Shortly before they were to leave, however, a cloud of dread came over her, and she refused to go, despite the protests of her incredulous parents. The nightclub was destroyed by fire that evening. The difference between her story and Winston Churchill's fortuitous urge to switch seats in his car was that Juliet knew something bad would happen at the club, although she could not specify the nature of the danger.

As these rather dramatic incidents suggest, intuition is an excellent warning device. But not all predictive intuitions are warnings. You might have a strong feeling that the person you just met will have a positive influence on your life or you might have a hunch that you should wait a week before investing because the price is going to fall. The better your intuition can predict, the more your actions will resonate with your desires.

Whether a prediction deserves to be called intuitive hinges on its precision and on whether it is likely to have been made by most people. Let's look at an example. Henry Kissinger once said, "The dilemma of any statesman is that he can never be certain about the provable course of events. In reaching a decision, he must inevitably act on the basis of an intuition that is inherently unprovable. If he insists on certainty, he runs the danger of becoming a prisoner of events." Suppose you had been working in the State Department early in 1977. If you had said, "I have a hunch something big will happen in the Middle East this year," you would have been greeted with polite indulgence at best if you bragged about it at year's end. If you had said, "There is going to be a diplomatic breakthrough between Israel and an Arab nation, possibly Egypt," you might have been called intuitive, and your colleagues might subsequently have turned to you for predictions. But if you had said, "Anwar Sadat is going to make a plea for peace before the Israeli parliament in November," you might have been nominated for Mr. Kissinger's old job.

We play guessing games with life. Those who guess well are called intuitive; those who are intuitive, however, don't think they are guessing.

ILLUMINATION

"When all the senses are stilled," say the *Upanishads*, "when the mind is at rest, when the intellect wavers not—then, say the wise, is reached the highest state. He who attains it is freed from delusion." What I am calling illumination has been given other names in different places across time: *samadhi*, *satori*, nirvana, cosmic consciousness, Self-realization, union with God. Certain readers might wonder why it is included at all. Some might see it as too exalted and sublime to be spoken of in the same breath as intuiting what stock to buy; some might be solely interested in how to use their intuition in the "real world" and thus consider this classification irrelevant.

This category transcends the other five functions. In fact, it transcends categories. It transcends words, concepts, thoughts, perceptions, and everything we think of as experience. It is, in fact, *transcendence*, one of the terms used for it in this book. But it is very relevant indeed. Understanding it helps us understand all forms of intuition, and cultivating it simultaneously cultivates the others. Most important, illumination itself represents the highest form of knowing, the realization for which we all thirst whether we know it or not.

Illumination, or transcendence, is different from the ordinary experience of knowing, which always has two components: a subject (the experiencer), and the object of experience, which can be something we think. In the state we are describing, that subject/object duality is dissolved. There is no separation of knower and known. There is no object of experience—not a sensation or a perception or even a thought.

In transcendence, the experiencer is conscious, but not conscious *of* anything; awareness alone exists. The knower knows, but there is no object of knowledge; knowingness alone exists. It is as if the film in a movie projector has run out but the projector light remains on, illuminating the screen. Previously, the viewer's attention had been on the changing forms and colors that to him constituted reality. Now he is aware of the screen itself, the silent, formless background on which the variegated experiences depend. In transcendence, the silent backdrop to experience is illuminated. This is pure consciousness.

It is also the Self, capitalized to distinguish it from the individuated self—the ego or changing personality with which we normally identify. Thus in the state of transcendence what is illumined is one's ultimate identity. We come to know that which we are. "Soundless, formless, intangible, undying, tasteless, odorless, without beginning, without end, eternal, immutable, beyond nature is the Self," say the *Upanishads*.

There are degrees of illumination, and the traditional Eastern texts make clear the stages of development: from a fleeting, perhaps hazy glimpse of the transcendent, as might occur spontaneously or in meditation; to permanent Self-realization, in which the transcendent is a silent continuum behind all experience; to supreme enlightenment, in which the Self is known to be truly one with creation. Over time, the seeker comes to know that his true nature is the boundless Absolute, the ultimate constituent of all the changing objects and patterns we perceive around us. Admiral Richard Byrd, to use a contemporary, secular example, had a glimpse of this union: "In that instance I could feel no doubt of man's oneness with the universe. . . . It was a feeling that transcended reason; that went to the heart of man's despair and found it groundless. The universe as a cosmos, not

Chaos; man was as rightfully a part of that cosmos as were the day and night."

Western science has not, as yet, reached this understanding, and it never will if it sticks to the constricting ideology of scientism. The pickax of rationality can't penetrate the Self, and the yardstick of empiricism can't measure it. "You ask how can we know the infinite?" asked the third-century A.D. Egyptian philosopher Plotinus. "I answer, not by reason. It is the office of reason to distinguish and define. The infinite, therefore, cannot be ranked among its objects. You can only apprehend the infinite by a faculty superior to reason, by entering into a state in which you are your finite self no longer—in which the divine essence is communicated to you. This is ecstasy. It is the liberation of your mind from its finite consciousness."

Rational thought uses symbols like words or numbers, and symbols have meaning only in relationship to particular entities. Since it has no attributes, the Absolute can't be compared to anything; since it is all-pervasive, it can't be separated from anything. Immanuel Kant did the world a service by demonstrating that all the arduous attempts of philosophers and theologians to prove or disprove the existence of God or an Absolute were pointless; with equal plausibility, we can construct an argument for either position. What Kant did not understand was that the Absolute was nevertheless knowable. It is knowable not through reason—although it can be expounded upon and elucidated with reason—but by direct experience. This is not the objective, sensory experience with which we are familiar, however, but a direct intuitive union.

As the empiricist philosopher David Hume found out, it is even more futile to try knowing the Self through objective experience as it is to deduce it. "When I enter most intimately into what I call *myself*," wrote Hume, "I always stumble on some particular perception or other, of heat or cold, light or shade, love or hatred, pain or pleasure. I never catch *myself* at any time without a perception, and never can observe anything but a perception."

And so Hume, like most of us, concluded that he was "nothing but a bundle or collection of different perceptions, which succeed each other with an inconceivable rapidity, and are in a perpetual flux and movement." The problem, of course, is that the Self is not an object, and so it can't be known the way we know objects. There is nothing to separate from the knower. Trying to know the Self objectively would be like the eye trying to see the eye.

Illumination can be considered the highest form of knowing because it tells us what we are and what the cosmos is, and establishes a genuine union between the two. It is also the most satisfying form of knowing; the state of consciousness itself has been called bliss, or *ananda*. For these reasons, supreme enlightenment has always been depicted as the end of ignorance, of alienation, of suffering. Even to the most pragmatic reader it should be clear that illumination has its own rewards. But it also has practical relevance in regard to our other categories. It is referred to throughout the book because it is a model for understanding the how and why of garden-variety intuition. Transcendence can be viewed as the exemplar to which all other forms of intuition can be related.

Furthermore, transcendence itself has a transformative impact on consciousness; those who experience it say that it upgrades all cognitive faculties. It is something like being on the roof of a building and then, once familiar with that vista, finding that the view from lower floors is somehow different. The expanded perspective becomes a reference point. And the actual process of going to the roof makes it easier to gain access to the other floors because of an overall familiarity with the terrain. In some way, illumination opens other intuitive channels, which is one reason why yoga and traditional consciousness disciplines made it their first order of business.

Most of this book is concerned with the first five functions of intuition, but we will return from time to time to transcendence. In Chapter 6 we will speculate about why cultivating the highest state may be the best way to cultivate the others. And in the next chapter we will see how illumination embodies the most significant features of all intuitive experiences, leading us to wonder if everyday intuition isn't in some way a microcosm or simulation of enlightenment.

4

The Intuitive Experience

When I am, as it were, completely myself, entirely alone,
and of good cheer—say, travelling in a carriage, or walking
after a good meal, or during the night when I cannot sleep;
it is on such occasions that ideas flow best and most abun-
dantly. *Whence* and *how* they come, I know not; nor can
I force them.

—Wolfgang Amadeus Mozart

The quote above, from a letter written by Mozart, elucidates
some of the central features of intuition with the impelling economy
of one of the composer's quartets. Like other great artists, Mozart not
only had uncommonly sharp intuition, but was sensitive to the elusive
event itself. As we discuss the when and what of the intuitive experience, much of the material will be drawn from creators.

Although they vary with the circumstances and the individual,
there are common elements in intuitive experiences. Your own might
not be as dramatic as some of those recounted here, but the basic features probably apply. Understanding the basic themes and your own
unique variations will help you become more sensitive to your intuition and take steps to develop it.

INCUBATION: THE PAUSE
THAT ENLIGHTENS

As Mozart's letter suggests, intuitive breakthroughs tend to occur
when the creator is away from the work itself. Graham Wallas in his
1929 book, *The Art of Thought*, which outlined the stages of the

creative process, called this apparently fertile period "incubation." It typically follows sustained preliminary work, which Wallas labeled the "preparation" stage, and is in turn followed by stages of "illumination" (the intuitive breakthrough) and "verification." Mozart mentioned three common incubators: conveyances, solitary walks, and beds. The Poincaré discovery mentioned in the preceding chapter occurred on a bus. The nineteenth-century German physicist Hermann Helmholtz said that his inspirations would come during "the slow ascent of wooded hills on a sunny day." The philosophy of Jean-Jacques Rousseau came to him as a multitude of "truths" in a flash while walking from Paris to Vincennes in 1754. And numerous accounts of innovative thinkers and achievers give the impression that great ideas are as likely to be conceived in bed as children.

The list is long of people who awoke to new knowledge, had it delivered to them in a dream, or were seized by it as they lay about idly. Linus Pauling, for example, realized the shape of the protein molecule when, resting in bed, a string of paper dolls dangled from his hand in the shape of a helix. When Conrad Hilton wanted to buy the Stevens Corporation, which was going to the highest bidder in a closed-bid auction, he submitted a sealed bid for $165,000. But when he awakened the following morning, the number 180,000 was in his head, so he promptly changed the bid. He secured the property, which eventually brought him a $2-million profit, because the next highest bid was $179,800.

Kitchen rituals seem to have a certain fecundity, too. One oil company executive does the family dishes every night even though he has a dishwasher because he has his best ideas at that time. Bathroom ablutions also seem to work. So many inspirations have arisen during shaving (Einstein, for one, remarked on it) that one wonders why artists and scholars keep growing beards. The poet A. E. Housman wrote, "Experience has taught me, when I am shaving of a morning, to keep watch over my thoughts, because if a line of poetry strays into my memory, my skin bristles so that the razor ceases to act."

Psychologists have proposed several theories to explain incubation:

> Elimination of fatigue. Like other organisms, we are self-regenerating systems; we normalize ourselves when given the opportunity. Getting away from taxing work might refresh a tired mind just as it rejuvenates tired muscles, thus making it more receptive to intuitive impulses.

Stress reduction. The strain of hard work and the frustration of not having found an answer might cause anxiety. That would work against intuition, which functions most effectively in relaxed conditions. High levels of arousal in the nervous system have been found to inhibit creativity, and at least one study of intuitive problem solving found that subjects placed in a state of anxiety did not do as well as a low-arousal group.

Set breaking. In *The Art of Creation*, Arthur Koestler speculated that incubation allows the mind to discard the "tyranny" of discursive thinking habits: "This rebellion against constraints which are necessary to maintain the order and discipline of conventional thought, but an impediment to the creative leap, is symptomatic both of the genius and the crank; what distinguishes them is the intuitive guidance which only the former enjoys." Innovative thinking can be blocked by habitual ways of viewing a problem. We tend to get into mental ruts. An incubation period might break those patterns, freeing the mind to entertain new possibilities.

Selective forgetting. Psychologist Herbert Simon suggests that in the early stages of problem solving we form a plan, which gets stored in short-term memory. While working we acquire new, pertinent information that we might overlook because our minds are dominated by the original plan. But the new information gets stored in *long-term* memory, Simon believes, and might become activated during an incubation period, when ineffective old ideas are selectively forgotten.

Nonconscious synthesis. Unlike computers, the mind is capable of doing many things at once. While we are sleeping, walking in the woods, washing dishes, or shaving, important work is being done outside our awareness. The factory of the mind continues to work while the manager is out, assembling diverse raw materials and putting them together in unusual ways to create new products. This is what William James meant when he said that we learn to swim in winter and skate in summer.

Incidental input. Nonconscious synthesizing, some psychologists believe, might be aided during incubation by the perception of objects or events that are analogous to the problem under consideration. A scientist who notices similarities between wildly different objects or processes might pursue the metaphor to connections that yield fruitful hypotheses. New products are invented when someone sees a functional link between unrelated phenomena; Gutenberg's mind merged three unlikely elements—the wine press, the process of minting coins, and the stamping of playing cards—to come up with the concept of movable type. And it is said that Mozart thought of a cantata for *Don Giovanni* when he saw an orange, which reminded him of a popular Neapolitan song he'd heard five years earlier.

Each of these theories seems to have validity, and perhaps each process occurs simultaneously during incubation.

Because of a shortage of experimental evidence, however, not all psychologists accept incubation as a necessary prelude to inspiration. Many studies have found no incubation effect at all, and most studies that *have* demonstrated it have never been duplicated.

One reason for this is the unrealistic nature of the testing procedures. Typically, subjects are asked to solve a problem that requires insight. One group is given a break while another works straight through. The results of the two groups are then compared. The subjects are generally given only a short period of time to work on the problem before incubation, and the incubation period itself is brief, perhaps only ten or fifteen minutes. The subjects are told when to incubate, and the type of activity they engage in during the break is determined by the researchers. These activities vary from test to test —waiting in an empty room, doing another demanding task, actively reviewing the problem, and so forth—but they are all artificial and imposed. Then there is the question of the subjects themselves: they are usually college students fulfilling a course requirement or getting a small fee.

As Robert Olton and David Johnson, whose study showed no incubation effect, put it, " 'Real life' accounts of the phenomenon describe a profoundly motivated person, a time period that often lasts for days or months, and a task that involves the use of a *well-orchestrated, highly developed repertoire of cognitive skills and abilities* appropriate to a specific body of knowledge."

The anecdotal evidence—not just from great creators but from average people in all walks of life who have come to know the value of "sleeping on it"—is rather compelling. Without exception, the people I interviewed said that their most significant intuitive experiences came when they were away from their work. Despite the lack of experimental proof, a well-timed incubation period seems to be good bait for intuition, a theme whose practical implications we will return to in later chapters.

However, I have a different objection to the incubation model as it is normally defined: it does not explain all those intuitions that *don't* come during breaks in activity. The intuitive functions we have called evaluative and operative are likely to fall into this category. And sometimes a fertile discovery or creative solution pops into mind when we are busy working on the problem itself. The executive who comes up with unusual decisions in the midst of chaos, the musician who takes off in uncharted directions during a song, the mathematician who suddenly deciphers a puzzle while scribbling symbols on the blackboard, the lover who knows what his or her partner *really* means as they converse, the parent who knows why a child is crying while wiping away tears—all are examples of how intuition can arise during the activity it addresses.

The way we now understand incubation—as an extended period of time away from the relevant activity—will probably be modified. Whatever takes place during those long stretches of time might also occur instantaneously during microscopic diversions of attention. In a meeting, for example, while someone else is speaking, you might miss a word or two. While working intensely on a task, your mind might wander ever so slightly. Such lapses, which we usually deplore, might actually represent momentary incubations, enough of an interlude to set up the right conditions for intuition.

This idea can be taken a step further. The mind can work on several levels simultaneously, although strictly speaking attention is in only one place at a time. Quite possibly, while attending to one aspect of a problem, another part of the mind is, in effect, incubating. For example, the mathematician at the blackboard might be writing down material thought of a moment earlier; while engaged in that sensory-motor activity (which is virtually automatic for him) he might be talking to a colleague or a class. As he writes or speaks, segments of his mind might be otherwise engaged. An instant later a solution might pop into his mind. This isn't quite the incubation that Poincaré had when he went off to military service, but perhaps it works in the same way.

This should not seem at all outrageous, given the fact that we are always doing many things at once. While driving we hum tunes, watch traffic, listen to a companion, and more, simultaneously. And in the midst of all that, we might have an inspired hunch about a work problem or a relationship. If that can happen, why couldn't we be fully involved in a task and have an intuition about another aspect of the same task? Thought always precedes action, and some nonconscious activity must precede thought, so in a sense some component of the mind is always a step ahead of what we are thinking and doing at any given moment. In some cases, the equivalent of a fertile incubation period might be occurring, even though there is no incubation in the usual sense.

Perhaps the truly salient features of incubation are on the psychophysiological level. Incubation should probably be thought of as a state of mind or a specific quality of consciousness, the details of which future researchers might be able to discern. Anecdotal reports suggest that a calm inner condition, with low arousal and a low signal-to-noise ratio (meaning that the mind is relatively quiet and free of unnecessary "static"), might constitute the most favorable ground for intuitive experience. Perhaps some forms of incubation, in the traditional sense, produce these physiological conditions. Further, the same or similar conditions might coexist with other states at certain times, enabling intuition to occur during active or more highly aroused periods.

If an incubationlike condition is a necessary prelude to all types of intuition, as I believe it is, then knowing what goes on in the central nervous system at the time might help us free our intuitive faculties. We will come back to this question in a later chapter. Here let's examine the intuitive experience itself.

THE PARADOXES OF INTUITION

"*Whence* and *how* they come, I know not," wrote Mozart, "nor can I force them." Echoed by intuitive people in all fields, this remark suggests the spontaneity and effortlessness of intuition. Intuition comes on its own. Whether a trivial hunch, a pragmatic business decision, or a discovery in a laboratory, it has the same quality that Keats referred to when he wrote, "If poetry comes not naturally as leaves to a tree it had better not come at all." Bach expressed much the same idea in response to a question about where he found his melodies: "The problem is not finding them, it's—when getting up in the morning and getting out of bed—not stepping on them."

You can no more force intuition than you can force someone to fall in love with you. You can prepare yourself for it, invite it, and create attractive conditions to coax it, but you can't say, "Now I shall have an intuition," just as, in Shelley's words, "A man cannot say, 'I will compose poetry.' The greatest poet even cannot say it: for the mind is as a fading coal, which some invisible influence, like an inconstant wind, awakens to transitory brightness."

There is a surprising quality to the experience, as if the intuiter were a magician pulling knowledge out of his own hat, shocking himself. That might be one reason a fortuitous intuition often brings with it a feeling of glee; like children, we love to be tricked. We also like a good joke, and intuition often has the qualities of a punch line. We laugh when the comedian surprises us with an illogical conclusion to a story. Intuition can defy expectation by suddenly veering off in a new direction, rearranging the material we have been working with, or bringing in something that seems entirely out of place.

Not that every intuition has an unanticipated twist. It might suggest a predictable course of action or confirm the choice of a rather ordinary alternative. What might be surprising in such situations is that we feel far more certain than we have any reason to—or that the intuition appeared at all. Intuition can be like one of those friends who shows up at the oddest times, even though all attempts to get him to call ahead or keep an appointment are in vain. Whether it is its content, its degree of certitude, or its timing, something about intuition is usually surprising.

At the same time, just as an absurd punch line somehow "fits" the joke, the content of an intuition may elicit what psychologist Jerome Bruner calls "the shock of recognition," a certain obviousness that, as soon as the surprise wears off, makes us think, "Of course—how could I not have seen it?" From that point on, it might seem absurd that we ever did *not* know what we now know. Mathematicians who wrestle with conundrums for long periods of time say that once the puzzle is solved they cannot remember what it felt like not to know the answer.

A young woman named Terri related a similar experience with a career change: "I had been unsatisfied in my work for three years and felt a strong urge to do something more meaningful. But the only thing I could come up with as an alternative was 'helping people.' That and dancing, which was ridiculous, since my dance training had been suspended ten years earlier, and I wasn't about to resume at age thirty-two. Then it suddenly dawned on me: become a dance therapist! It was a total shock. But from that moment on, it seemed absurd that I ever considered anything else."

In a typical intuitive experience there is a sense of being a recipient as opposed to an initiator. Creative people often describe themselves as "agents" or "channels" for some other source. In a religious context this is known as being an instrument of the Divine, or having God work His will through you. Milton wrote that the Muse "dictated" to him the whole "unpremeditated song" that we know as *Paradise Lost*, and Bach said, "I play the notes in order, as they are written. It is God who makes the music." The more secular-oriented, like Joseph Heller, just say, "I feel that these ideas are floating around in the air and they pick me to settle upon. The ideas come to me; I don't produce them at will."

When the intuitive mind is working with particular fluency, the actions of hands, feet, and tongue seem to occur without deliberation or conscious thought. Athletes and musicians often say they can almost watch themselves perform as if they were in the audience. The great running back Hershel Walker said, "I surprise myself. I don't even know what I'm doing to do. I don't have real control. I'll start running and I don't know what's coming next." Try to convince his opponents that Walker doesn't know what he's doing.

Writers often experience what one described as being "part of the typewriter, trying to keep up with whatever is giving the orders." You commonly hear novelists and playwrights say that characters "take over," acting on their own, speaking dialogue, changing the plot irreversibly. Here is Henry James describing how he came up with the plot components of *The Ambassadors*: "These things continued to fall together, as by the neat action of their own weight and form, even while their commentator [James] scratched his head about them; he easily sees now that they were always well in advance of him. As the case completed itself he had, in fact, from a good way behind, to catch up with them, breathless and a little flurried as best he could."

This self-propelling quality of intuition should not be mistaken for the automaticity of habit or physical instinct. Routinely, we act without thinking through the steps, responding mechanically, with well-rehearsed patterns set in motion by an outside stimulus. A driver automatically swerves when a car cuts him off, an editor automatically corrects a spelling error, a mechanic automatically turns the right screw, a dentist automatically diagnoses a toothache. These acts are not the same as the sudden appearance of something new: the driver has a hunch to make a detour and finds a shortcut; the editor gets a great idea for reorganizing the book; the mechanic hits upon why a car won't start when no one else can figure it out; the dentist senses complications beyond the obvious diagnosis.

So it is that a fact might appear to be a message, a decision might seem to be a command, an idea might seem to be a gift. With intuition you, the magician, are surprised by the rabbit, which seems to be in the service of another, superior sorcerer.

Yet—another paradox—it is your hand pulling out the rabbit, and you feel deeply involved in the process. Again, artists embody the dramatic example. They typically report that, in addition to being a "channel," they are so absorbed with the objects of their imagination or the tools of their trade as to feel at one with them. As William Butler Yeats expressed it, they are "self-possessed in self-surrender" at the moment of revelation.

The attached, involved side of the equation recalls the "intimacy" discussed in Chapter 2, that sense of merging with the object of knowledge. The French philosopher Henri Bergson called intuition a "kind of intellectual sympathy by which one places oneself within an object in order to coincide with what is unique in it and consequently inseparable." By thus "entering into" the object, we can know it perfectly and absolutely, Bergson maintained. He contrasted this with intellectual analysis, which he called a "translation" and a "representation" in symbols.

Hence the intuitive experience contains contradictions: it is unexpected, but somehow fits; it comes from within, but at the same time from some unnameable *other*; we produce it, but it also seems to happen *to* us; we are involved but uninvolved, absorbed but detached.

THE HOLISTIC NATURE OF INTUITION

The word *holistic* has often been ascribed to intuition. It has been taken to mean that intuition gives knowledge of wholes as opposed to just parts. But that can be misleading because it focuses on *what* is known. It is difficult to determine whether something one knows is a whole or a part, since, as systems theory tells us, every part is a whole made up of smaller parts, and every whole is a part of a larger whole (cells are wholes that are parts of organs, which are parts of organisms, and so on). The only object of knowledge that can truly be called holistic can't really be called an object: the Absolute is wholeness itself; it contains everything and is contained in everything.

The actual holistic quality of intuition has to do with two things. It is axiomatic that a whole is greater than the sum of its parts. The parts and their sum can be discerned through rational analysis, but the *greater* can be apprehended only through intuition. It is experiential rather than conceptual, a realization and a feeling, an intimate identification with the wholeness, not an inference or a fact to be imparted verbally.

The second aspect of intuitive holism has to do with the experience that Mozart seemed to be referring to when he wrote, "Nor do I hear in my imagination the parts *successively* but I hear them, as it were, all at once." We think of intuition as a flash that comes and goes instantaneously. In that instant might be contained an extraordinary amount of information. If a picture is worth a thousand words, then an intuition might be worth a thousand pictures. It is like a train speeding past your field of vision: you don't see any details, just a blur accompanied by sounds—and yet in that instant you know, at the very least, that it was a train. Time seems to be compressed, and so, in some mysterious way, is meaning.

We normally experience and conceive of meaning in a linear fashion, as a sequence of symbols and concepts strung together. An intuitive experience, however, may contain no clear boundaries, no obvious demarcations, no sequential arrangement. It might contain the essence of the knowledge, the way a seed contains the essence of a tree, or it might contain some details; it might be a fragment of the whole, or almost complete. It will usually contain a richness of meaning that will take an eon to articulate compared to the time it took to apprehend.

FLASH IN THE MIND

Intuition is often so concentrated that it flashes by before we can seize it. We have all had the frustrating experience of having a solution dash past our awareness, leaving us to bemoan, "What was that? I had the answer!" It is like trying to capture a snowflake; as soon as it hits your warm hand it is no longer a snowflake. This sense of loss is what makes artists feel that what they produce is just a drop of water, not a snowflake. Said Shelley, "When composition begins, inspiration is already on the decline, and the most glorious poetry that has ever been communicated to the world is probably a feeble shadow of the original conception of the poet."

But that is not always the case. "The committing to paper is done quickly enough," Mozart's letter continues, "for everything is . . . already finished; and it rarely differs on paper from what it was in my imagination." Perhaps the difference is in the intuiter's ability to sustain the intuitive moment so that its features and its essential message can be clearly apprehended. The impact of an intuition may in some way be related to the clarity with which it is perceived, and the clarity may have something to do with extension in time, or with a kind of *suspension* of time. Look at this part of Mozart's letter: "My subject enlarges itself, becomes methodized and defined, and the whole, though it be long, stands almost complete and finished in my mind, so that I can survey it, like a fine picture or a beautiful statue, at a glance."

Initially, Mozart seems to be describing nothing more than good imagination. But his use of such phrases as "enlarges itself" and "becomes methodized" suggest that he is still an uninvolved witness. Sometimes the intuitive moment can be kept alive undiluted, as if the passing train were to slow down—or time were to stand still—enough for us to appreciate a face in the window or a sign on the side of the locomotive. This would not always be necessary, of course, but at times intuition might contain the germ of further knowledge or richer detail.

It is often advantageous to stretch intuition or hold it still for an instant longer. It is also advantageous to recapture at will the intuitive experience—not just to remember its essential features but to actually reenter the state in which it was captured. Many of us have to get back into the mood of the previous day's work in order to proceed with any continuity. This ability should grow as our intuitive capacities develop.

THE LANGUAGE OF INTUITION

Like thought in general, intuition can take on different forms. Every sense modality has corresponding mental properties. In fact, Indian philosophy maintains that every thought contains qualities associated with each of the senses, just as any material object could, if our senses were acute enough, be seen, heard, tasted, smelled, and touched.

That the mind can operate in each sensory mode is obvious from the common experience of memory. When recalling a particular event, you might, in your mind, hear a person speaking or a melody played; see a face or a scene; smell the jasmine; taste an apple pie as if it were in your mouth; feel the brush of wind or the touch of a hand on your skin. In the same way, some people can imagine objects they have never actually experienced.

The mind shifts from one modality to another just as we can shift our focus from one sense perception to another. Where the focus rests depends on both the situation and the propensities of the experiencer. We seem to prefer one way of perceiving over another. Painters, for example, might see things in a scene that a musician would not, whereas the musician might be tuned to the sounds around him. In a wooded clearing one person might focus on the feel of the grass underfoot, another on the scent in the air, and still another on the taste of a blackberry.

The same kind of propensities seem to hold in thought as well, and the form our intuition takes will usually correspond to these preferences. Some people tend to think in words, others more visually (these seem to be the predominate modes). There are situational variations, of course. No matter how visual a person normally is, he will think in words when deciding how to address the boss. A verbal person will think in visual images when deciding how to decorate a room.

It is often said that rational thought is verbal and intuition is nonverbal. Like many declarations about intuition, this one has some validity but is overstated. I for one frequently have intuitions in linguistic form; when writing, the right word or phrase might pop spontaneously to mind. In routine instances, this might be attributed to memory, as if my mind had scanned some stored vocabulary list. But when the product is an unusual phrase or an imaginative combination of words, it is every bit as intuitive as a business hunch or scientific discovery.

When Samuel Taylor Coleridge awoke with the "distinct recollection of the whole" of "Kubla Khan," the famous unfinished poem that composed itself in a dream, "all the images rose up before him as *things*," he said, speaking of himself in third person. But the words were also there. Coleridge said there was "a parallel production of the correspondent expressions without any sensation or consciousness of effort."

It is not just writers, however, to whom intuition comes in verbal form. Others refer to inner messages as coming to them in explicit language. For example, a psychotherapist said that when working with a particular patient the word "father" kept popping into her mind, although at the time the patient was discussing a problem with her job. Finally the psychologist yielded to the persistent voice and said, "Tell me about your father." It turned out that the patient's boss reminded her of her father, who had raped her when she was a teenager, a crucial bit of suppressed information.

Thus while it is frequently nonverbal, intuition can speak our language without losing its essential character. Similarly, while we normally reason verbally, this is not always the case. Psychological instruments that test reasoning ability often use sequences of pictures, not words. For example, a comic-strip artist or filmmaker works with logical sequences of images. A composer reasons with pure sound. When we manipulate objects in space, including our own bodies, we might be reasoning spatially without verbally constructing each proposition.

On the other hand, intuition will often come in visual images, particularly when the subject matter calls for it, as in art or architecture. An electronics technician said, "On the train home or in the middle of the night I might suddenly see before me in minute detail a wiring diagram that I had been working on that day. Sometimes key connections are moved around, solving a problem that had been driving me crazy." His account is reminiscent of the experiences of Nikola Tesla, the inventor of, among other things, the AC generator and fluorescent lighting. Tesla said that he was capable of such minutely detailed visions that he could actually perform "tests" by mentally running machines for weeks and then looking for signs of wear.

The intuition of scientists can often be as visual as that of poets and painters. One of the most interesting visual intuiters—and one of the more important—was the nineteenth-century British physicist Michael Faraday. Among other things, Faraday developed the first dynamo and electric motor, ideas that originated in his mental vision of the universe as a composite of curved tubes through which energy radiated. Faraday also laid the foundations of modern field theory with ideas that developed out of his images of "lines of forces" surrounding magnets and electric currents.

Other examples of predominantly visual intuitions include that of Mendeleev awakening with the image, virtually in its entirety, of the Periodic Table of Elements that now adorns chemistry classrooms all over the world. And of course there is the famous dream of Friedrich August von Kekulé:

> I turned my chair to the fire and dozed. . . . Again the atoms were gambolling before my eyes. This time the smaller groups kept modestly in the background. My mental eye, rendered more acute by repeated visions of this kind, could now distinguish larger structures, of manifold conformation; long rows, sometimes more closely fitted together; all twining and twisting in snakelike motion. But look! What was that? One of the snakes had seized hold of its own tail, and the form whirled mockingly before my eyes. As if by a flash of lightning, I awoke. . . . Let us learn to dream, gentlemen.

In this way did Kekulé discover a revolutionary idea that was to become a cornerstone of modern chemistry: the molecules of certain organic compounds are not open structures but closed rings.

Kekulé's vision brings up an interesting point: intuition is often symbolic. Carl Jung tells us that a snake biting its own tail is a universal symbol that has taken on different meanings in different cultures. It is not clear how Kekule knew the snake referred to his laboratory work rather than to something else. Sometimes the meaning is obvious, but at other times it has to be figured out, which might require additional intuitive input as well as analysis. This holds not just for visual images but for any intuitive message. In a remote-viewing test performed at Stanford, subjects in a lab were asked to describe the location of another person. Their hunches were remarkably accurate, but often misinterpreted. For example, they might feel the presence of an "august" or "solemn" building and say it was a library when it was actually a church.

At times the verbal and visual modalities are combined. Coleridge saw the images *and* heard the words to "Kubla Khan." When I had the idea to write this book, what came to me was an image of a bulging file folder filled with an eclectic assortment of notes and clippings. I had been accumulating material for a book, but I could never figure out what the book would be about. When the realization came, I saw that folder, accompanied by some subtle sense of the word *intuition*. I can't even be sure it was a sound, but the meaning was clear.

In a survey of mathematicians, Jacques Hadamard found that most of them think visually—although not necessarily in mathematical symbols—but also kinetically. Einstein's reply was: "The words or the language, as they are written or spoken, do not seem to play any role in my mechanism of thought; the physical entities which seem to serve as elements in thought are certain signs and more or less clear images which can be 'voluntarily' reproduced and combined. . . . The above-mentioned elements are, in my case, of visual and some of muscular type. Conventional words or other signs have to be thought for laboriously only in a secondary stage."

The word *muscular* is clearly an indication of the involvement of a kinesthetic element, which is probably mediated by the sense of touch. Einstein added that vague "combinatory play" with these elements is the "essential feature in productive thought—before there is any connection with logical construction in words or other kinds of signs which can be communicated to others."

As expressions like "I felt it in my bones" and "I had a gut feeling" indicate, physical sensations are often associated with intuition. Often they are global feelings that seem to radiate all over. People describe them as a "glow," a "burning sensation," a "cold chill," "tingling," or "electricity running through me." Sometimes they are localized and can be pinpointed with precision. Describing what happens when a line of poetry comes to him, A. E. Housman wrote that his skin bristled. He added: "This particular symptom is accompanied by a shiver down the spine: there is another which consists of a constriction in the throat and a precipitation of water to the eyes; and there is a third which I can only describe by borrowing a phrase from one of Keats's last letters, where he says, speaking of Fanny Brawne, 'everything that reminds me of her goes through me like a spear.' The seat of this sensation is the pit of the stomach."

Eugene Gendlin, a psychologist/philosopher whose research on people undergoing psychotherapy led to the technique and book called *Focusing*, found that successful patients were those who were able to derive meaning from what he terms "the felt sense"—what the body knows of a particular situation or problem. This "fuzzy, murky" sense, Gendlin found, seems to occur around the middle of the body, along the central axis, anywhere from the navel to the throat, and most often the stomach. This could possibly have something to do with the subtle energy centers called *chakras* that Indian philosophy places at seven points along the spinal column. In any event, the experience of knowing does not seem to be confined to the head. I am reminded of the Zen story in which a monk is asked where he thinks: he points to his stomach.

Physical sensations can interact with intuition in several ways. They might, for example, be raw data that provide information about the body itself. Someone who is sensitive to bodily signals might intuit the presence of a disorder before it can be diagnosed through ordinary methods, or he might know precisely what foods to eat. Here is an example of a good hunch precipitated by the body: A salesman was bothered for some time by a shooting pain in his left leg, especially when he sat. On his way to see a physician, his leg in pain, he had a sudden flash and knew what the problem was: sitting on a wallet bulging with credit cards. The skeptical doctor checked for everything else but found nothing. A switch of pockets was the cure.

As an intermediary between the environment and the intuitive mind, the body might provide behavioral instructions. Sudden muscular tension, a quickened pulse, or a fluttering sensation in the stomach might alert you to a real danger—the equivalent of "Don't believe a word this guy says" or "Get out of this place fast." Quite often there will be no discernible message, just a strong physical urge that is difficult to resist. A female executive tells this story: "I entered the lobby of a building and got on an elevator. A man stepped on behind me. Just before the doors closed, I felt impelled to leave, as if I were being swept back into the lobby by an outside force. I went into a phone booth, and while I was dialing the man stepped out of the same elevator. That was the first time I was consciously suspicious. Sure enough, the guy waited in the lobby until another woman got on an elevator alone. He was apprehended and turned out to have a record."

Physical sensations are not always warnings, of course. They also accompany positive feelings, such as comfort in the presence of a particular person. They might also alert us to an impending intuitive experience. Quite often there is a kind of halo, an intimation that precedes intuition. Unlike a trumpet-blowing herald, this intimation might be just a faint body sense, some barely perceptible shift in how you feel, like a small child tugging at your sleeve. A receptive person will pay attention instead of trudging on to some other concern and thus missing the intuition entirely. Think of it as hunting: when you pick up the scent of your prey, or hear rustling in the underbrush, you freeze, taking care not to frighten it away.

Bodily sensations might also be part of the feedback loop that helps us evaluate a particular intuition. A decision, a solution, or an operative prompting might be accompanied by a perceptible physiological change. The strength, persistence, and quality of the feeling might be a clue to how seriously to take the mental content. Frances Vaughan quotes physicist Carson Jeffries, who noted that when a sudden spark of insight is true it gives him " a warm, sensual body pleasure." He said he could tell when an idea was good because "it excited me and made me happy."

It would seem that part of becoming more intuitive would be an ability to recognize and decipher the body's messages. This requires a certain sensitivity and a good deal of self-awareness. There are no rules for interpreting bodily sensations in this regard; they are strictly individual matters that can be sorted out with repeated experience. The signals are often quite subtle, reaching awareness only when they exceed a certain threshold of intensity. Also, it is easy to attach too much cognitive significance to them. Much has been made of the connection between intuition and the body, and we have to be wary of overdoing it. Some people go so far as to suggest that intuition *is* body awareness, and that *the* way to be more intuitive is to "get in touch with your body," as if flesh and blood were the exclusive repositories of wisdom. It is important to acknowledge that the body contains information and transmits messages, but we should not elevate every physical impulse to the level of an epiphany.

The verbal, visual, and kinesthetic forms we have discussed are the most common ways intuition is expressed *when it is vivid*. Most of the time, however, it is difficult to categorize the form. People get flustered when pressed for a description and end up saying, "It was just a thought" or "It was a feeling." Typically, such responses seem unsatisfactory; we feel we ought to be able to describe the experience more objectively. But the fact is that intuition *is* thought, and thought is frequently a faint, ephemeral, smoky abstraction that can only be described as a feeling.

There is good reason to believe that thought originates in a more abstract, feelinglike form and takes on concrete, symbolic qualities in a subsequent state of development, particularly when communication is necessary. The feeling level is actually deeper and closer to the source than the more tangible manifestations of sound, sight, and touch. This would seem true of ordinary speech: first you know something, then you find words to convey that meaning, and sometimes there is no way to capture it adequately. A flustered TV character once said of a garbled statement, "You should have heard it before I said it." We might speculate that many intuitions appearing in a specific form, especially a verbal form, are actually adulterated versions of the original, and perhaps some depth of meaning or emotion has thereby been sacrificed.

This is important to keep in mind; often when we have an intimation of intuition, or some faint feeling, we try to force it into a palpable structure, usually a verbal message, even though doing so might create distortions by filtering it through layers of other psychic content. Those faint feelings are actually a deeper, purer level of mind than verbal, visual, or kinetic modes. Part of cultivating intuition, therefore, might entail learning to tune into earlier developmental stages of the impulses, a notion we will return to in subsequent chapters.

THE EMOTIONS OF KNOWING

As the use of "feeling" to indicate both an emotion and a physical event suggests, there is a strong connection between the two realms of experience. Perhaps both are mediated by the sense of touch. As with bodily signals, emotions may be the subject matter of intuition (or of rational analysis, for that matter), as when you have an insight into why you have been feeling sad, restless, or sentimental. They might also be clues that feed data about the environment to intuition—you get a positive, happy feeling about a prospective employee and hire him even though he is less qualified than the candidate who made you feel hostile. You can't figure out why you get uncomfortable when you're with a certain person, and you suddenly realize he is keeping something from you. Or an emotion might be a simultaneous expression of an intuition, a clue to its meaning or veracity. That is the context in which we will discuss it here.

Knowing feels good. There is a certain tension created by ignorance, an incompleteness in an unresolved problem. This has physiological and emotional counterparts. When the answer comes, there is a feeling of restoration. Wholeness is restored, and that feels comfortable, like filling in a circle that had a missing section. This might precipitate a sense of exhilaration, joy, or overpowering ecstasy, often accompanied by a burst of energy or heightened sense perception.

In *The Courage to Create*, psychologist Rollo May discusses a sudden breakthrough: "The moment the insight broke through, there was a special translucence that enveloped the world, and my vision was given a special clarity. . . . The world, both inwardly and outwardly, takes on an intensity that may be momentarily overwhelming." He also writes, "I experience a strange lightness in my step as though a great load were taken off my shoulders, a sense of joy on a deeper level that continues without any relation whatever to the mundane tasks that I may be performing at the time."

They are not always so powerful, of course, but the emotional correlates of accurate and important intuitions seem to center around happiness, harmony, and beauty. It is often said that suffering is necessary in order to create. The fabled cases of suffering artists, however, reveal that anguish and misery came when for one reason or another they could *not* create. It is a dramatic expression of the tension, frustration, and sense of incompleteness that accompanies ignorance. When actually creating, those suffering artists were in bliss, a heightened version of the rapture you or I might feel when we come to a realization about a person or problem. Mozart, who suffered intensely, wrote of the intuitive inspiration, "All this fires my soul," and in the same paragraph, "What a delight this is I cannot tell! All this inventing, this producing, takes place in a pleasing lively dream."

One of the central emotions of intuition, and a major clue to the quality of the revelation, is a sense of esthetic pleasure. As Keats wrote, "Beauty is truth, truth beauty." That sense of beauty and harmony informs artist, scientist, businessman, and lover alike. Something in true intuition elicits the same response as a painting, a song, or the resolution of a well-told tale. It has a certain symmetry and coherence, a sense of balance and inevitability. When an idea doesn't quite fit it is like a dab of the wrong color on a painting or the wrong line of dialogue in a play. It projects dissonance.

When people are asked how they can distinguish the exceptional intuition from the mediocre, it is beauty that comes up consistently. Paul Dirac, who predicted the existence of antimatter two years before it was proven, wrote, "It seems that if one is working from the point of view of getting beauty into one's equations, and if one has really a sound insight, one is on a sure line of progress." Writing in *Newsweek*, Horace Freeland Judson recalls asking Dirac how he recognizes beauty in a theory. "Well—you feel it," Dirac answered. "Just like beauty in a picture or beauty in music. You can't describe it, it's something—and if you don't feel it, you just have to accept that you're not susceptible to it. No one can explain it to you."

Henri Poincaré felt that exceptional mathematicians, those who become creators, are capable of an "intuition of mathematical order that makes us divine hidden harmonies and relations." Like other mathematicians, he spoke of the elegance created by mathematical entities "whose elements are harmoniously disposed so that the mind without effort can embrace their totality."

Despite a great deal of opposition, Johannes Kepler held to his revolutionary astronomy because, he wrote, "I have attested to it as true in my deepest soul and I contemplate its beauty with incredible and ravishing delight." As in art, simplicity seems to be a key to the esthetic of truth. According to the contemporary physicist Richard Feynman, we are able to recognize scientific truth by its simplicity and beauty: "What is it about nature that lets this happen, that it is possible to guess from one part what the rest is going to do? . . . I think it is because nature has a simplicity and therefore a great beauty." For that reason, scientists are trained to look for the simplest hypotheses consistent with the facts.

What is most intriguing about this connection between beauty and knowledge—and its relation to the day-to-day reality of making decisions and solving problems—is that the same qualities are associated with practicality. Rollo May said of psychotherapy, "Insights emerge not chiefly because they are 'rationally true' or even helpful, but because they have a certain form, the form that is beautiful because it completes an incomplete Gestalt." Perhaps the executive's declaration of "Beautiful!" when he hears a good idea has something to do with Poincaré's most telling remark about mathematics: "The useful combinations are precisely the most beautiful."

THE TRANSCENDENTAL EXEMPLAR

In the preceding chapter, I suggested that illumination, or transcendence, is a prototype of the more familiar varieties of intuition, and that it might serve as an explanatory model. Let's look at it in terms of the characteristics we have discussed in this chapter.

Spiritual disciplines have made a way of life of what we call incubation. Seekers who adopt the path of the recluse renounce worldly affairs for a monastic way, which can be regarded as one long incubation. Those who follow the householder path incorporate periods of incubation into their routines—daily meditations, rituals, secluded retreats. The phase of conscious work that precedes classical incubation can be likened to that portion of the seeker's pursuit when he studies sacred texts, ponders eternal riddles, performs service, listens to learned discourses, and so forth. But it is during the incubatory phases that illumination occurs. Indeed, it could be said that transcendence itself is the ultimate incubation, since it leaves behind even mental activity.

From what we know of the physiology of meditation, transcendence is a state of least excitation, of deep inner silence, along with heightened alertness. This corresponds to the postulated physiology of incubation. And, as the seeker progresses, the core of inner silence is maintained along with thought and action; this is reminiscent of the proposed incubatory state that can coexist with focused mental activity. Perhaps some physiological configuration accounts for the ability to prolong the intuitive moment as well as the range of illumination, which can be experienced as anything from a fleeting glimpse of pure awareness to the permanent awakening of enlightenment.

Despite the arduous discipline associated with mysticism, illumination itself is effortless and spontaneous. As is true with artists, despair is often the lot of seekers, but that is the passionate agony of frustration and restless anticipation. Illumination itself simply occurs, when it occurs, and is described as grace—a divine gift. It arrives like a bud in springtime, but without the predictability, when the seeker is adequately prepared. In fact, as with artistic inspiration and the everyday hunch, transcendence is actually inhibited by too much effort, and seekers are exhorted to "try without trying."

Like ordinary intuition, illumination has a paradoxical quality. It is an "inner" event, and yet it seems to descend like an offering from an outside source. As the seeker advances and the pure, undifferentiated Self is increasingly realized, he might experience the twin sense of being separate from his thoughts and actions—as if silently witnessing them—and at the same time in full control. He will apprehend both the changing, localized self and the universal, boundless Self; he will perceive the world as both part of him and apart from him; he will see reality as the One and the Many. These paradoxes cannot be resolved rationally, but are reconciled by the intuitive experience of illumination.

The holistic quality of intuition—the concentration of vast knowledge into a single instant—and the intimate union with what is known are both exemplified in illumination. There is no *object* of knowledge as such, but in that state the knower is one with all that is. When the experience is vivid, mystics have reported, they feel that they "know everything," and this is accompanied by a sense of perfect simplicity (nothing could be simpler than that which has no duality) along with undiluted certainty. In the *Paradiso*, Dante described it this way: "Within its deep infinity I saw ingathered, and bound by love in one volume, the scattered leaves of all the universe."

Not much can be said about the language of illumination, since transcendence is beyond form, sensation, and symbol. Upon emerging from the experience, however, floods of images and words have been known to erupt, giving us immortal poetry, hymns, sacred books, and other expressions of divine revelation. This sequence from pure, content-free knowing to individuated expression is parallel to ordinary intuition, in which wordless, imageless feelings might quickly translate to form and substance. Illumination is also beyond emotional states. But the surges of ecstasy, happiness, calm, and energy that have been associated with intuitive inspirations of all kinds are reported in stellar form by the illumined. This can be attributed to certain properties of the Absolute, which are variously described as pure and unmanifest energy, concentrated universal love, absolute peace, and *ananda*, or bliss.

Special attention is drawn to these parallels to support the contention that all intuitive experiences can be viewed as microcosms of the highest intuition, that of mystical union. Ordinary intuition is, in some way, a special case of transcendence. The practical implications of this will be discussed in Chapters 7 and 8.

PERSONAL REFLECTION

To help make the material in this chapter personally meaningful, you might want to reflect on the hallmarks of intuition in light of your own experience. Think back to your most memorable intuitions.

Did they tend to come when you were involved in the subject of the intuition or when you were engaged in something else?
Did they come during restful, relaxed moments?
Did they come spontaneously, as though they were delivered to you?
Were they surprising in content, form, or timing?
Have you ever *tried* to be intuitive? Did it work?
Are your intuitions generally flashes or are they sustained, as in a reverie?
Are they detailed or a patterned sense of a whole?
Do you normally think in words or images? Are most of your intuitions the same?
Can you recall physical sensations and emotions associated with the intuitions?

5

Who Is Intuitive?

The obvious answer to this question is, "Everybody." We are all intuitive. Yet some people seem to be more so than others. They are right every time; they make the smartest decisions and solve the most intractable problems without much ado. If everyone is intuitive, it is tempting to call them "very intuitive" or "exceptionally intuitive."

"Who is intuitive?" is an interesting question, as likely to start an argument as "Was that experience intuition?" It is an important question, too. Intuitive people are valuable commodities, particularly in certain situations—where problems are not clearly defined and the method of approach can't be structured in advance, where the information base is small and uncertainty is high. Weston Agor, a public-administration professor at the University of Texas, El Paso, believes that intuitive decision makers are especially effective when new trends are emerging, when interpersonal judgment is valued, and when it is necessary to challenge assumptions. Agor would like to see organizations single out intuitive people for certain roles and team them with colleagues whose analytic talents are complementary.

The question has personal relevance as well. No doubt you have already determined whether you are intuitive, and you are probably hoping for confirmation from this chapter. You should be closer to an answer by the end of the chapter, but some of the information may surprise you, and along the way you may find that it is not an easy question to answer. For one thing, self-assessments and appearances can be deceiving, as the following stories illustrate.

George has been an entrepreneur ever since he shined the shoes of soldiers during World War II. With no formal training, just a high school education and a barrel of street smarts, he has managed a string of successful businesses over the past thirty years. Mutual friends had told me that George was an uncanny hunch player, so I interviewed him in the handsome offices of his latest successful enterprise. He began by telling me he was not a very intuitive person. We discussed his current venture, which is now being franchised. One of George's functions is to decide who gets a franchise. I asked him how he makes those decisions.

"The applicant has to have sound financing and some management experience," he said.

"Is that all?"

"No, he has to have . . . well, the right stuff."

"How do you determine that?" I asked.

"I can tell you in less than a minute if the guy's got it." George paused, looked at me quizzically, and said, "Is that intuition?"

Contrast that with John, a philosopher. Trained in mathematics, he is known for his orderly, systematic, impeccably logical arguments. Colleagues say that if John is on the other side of a disagreement you have your hands full. He was the last person I would have thought of as intuitive. Yet he told me, "I've always been extremely intuitive. My mind is always making wild leaps that turn out right."

When I reminded him of his reputation as a quintessentially rational thinker, he said, "I've learned to construct arguments. But they always come afterward."

INTUITION CAN BE CIRCUMSTANTIAL

One factor than can taint the picture is ideology. Jack might believe in intuition and accept it as a legitimate and valuable way of knowing. He plays up his own intuition, even brags about it. On the other hand, Jill has a strong rational-empirical ideology and belittles the value of intuition. The two minds might work in virtually the same way, but in describing his method of operation Jack emphasizes his acute intuitive skills, while Jill stresses her superior logic, her ability to organize and analyze data, which Jack considers derogatory. Jill says she figured it out; Jack says he "flashed on it."

Then there is the related question of social milieu. In certain circles you would not brag about being intuitive; in others, intuition is a badge of honor. Several scientists and executives have confided that they value their intuition highly but never mention it to colleagues. "Before I commit myself," one told me, "I gather all the data I can and describe my proposition so as to make it appear logically derived." In many spiritual and artistic communities, people express mundane observations and deductions so as to make themselves appear to have esoteric powers.

We must also consider the context. Someone who is especially intuitive in one domain might not be so in others. The intuitive physician might bungle his personal finances by following consistently bad hunches about investments. The intuitive personnel director who never hires the wrong person might create catastrophes by misjudging lovers and friends. The intuitive mathematician who awes academic colleagues may be way out of touch with his inner needs and motivations. Even psychics who pride themselves on their intuitive abilities have their specialties: diagnosing illness, predicting the future, uncovering the past, and so forth.

Individual and situational differences can be explained in part by experience. We acquire fluency in an area by internalizing certain activities and making them automatic. Novices have to pay attention to each little detail, just as we have to concentrate on every step when learning a new dance. Veterans don't have to attend to minutiae, so their minds are free to dart about making intuitive leaps.

Paul E. Johnson, a psychologist at the University of Minnesota, has studied expert physicians, engineers, lawyers, and commodity traders. He found that they are faster and better than beginners at solving problems in their fields and that they usually can't explain how they do it. "It just comes to me," is a typical response. Johnson found that, over time, experts make subtle refinements in their formal training. They acquire a "high-altitude overview" that tells them what information to gather and what to ignore, along with "specifically tailored tricks" that link information in nonobvious ways. Johnson believes that these factors create the kind of automatism that fosters creativity.

The experience factor is often used to explain away intuition. In fact, George, the entrepreneur attributed his own savvy to "learning from experience." But that does not explain why two people with equal experience and the same degree of professional training will differ radically in the quality of intuition and their inclination to use it.

Expertise can actually work against intuition, because it can make us overly dependent on a particular frame of reference or on a stylized, orthodox approach. Old hands often suffer from what psychologists call "problem set," habitually dealing with problems in ways that worked in the past. Thus the internalized operations that can free an experienced person to skip steps and make quick connections may also inhibit the kind of intuition needed to deal with novelty and ambiguity. Fresh, nonhabituated minds are often the most innovative because they dare to question assumptions and ask ridiculous questions.

Other circumstances can make us seem more or less intuitive. Intuition seems to work best when we are highly motivated, confident, and deeply involved in the subject matter. You are more likely to have an intuitive insight about your spouse than you are about an acquaintance, or about a major professional commitment as opposed to a casual hobby. This is because we are constantly asking ourselves questions about people and situations that are important to us, and the intuitive mind is programmed by the desires and goals we communicate to it.

Circumstances also affect how we respond to intuition. Most people notice that there are times when they welcome their intuitions and are willing to heed them. At other times they force themselves to be rational and are circumspect about their intuitive impulses. There are many reasons for this. One is confidence; we tend to have more faith in our inner voices in some situations than we do in others, perhaps depending on our level of experience and familiarity. Perhaps a more important factor is risk. Trusting in our intuition implies a willingness to take risks with the unprovable products of our own minds. When the stakes are high, someone who would normally act intuitively might adopt a more conservative, hesitant strategy, searching for facts and reasons before acting. Unfortunately, taken to extreme, this attitude can backfire, stifling intuition when it is needed most, and causing us to reject intuitions that should be heeded.

Executives have noticed that their readiness to heed their intuition depends on several variables: how much money is at stake, whether a wrong decision will affect their jobs or personal reputations, and the impact of the decision on other people. Interestingly, money does not seem to be as important as the other two factors. According to Ralph Keyes, author of a forthcoming book on risk taking, looking foolish or being humiliated is, to most people, the biggest risk of all. Keyes feels that many executives gather hard data not so much to help them make decisions but to obtain support for an intuitive idea and to defend themselves in case it doesn't pan out. Along the same lines, a study by social psychologist George Cvetkovich found that, in the researcher's words, "decision makers shift to a form of thinking that is analytic and easily described to another person when they believe that they are personally accountable for their judgments. In contrast, persons making judgments for themselves or for someone not having a legitimate reason to question their thinking . . . evidently shift to a form of thinking that is rapid, 'intuitive,' and difficult to describe."

But the potential impact of the intuition on others may be the most important factor of all. Most of the decision makers I interviewed said that when a colleague or loved one stands to be hurt by a wrong decision or a misguided solution to a problem, they tend to become very cautious and excessively analytic.

MATTERS OF STYLE AND SUBSTANCE

When we ask the question "Who is intuitive?" do we mean who functions intuitively or whose intuition is better? The distinction between style and substance is crucial.

As was mentioned earlier, problem-solving studies often distinguish between two modes of functioning: one is relatively loose and flexible, while the other is more orderly and is usually labeled rational or analytic. Psychologists James McKenney and Peter Keen, of Harvard and Stanford, respectively, find that persons whom they call systematic thinkers tend to begin by explicitly defining the problem and deciding exactly how it should be solved. They are conscious of planning, conduct an orderly search for information, and increasingly refine their analysis as they aim for predictability and a minimum of uncertainty.

Intuitive problem solvers, by contrast, avoid committing themselves to a particular strategy. They act without articulating their premises or procedures, and they enjoy playing with unknowns in order to get a feel for what is required. While they are considering a number of alternatives and options simultaneously, intuitive thinkers keep the overall problem continuously in mind. They tend to jump in and try something, and then switch to another method or a new definition of the problem if it doesn't work out.

But intuitive *style* and intuitive *quality* are two different things. Someone who functions intuitively might simply be a wild guesser or a disorganized, lazy thinker. On the other hand, someone like John, the philosopher described earlier, might approach a problem in a very systematic, orderly manner but still bring a sharp intuitive sense to bear within that context. Such a person might seem nonintuitive because he is trained to communicate a certain way, because he is conservative in evaluating intuitions once they arise, or because the particular situation demands precision. Two accountants or statisticians, for example, might take the same systematic approach to a particular task but, when the information is in, one of them might intuit a meaning in it that the other does not. As advertising executive Joan Rothberg put it, "Some people know how to make the numbers dance."

With an intuitive stylist, we must take into account how often the approach pays off. Validity and accuracy are the only ways to gauge quality, although consistency is also a crucial consideration. Some people are erratic, amazingly intuitive sometimes and miles off target at other times.

Despite these caveats, intuitive stylists probably do have higher-quality intuition, on the average, and so would people who believe in and value intuition. There is a circular relationship among values, style, and intuitive ability. For example, someone might come to value intuition for social or ideological reasons and as a result might begin to function in a more intuitive mode. This alone should improve the quality of his intuition, since half the battle is becoming more confident in it and more sensitive to its nuances.

Psychic researchers have found that belief and willingness definitely affect performance. Russell Targ and Harold Puthoff of the Stanford Research Institute had been conducting remote-viewing experiments with acknowledged psychics when they decided to see how ordinary people compared with their subjects. They found that nonpsychics could become just as adept in a short period of time. "What seemed to be important," the researchers noted, "was a general willingness and openness to exploring in greater depth some of the faint images and hunches that often pop up in the mind which we ordinarily might reject as spurious or irrelevant."

Alternatively, the cycle might begin with a tendency to function in an intuitive mode that is either innate or acquired, perhaps by following the example of a teacher or mentor. Success might then lead to stronger convictions about intuition, greater faith in it, and more awareness of it. This in turn would improve the quality of the intuition, which would reinforce the tendency to choose an intuitive approach, and so forth.

For these reasons, in the absence of a definitive way to judge the quality of intuition, a certain style might be a reasonable barometer, and so would confidence and belief.

STEREOTYPES OR INTUITIVES?

Certain types, or categories, of humanity are often portrayed as exceptionally intuitive: women, Easterners, and people from nonindustrial cultures. One might argue that there are innate differences in mental styles and abilities, a view that can be interpreted in one of two ways, depending on the point of view: either some groups are inherently gifted with intuitive power or they are inferior when it comes to rational thought. Most people would argue for a cultural interpretation, which does indeed seem more plausible. It strikes me as significant that these allegedly intuitive groups have certain things in common. They are relatively powerless—some might even say oppressed—and they are often treated as if they were members of yet another group that is thought of as intuitive: children.

Certainly this has something to do with the fact that the dominant value structure of white, male, adult Westerners is rational empiricism. Perhaps, because their natural intuitive ability is undervalued, some other groups are treated as inferior. Or perhaps, because of their social status, some groups do not have the opportunity to develop and use their objective, analytic skills and so have either *become* more intuitive or are *perceived* as more intuitive. These and similar questions—for example, do they have better intuition, or do they function with an intuitive style?—make this a difficult and provocative area. Let's explore it more deeply.

WOMAN'S INTUITION

Nick and Nora go to a party where they meet some new people. On their way home, Nick says, "The Carters are a great couple, aren't they?"

"I liked them," says Nora, "but I think their marriage is in trouble."

"Nonsense, they're terrific. I may do some business with Carter."

"I wouldn't trust him," says Nora.

Later, it turns out that Nora was right on all counts. And so, through such common experiences, the folklore of feminine intuition is reinforced.

It goes back a long way. You will often see the words *feminine* and *intuitive* under the ancient Taoist symbol of yin, which represents the soft, yielding, receptive, passive, inner side of nature. Under yang, the hard, dynamic, active, dominant side, you will see *masculine* and *logical.* This seems to lend authenticity to the labels, giving them the sanction of antiquity and cosmic order. And, indeed, there *is* something yinlike about intuition. But is it true that women are really more intuitive than men? And if they are, is it a biologically determined trait or a culturally acquired one?

Direct attempts to study this matter have been inconclusive, mainly because it is so difficult to measure intuition. As for style, some problem-solving studies have found women to be more intuitive; others have found the opposite. A look at gender differences on performance and behavior measures might indirectly shed some light on the question.

Research strongly suggests that men do better on tests of spatial visualization—dealing with maps, mazes, and three-dimensional objects—and at mathematical reasoning, particularly when it involves spatial organization, as in geometry. When solving problems, men focus more narrowly and are less dependent on situational variables. Women, by contrast, are more sensitive to context; they pick up peripheral information not directly related to the task at hand. Women process information faster, are better at understanding nonverbal information and reading facial expressions, and are more sensitive to slight variations in sound and odor.

If, as the evidence suggests, women are more receptive to peripheral and subliminal material, they might acquire more of the raw material that the mind processes into an intuitive insight. The male orientation to tangible objects, which seems to begin in infancy, might predispose them to a rational, quantitative style of thought, since material objects can be dealt with in that manner. This might explain the party scene; although she was unaware of them, Nora picked up on subtle cues that did not even register subliminally with Nick. It might also help explain why, when driving through a strange city, a woman might later remember the attractive restaurant they passed or respond to the mood of the environment, while a man is figuring out a better route.

These known gender differences are relatively small, however, and they are *average* differences. On the average, men or women score better on certain tests—men on math, women on language, to cite another example. That, of course, does not mean that all men are better than all women at math, or vice versa with language, any more than all men are taller than all women. Further, the magnitude of difference *within* each sex is greater than that *between* the sexes. On the whole, behavioral tests provide no evidence for women's intuition; at best they constitute a partial explanation *if* the phenomenon exists.

No one knows if behavioral differences between the genders are a matter of nature or nurture. Controversy abounds, and objectivity often takes a backseat to politics, which makes it difficult for scientists to indulge in public speculation. It is currently fashionable to assume that sex differences can be attributed to environmental conditioning. Scientists who merely stumble upon evidence to the contrary run the risk of being labeled sexist regardless of their political or social convictions.

What little evidence there is suggests that the debate will continue for a long time and may be resolved no sooner than the chicken/egg problem. Some researchers believe there are structural and organizational differences in male and female brains, but there is no conclusive evidence for this. We do know that there is a connection between behavior and sex hormones. Females with excessive male hormones in the prenatal period will show greater interest in athletics and career, less interest in dolls, clothing, and motherhood; males with excessive female hormones develop with below-average athletic skill and less aggressiveness and assertiveness. But neurological research is just beginning, and whether the data relate to intuition is anyone's guess.

What about the two hemispheres of the brain? Trying to make sense of popular writing on sex differences and the hemispheres can drive one to drink. I have read that men are left-brain oriented and women are right-brain oriented because mathematical reasoning is primarily a left-brain function and reading facial expressions is more right brain. But I have also read the opposite: women are left-brained because they excel at verbal skills, a left-hemisphere responsibility, and men are right-brained because of their superior spatial perception, which seems to take place in the right hemisphere. When I posed the question to biopsychologist Jerre Levy, a prominent figure in split-brain research, she shared my consternation. "The whole idea that each sex operates with an opposite side of the brain," she said, "is a silly notion backed by no evidence even in psychological data."

Both sexes display the usual differences in function between the two hemispheres of the brain, but men tend to specialize more. Women seem to have a greater ability to switch from one side to the other, and are more likely to have either hemisphere perform the same task. If, as I suspect, intuition involves a kind of interhemispheric synchrony, this might support the idea that women are more intuitive. But that, too, is conjecture, and if there are hemispheric differences between the sexes, the cause can just as easily be environmental—that is, patterns of hemispheric usage might be determined by social roles.

Perhaps men and women are equally intuitive, but cultural factors have led us to believe otherwise. Given their traditional roles as nurturers, women have to be good judges of people. They have to know whether someone is sincere or is hiding something. They have to know when someone is ill, or afraid, or worried, or angry. Like experts in other fields, they might develop an acumen for their subject matter and learn to respond appropriately without rational deliberation. Men, on the other hand, learn to deal with mechanical objects and mathematical symbols. Certainly they have to read people, too, but usually in the context of pragmatic or strategic concerns that can be dealt with in a more calculated way. Women's traditional concerns are emotions, and in that realm judgments are usually understood to be intuitive. This is not so when a businessman says, "Buy it," or a carpenter intuits a unique way to add space to a kitchen. Men may be just as intuitive, but much of their work can be explained as the product of pure reason.

The situation is compounded by cultural connotations that make most men want to appear logical; intuition is somehow linked to emotionalism, fantasy, fey spaciness—and femininity. Male pride has to do with being in charge, and that usually means being objective and unemotional. Men become good at arguing logically because it fits the dominant masculine values, it is encouraged by parents and teachers, and their traditional tasks lend themselves to rational exposition.

It could be argued that cultural factors have actually made women more intuitive. Intuition comes most readily to a receptive, patient mind, one that yields to it. Perhaps the conditioning that makes women more passive also cultivates more openness to intuition, to letting things happen rather than trying to make things happen. They might also develop intuition simply because it is considered acceptable for them to do so. Women have not been discouraged from having feelings, either the emotional kind or the cognitive kind. Until they enter traditional masculine domains, they have less motivation to be analytic and objective and less need to argue logically.

Or it could be argued that women just *appear* to be more intuitive because they don't hesitate to express their intuition and because their roles don't demand quite the same degree of rationality. Perhaps both sexes are equally intuitive, but in different realms because of contrasting interests and concerns. What we have called feminine intuition really has to do with interpersonal situations, and as sex roles become less rigid we may find that the apparent differences diminish. Indeed, there is evidence that this might be so. According to Frances Vaughan, studies by psychologist Judith Hall found that women interpreted nonverbal cues such as expressions and gestures more accurately than did men, but liberal men scored higher than traditional men and traditional women scored higher than their liberal counterparts.

BOWING TO THE EAST

Are people from the East and nonindustrial societies more intuitive than white Europeans? In many ways this question is as enigmatic as the one about women, and just as volatile. The arguments are also parallel. If some ethnic or racial groups are more intuitive than others is it because of biological or cultural factors? Are they really more intuitive, or do they just appear so?

In exploring this aspect of "Who is intuitive?" we have to be careful of cultural stereotyping. Lumping most of the world's population into a category such as non-Western is absurd. The term covers a vast range of racial and national diversity. Are Indians more intuitive than Japanese? Are Africans more intuitive than South Americans? If there is no reliable way to measure intuition in individuals, it is even more difficult to measure it in relation to entire cultures or nationalities.

In some ways it would seem reasonable to assume that non-Western people are more intuitive. Their cultures have more respect for the inner dimension, the nonphysical, the wisdom of symbols, dreams, and rituals, and they revere gifted channels of divine wisdom such as priests, gurus, and shamans. They might be more open to intuitive knowledge, trust it more, and look for it more. Their lifestyles might also be more conducive to intuition. It is not uncommon, for example, to see Japanese or Indian businessmen take a meditation break during the workday or check into a monastery for a retreat. They attend to the inner life. Also, because they are not bound by an ideology that raises rational empiricism to religious status, they might be less likely to interfere with their intuition. Non-Western philosophies are more oriented toward letting things happen, to acknowledging the interplay of the worldly and the divine, and to respecting things unseen.

It is also true that, in general, non-Western philosophies prize intuition and recognize it as the only route to ultimate reality. But we must take care not to go overboard. Some Eastern cultures value rationality very highly indeed. Even in ineffably spiritual matters, most Eastern texts are exemplary for their rational exposition. Misinterpretations have led us to suppose that they advocate the abandonment of reason. But such injunctions are made in the context of actual spiritual practices such as meditation, not as a prescription for everyday life. Further, Eastern scholars and scientists value logical inquiry and rigorous analysis as much as their Western counterparts; branches of Indian philosophy such as *nyaya* and *sankhya*, for example, are extraordinary expressions of disciplined rational argumentation.

Finally, even though non-Western cultures are ideologically more accepting of intuition, it does not necessarily follow that non-Western people are more intuitive—any more than an openly religious person is inherently more moral or that someone who loves poetry is therefore a good poet. One interesting line of inquiry would be to compare Western and Eastern persons in the same occupations to see if, as a group, one is more intuitive than the other. It has been suggested, for example, that one of Japan's big advantages—despite its exceptionally orderly, even punctilious values—is the openness of their executives to intuition. "Our company's success," notes Shigem Okada, head of Mitsukoshi, Japan's largest department store, "was due to our adoption of the West's pragmatic management combined with the spiritual intuitive aspects of the East."

Weston Agor, from whom I got that quote, distributed questionnaires to members of the American Society for Public Administration. The test was designed to determine what Agor calls the "brain style" of the respondent—intuitive, rational, or integrative. From his 1,679 returned questionnaires, Agor found, among other things, that managers with Asian backgrounds scored higher on the intuitive and integrative scales. A self-descriptive instrument, Agor's test does not measure the quality of intuition, just one's preference for that style. The percentage of Asian respondents was admittedly low, but the results are interesting to contemplate, and it is hoped that other studies will follow.

Quite possibly some genetic or cultural traits can make one group of people more inclined toward intuitive thinking than others. While we should be open to such possibilities, we should avoid jumping to stereotypical conclusions.

IS INTUITION KID STUFF?

Like the other contentions we have been examining, the children-are-intuitive argument has been overstated and underexamined. But it also contains a grain of truth.

To jaded adults, there is a special charm in the curiosity, freshness of perception, and wonder of children. We get quite wistful, even envious, wishing we could recapture that joy and innocence. But, in our longing, we often romanticize childhood and attribute to it powers that may not actually exist. Many people think children have access to special or unusual modes of knowing; even brilliant thinkers have fallen prey to hyperbole in this regard. The biologist and philosopher Lyall Watson, for example, writes in *Lifetide*, "Every child of five knows everything there is to know; but when children turn six we send them to school, and the rot sets in." Anyone sensitive to the abuses of education knows what such a statement is driving at, but such a celebration of the "wisdom of childhood" is extreme. It is also widespread.

On a simple dichotomy of intuition/rationality, we would have to say that children are more intuitive than adults, at least in terms of the proportions in which they use either faculty. Kids, after all, don't acquire the capacity for formal reasoning for some time. As with women and non-Westerners, if we assume that less logic means more intuition, the argument is over. But it is not that simple. To say that children have better intuition than adults is absurd.

We generally view cognitive development as a process in which the capacity for reason gradually emerges. To some, this acquisition is lamentable, since it allegedly destroys native intuitive abilities and shuts off the enchanted world of myth and magic. To others it is the apex of human development. Among the latter was the celebrated Swiss psychologist Jean Piaget, whose painstaking studies did for cognitive development what the early naturalists did for flora and fauna—identified, classified, and labeled its components and placed them in a coherent framework.

According to Piaget's model, we move through four stages of cognitive growth. In the *sensory-motor* stage (birth to 1½ or 2 years old), infants live instinctively, with no images or symbols, no awareness of past or future. Then, in the *preoperational* stage (from about 2 to 7), symbols, concepts, and images come to stand for real objects and events and can be used in thinking on a rather primitive scale. Piaget actually used the word *intuitive* to describe these two preoperational stages.

In the stage of *concrete operations* (ages 7 to 11 or 12), children begin to manipulate mental contructs. They know that the category "horses" is larger and more encompassing than "white horses." Now less egocentric, the child knows there are causes outside the self for observed events. Finally, in the stage of *formal operations* (some time between 11 and 15), emerging adolescents can think about abstract entities and relationships. They can judge the validity of a proposition by the way an argument is structured. They can also contemplate abstract concepts, hypothesize, think about thinking, and solve problems systematically, making plans before taking action.

Piaget's theory has been modified in recent years, in some ways contradicted and in others confirmed. Research indicates that preoperational children might be more logical than Piaget believed; they are just unable to express their reasoning verbally. Conversely, adolescents and adults can be less logical than Piaget's model would predict. And cross-cultural studies indicate that Piaget's formal operations might not be universal but something we learn in Western schools. For all his brilliance, Piaget may have been overly tied to a rational-empirical model of the mind; he saw formal operations as the end point of growth, a kind of oak toward which all we acorns are impelled. Like Freud, Piaget did not go far enough. There is no room for higher states of consciousness in his work, nor for the possibility of developing intuitive faculties.

As in our previous discussions, part of the problem is the bugaboo of extreme dichotomies. We see formal logic and assume the absence of intuition; we see the absence of formal logic and assume the presence of intuition. Certainly adults use reason more than children, but intuition isn't entirely annihilated by adulthood. As we have pointed out repeatedly, intuition is an integral part of rational thinking. Indeed, some of the talents that Piaget and others have attributed to formal operations—hypothesizing, imagining new possibilities—can easily be credited to intuition.

The emphasis on formal thought at a certain time of life might overshadow the intuitive mind and even retard its development, but it doesn't eliminate it. More than likely, the capacity for intuition continues to grow, albeit not to its full potential. But, then, neither does rationality. Formal operations could, in fact, be viewed as an additional contributor to intuition, providing more information, new symbols and concepts, wider applications, and a rigorous way of testing its products. The intuition of the child is based on crude sensory information and rudimentary images and symbols. True, they frequently startle us with their impossibly insightful leaps, but only because they are children. To elevate fertile imagination and unpredictable sagacity to the level of wisdom does justice neither to children nor to adults. It is like watching children splash around randomly with paints and comparing them to Picasso.

Some writers have suggested that children's intuitive knowing and unprogrammed perceptions are the same as those of saints and yogis. Infancy, after all, is a state of unity of self with environment and of the absence of ego awareness. That sounds like transcendence. But confusing infant consciousness with cosmic consciousness is actually a flagrant form of what Ken Wilber, author of *The Atman Project* and editor of *Re-Vision* journal, calls the "pre/trans fallacy." Infancy, says Wilber, is "pre-subject/object differentiation, which means the infant cannot distinguish subject from object. But the mystic union . . . is trans-subject/object, which means that it transcends subject and object while remaining perfectly aware of that conventional duality." To say that childhood intuition is the same as the intuition of enlightenment is like saying that infants are exactly like kings because they get everyone to serve them.

The pre/trans fallacy can work in either of two ways: it can either elevate infancy to the status of higher consciousness or reduce higher states to a condition of infantile regression. Both misconceptions fail to recognize the evolution of consciousness. Enlightenment is not just a recapturing of the wisdom of childhood, but a higher goal toward which we evolve.

And yet there is something to the contention that intuition loses out in adulthood. Educational institutions do, in fact, stifle our natural intuitive abilities, as many educators have pointed out. Not only are systematic, logical thought patterns demanded to excess, but intuition is ignored, even discouraged. We tell children in many ways that the inner voice is not worth listening to. A child's intuition is no more fully developed than his muscles and bones. What children have is intuitive potential and—until we get our hands on them—certain natural qualities that aid intuition: curiosity, receptivity, innocence, and wonder. Children have a natural way of surrendering to experience and are not constrained by the need to be right. Those qualities are worth recapturing, for they open the mind to intuition and extra-rational discovery. In that sense, we would all do well to be more childlike.

THE INTUITIVE PERSONALITY

Of all the influential theorists in modern psychology, Carl Jung seems to have taken intuition most seriously. To him, it was "neither sense perception, nor feeling, nor intellectual inference, although it may also appear in these forms. In intuition a content presents itself whole and complete, without our being able to explain or discover how this content came into existence. Intuition is a kind of instinctive apprehension, no matter what the contents."

According to Jung's theory of psychological types, personality and behavior can be understood in terms of four distinct functions—thinking, feeling, sensation, and intuition. These functions are then divided into pairs of polar opposites, with thinking and feeling on one axis and sensing and intuition on the other. (We must be careful not to confuse Jungian terminology with our colloquial use of these terms. Ordinarily we might think of intuition and "thinking" as a dichotomy, and associate "feeling" with either one of our senses—touch—or with intuition, as in the expression "I have a feeling." In order to grasp Jung's model, it is best to stick closely to his definitions.) Jung summarized the four functions this way: "Under sensation I include all perceptions by means of the sense organs; by thinking I mean the function of intellectual cognition and the forming of logical conclusions; feeling is a function of subjective valuation; intuition I take as perception by way of the unconscious, or perception of unconscious contents."

The four functions are rarely distributed uniformly; we are basically oriented one way or the other on each dichotomy. A person's preference is more or less determined at birth and strengthened through use, since the favored mode is exercised and the less favored is neglected. According to the Jungian framework, each of us would be located at a certain point on each axis, and would fall into one of four quadrants (see Figure 1).

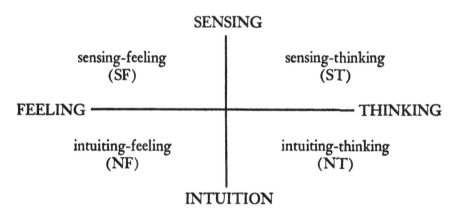

Figure 1. *Jung's Psychological Types.*

Jungians view sensing and intuition as *perception functions*, and they view thinking and feeling as *judgment functions*. Perception determines what we know; judgment determines what we do about what we know. On the perceptual axis, sensing makes us aware of things as they appear; it is a fact gatherer, bringing in information from the outside world. Intuition supplies information from within; it looks beyond appearances to inner meanings, relationships, interpretations, and possibilities.

According to Robert Hanson, a Jungian psychologist, those who favor sensing "grow expert at observation, tend to be very practical, realistic, good at remembering and working with things and facts, such as tools, machinery, dates, quantities, scores, places, and events." The sensing type is interested in the here and now. By contrast, the intuitive person, says Hanson, "tends to perceive things in terms of possibilities, meanings, and relationships. The intuiter has an active imagination, is continually coming up with new ideas, is often inspired, and enjoys tackling new and unresolved problems."

Sensing types focus on practical, concrete, tangible realities; they lean toward standardized procedures and are not comfortable with complexities and ambiguities. Intuiters, by contrast, are stimulated by abstract ideas and by implications and relationships among concepts; they like doing things their own way; the unknown, the complex, and the novel attract them.

The two perception functions work along with the judgment functions—thinking and feeling—which in Jungian terminology are both deliberate, conscious ways of deciding. Again, Jung used "feeling" in a specific way, as a "judgment of value—for instance, agreeable or disagreeable, good or bad, and so on." Feeling types base decisions on personal, subjective factors—how they feel about something; thinking types are logical and impersonal. As the late Isabel Briggs Myers, a leading figure in Jungian psychology, wrote, "If, when one judges these ideas, he concentrates on whether or not they are true, that is thinking-judgment. If one is conscious first of like or dislike, of whether these concepts are sympathetic or antagonistic to other ideas he prizes, that is feeling-judgment."

In this model, an intuitive person would know something intuitively and then judge it in one of two ways: by organizing information in an orderly fashion, looking for facts and verifiable information, and thinking it through objectively (the *thinking* type); or by acting more spontaneously, subjectively, and perhaps emotionally, according to personal likes and dislikes (the *feeling* type). The former would be an NT (Jungians use "N" to stand for intuition because another category, introversion, usurped the "I") and evaluate with the head; the latter would be an NF and evaluate with the heart. The NT might be an ingenious problem solver, the NF an inspired teacher or communicator; the NT is interested in ideas and truths, the NF cares more about people and values.

Jungian psychologists have used these classifications in a variety of settings. More than twenty years ago Isabel Briggs Myers designed the Myers-Briggs Type Indicator (MBTI), an empirical instrument designed to classify people according to the Jungian types. The

MTBI (which gets quite complicated, since the four functions are further fleshed out by other dimensions) and offshoots of it have been widely validated and applied in business, counseling, and educational settings. A variation of it, the Learning Preference Inventory, designed by the consulting firm of Hanson, Silver & Associates, assesses an individual's favored style of learning. The instrument, which has been used in classrooms to gear teaching procedures to individual differences, contains thirty-six items. Here are two examples:

I prefer questions that ask me
to come up with original ideas.
how ideas are related to one another.
to select the correct answer.
how I feel about things.
When I'm faced with a difficult assignment I like to
talk with others to see what needs to be done.
be told exactly what needs to be done.
think things through for myself before someone tries to
explain it to me.
find new or different ways of completing the assignment.

Each item is ranked in order of choice, and the scoring procedure places the individual in one of the four Jungian quadrants. An intuitive-feeler (NF), for example, according to the Hanson-Silver manual, is curious, insightful, imaginative, and creative, someone who dares to dream, is committed to his values, open to alternatives, and constantly searching for unusual ways to express himself. Also, NFs are "eager to explore ideas, to generate new solutions to problems, and to discuss moral dilemmas." They are motivated by their own interests, sensitive to beauty, and independent. Tolerant of ambiguity, they trust their insights, prefer not to follow step-by-step procedures, and take circuitous, inexplicable routes to solutions. Flexible, adaptable, seemingly scattered and chaotic, NFs are comfortable working with a minimum of directions. Their unusual, unique, inventive responses look beyond the facts to the big picture. But NFs are sometimes unrealistic and unable to plan or organize; they might become so enthusiastic that they start more projects than they can complete.

Although intuitive-thinkers (NTs) have much in common with NFs, they are more theoretical, intellectual, and knowledge-oriented. Their judgment tends to be more analytical, logical, critical, and, usually, impersonal. More organized and systematic than NFs, they tend to plan and think things through before beginning work. NTs enjoy arguing a point logically, are geared toward theory, and like to play devil's advocate. Their primary concern is conceptualization rather than detail. As for weaknesses, NTs can be overly critical, unconcerned about feelings, intolerant of disagreement, and might monopolize conversations.

At first glance, the NT might seem very nonintuitive. But keep in mind that these are relative preferences. One NT may be dominated by the intuitive component, while another NT may be more thinking-oriented. Also, both are markedly different from the sensing type, who thrives on systematic, concrete, programmed conditions and is attracted to numbers, details, and facts. By adding the feeling-thinking dimension, the Jungian model allows us to broaden the view and subdivide intuitive types. It helps, for example, account for John, the philosopher mentioned earlier, a classic NT. The NF is the kind of person who might be assumed to be intuitive, since he evaluates in a less rational manner; the NT might give the opposite impression but nevertheless be equally intuitive.

As with most psychological tests, the Jungian instruments must be approached with some reservation. They are self-evaluations, indicating our stated preferences and observations about our own behavior. Quite possibly, someone might answer as an intuitive or feeling type because there is a romantic, sensitive ring to certain questions; someone else might answer as a senser or thinker because certain questions suggest competence and leadership qualities. It should also be noted that the Jungian model tells us about style, not about intuitive *ability* or the *quality* of a person's intuition, except to say that intuitive types would tend to use, and therefore develop, their intuition.

Approached with some caution, Jungian testing devices can be useful tools for self-understanding, and they can be applied to occupational choices, job assignments, personnel selection, and training and teaching methods. They can be personally revealing. Quite often, for example, a person will discover a preference for an intuitive style of functioning, and realize either that he has been suppressing this tendency in order to project a certain image or that his current job conditions force him to stifle it.

Testing instruments have been devised for a variety of settings, and psychologists have correlated the MBTI with other data. If you wish more information or the instruments themselves, write to: The Center for Applications of Psychological Type, Inc., 414 SW 7th

Terrace, Gainesville, FL 32601, a clearinghouse for information on the MBTI; The Consulting Psychologists Press, 577 College Ave., Palo Alto, CA 94306, publisher of the MBTI; Hanson, Silver & Associates, Inc., Box 402, Moorestown, NJ 08057, consultants who design and apply Jungian instruments on the East Coast. Weston Agor used MBTI questions in his study, which is written up in his forthcoming book, *Intuitive Management*.

WESTCOTT'S INTUITIVE PROBLEM-SOLVING SCALE

The most extensive empirical research on intuition was done by Malcolm Westcott in a series of studies that spanned a decade ending in the late 1960s. Admittedly predisposed to the intuition-as-inference model, Westcott, now at York University in Toronto, attempted to define intuitive people not only by style of behavior but also by actual performance. He then used standard personality tests to determine what intuitive people are like.

Westcott had subjects solve problems involving series and analogies, both verbal and numerical. Each problem had a single answer, which would be obvious to anyone who had all the clues. For example, the subject has to fill in the missing number in the ratio, 16:——. The clues, revealed in order upon request, are: 4:2, 9:3, 25:5, 100:10, 64:8. The answer, of course, is 4.

Westcott looked at two variables: first, how many clues the subjects required before they were willing to make judgments; and, second, how correct the conclusions were. He reasoned that the two measures were relevant to the standards by which we commonly judge intuitive people—those who leap to accurate conclusions more rapidly than expected. He found that people fell along two separate continuums: one ranged from very accurate to inaccurate, the other from needing few clues to needing many. On the basis of test scores, Westcott divided each of the 1,097 subjects in his eleven studies (197 men, 900 women, all students) into four groups:

1. Intuitive thinkers; little information, highly successful in finding solutions.

2. Wild guessers; little information but typically unsuccessful.

3. Cautious successes; excessive information and highly successful.

4. Cautious failures; unsuccessful despite excessive information.

Using a variety of personality tests and interviews, Westcott and his colleagues found that intuitive people tend to be:

unconventional and comfortable in their unconventionality.

confident (they were more sure of their answers on the test than those who waited for more cues).

self-sufficient (they didn't base their identities on membership in a social group).

emotionally involved in abstract issues, either in intellectual, academic terms or in human values (the distinction might be similar to the Jungian NT and NF).

willing to explore uncertainties and entertain doubts, and able to do so without fear.

willing to expose themselves to criticism and challenge.

able to accept or reject criticism as necessary.

willing to change in ways they deemed appropriate.

resistant to outside control and direction.

independent.

foresighted.

spontaneous.

There were clear personality differences between intuitives and wild guessers, both of whom appeared to have an intuitive style in that they required relatively few clues. The wild guessers—who were not good at solving the problems—were self-absorbed, cynical, and had a high degree of physical and emotional disorders. There was also a clear distinction between intuitives and cautious successes, who had correct answers but needed a lot of information. The latter stood out in their preference for order, certainty, control, and respect for authority. More conservative, they function best in situations where expectations are clearly established. These differences correspond with the usual distinction between intuitive and rational styles.

We must be circumspect when attempting to generalize from Westcott's studies. He used student subjects in highly artificial situations where there was little intrinsic motivation. And he was testing intuition of a specific type—if, in fact, it *was* intuition—that may not be comparable to the intuition associated with innovative break-through, creative inspiration, penetrating interpersonal insights, or spiritual revelation. Nor did the setting resemble real life: each problem had a single right answer; the problems and the ingredients needed for solution were clearly defined; and the answers could have been obtained with pure deduction.

Nevertheless, the personality portraits that emerge from the Westcott studies (which are documented in Westcott's 1968 book, *Toward a Contemporary Psychology of Intuition*) correspond nicely with the Jungian data on the intuitive type. And both fit well with data on problem-solving styles and with measures of qualities associated with intuitive people—creativity, originality, and independence of judgment. The portraits describe a constellation of features: self-assured, highly motivated nonconformists who can tolerate ambiguity, change, and uncertainty and are willing to risk looking foolish or being wrong.

There are no easy answers to the question "Who is intuitive?" But, used with caution, the available tests and personality portraits can help us recognize intuitive people. When a situation calls for an intuitive approach, people who fit the portrait just might, on average, be more suitable. While it is no guarantee, the chances are that independent, confident, flexible people will have learned to use their intuition better than most. In fact, it is probably true that one reason they *have* these characteristics is that at some point they learned to trust their inner voices.

When faced with uncertainty and ambiguity, people without such traits might try to restore equilibrium by imposing as much predictability as they can, adhering like glue to rigid rules and procedures, or seeking the often false security of statistics. They might define problems in an overly simple way, gather information from only obvious places, and consider only safe, predictable alternatives. In this way they discourage their intuitive minds from functioning effectively. Those who enjoy, or at least tolerate, uncertain conditions and who are adaptable and independent are more likely to encourage their intuition and give it room to operate.

It might be tempting for anyone who wants to become more intuitive to try cultivating the attributes and style of the intuitive personality. This should be approached with caution, however. It is dangerous to adopt certain external behaviors in hopes of becoming transformed internally. The strain of trying to be something you are not can be a bigger barrier to intuition than behavioral traits. Certain aspects of the intuitive personality and the intuitive style can, however, be adopted without excessive contrivance or the sacrifice of our natural propensities. Doing so can be a definite boon to intuition. We will return to this in Chapter 8.

ARE YOU INTUITIVE?

If that question refers to the quality of intuition, it can only be answered through careful auditing of your experiences, which can be accomplished systematically with the journal described in Chapter 10. In the meantime, here is a questionnaire that will help you assess your basic style of approaching problems and decisions. To the degree that there is a correlation between intuitive style and the quality of intuition, your score might reflect on the latter as well. For each item, choose the alternative, A or B, that best applies to you.

1. When I don't have a ready answer, I tend to be:
    A. patient.
    B. uneasy.

2. When faced with uncertainty, I usually:
    A. become disoriented.
    B. remain comfortable.

3. In challenging situations, I am highly motivated and deeply committed:
    A. most of the time.
    B. infrequently.

4. When my intuition differs from the facts, I usually:
    A. trust my feelings.
    B. follow the logical course.

5. When working on a difficult problem, I tend to:
    A. concentrate on finding the solution.
    B. play around with possibilities.

6. When I disagree with others, I tend to:
    A. let them know about it.
    B. keep the disagreement to myself.

7. Generally speaking, I:
    A. prefer the safe way.
    B. enjoy taking risks.

8. When working on a problem I change strategies:
    A. seldom.
    B. often.

9. I prefer to be told:
    A. exactly how to do things.
    B. only what needs to be done.

10. When things get very complicated, I:
    A. become exhilarated.
    B. become insecure.

11. When faced with a problem, I usually:
    A. create a plan or outline before getting started.
    B. plunge right in.

12. In most cases:
    A. change makes me nervous.
    B. I welcome unexpected changes.

13. My reading consists of:
    A. a variety of subjects, including fiction.
    B. factual material mainly related to my work.

14. When my opinion differs from the experts, I usually:
    A. stick to my beliefs.
    B. defer to authority.

15. When faced with a number of tasks, I:
    A. tackle them simultaneously.
    B. finish one before going on to another.

16. When learning something new, I:
    A. master the rules and procedures first.
    B. get started and learn the rules as I go along.

17. At work I prefer to:
    A. follow a prearranged schedule.
    B. make my own schedule.

18. At school I was (am) better at:
    A. essay questions.
    B. short-answer questions.

19. Basically, I am:
    A. an idealist.
    B. a realist.

20. When I make a mistake, I tend to:
    A. second-guess myself.
    B. forget it and go on.

21. The following statement best applies to me:
    A. I can usually explain exactly why I know something.
    B. Often I can't describe why I know something.

22. When offering a description or explanation, I am more likely
    to rely on:
    A. analogy and anecdote.
    B. facts and figures.

23. I can usually be convinced by:
    A. an appeal to reason.
    B. an appeal to my emotions.

24. When I am wrong, I:
    A. readily admit it.
    B. defend myself.

25. I would rather be called:
    A. imaginative.
    B. practical.

26. When faced with a difficult problem, I am likely to:
    A. ask for advice.
    B. tackle it myself.

27. Unpredictable people are:
    A. annoying.
    B. interesting.

28. When setting an appointment for the following week, I am likely
    to say:
    A. "Let's set an exact time now."
    B. "Call me the day before."

29. When something spoils my plans, I:
    A. get upset.
    B. calmly make a new plan.

30. When I have a hunch, I usually react with:
    A. enthusiasm.
    B. mistrust.

31. Most of my friends and colleagues:
    A. believe in the value of intuition.
    B. are skeptical about intuition.

32. I am best known as:
    A. an idea person.
    B. a detail person.

Scoring

Give yourself one point if you answered A on the following items: 1, 3, 4, 6, 10, 13, 14, 15, 18, 19, 22, 24, 25, 30, 31, 32.

Give yourself one point if your answered B on the following items: 2, 5, 7, 8, 9, 11, 12, 16, 17, 20, 21, 23, 26, 27, 28, 29.

If your total score is 24 or above, you tend strongly toward an intuitive approach to decisions and problems. More than likely you trust your intuition, as well you should, since it is probably highly accurate.

If your total is between 16 and 23, you tend to vary in style but are more intuitive than analytic or systematic. Your intuition is probably correct more often than not.

If your total is between 8 and 15, you tend to mix styles but lean more toward the analytic and rational than the intuitive. Your intuition might be erratic.

If your total is below 8, you lean heavily toward a systematic, rational approach to problems and decisions. Chances are you do not trust your intuition very much, perhaps due to past experiences when it has been wrong.

In evaluating these results, do not regard this test as a definitive measure of your intuitive capacity. For one thing, there are no universally accepted standards for making such judgments; no systematic attempt to determine either intuitive ability or style, including this one, has been validated with long-term use. Also, keep in mind the points made in this chapter: you are likely to be more intuitive, and to trust your intuition more, in some situations than in others. A high score on the questionnaire is a good indication of positive, intuition-enhancing behavior. In that respect, the questions can also serve as a tool for introspection and improvement.

6

Right Brain, Wrong Theory

While no one quite knows how intuition works, many people think they know *where* it works: in the right hemisphere of the brain. Popular magazine articles of recent years, and even some scientific journals, make it seem an established fact. It is not. The split-brain research that won Roger Sperry a Nobel Prize, and that is being continued by outstanding scientists, has opened new doors in the quest for understanding the brain. In their early findings are perhaps the seeds of what might someday become a neurological description of how intuition works. But at this point there is no justification for concluding that intuition is a property of the right brain alone.

At one time the right brain was considered the "silent" or "minor" hemisphere. Then, when it was learned that the right hemisphere did things the "dominant" left hemisphere did not do, a minor craze was triggered. In 1977 Daniel Goleman wrote a sober assessment in *Psychology Today* titled "Split-Brain Psychology: Fad of the Year," in which he noted that fads can inspire both new, important research and misleading popularization. In the case of the split brain, both happened. The fad amounts to taking observable dichotomies—such as analytical people and intuitive people—and carelessly plugging them into the two-hemisphere model. Eventually the scientific community pulled in the reins on overstatement, but the general public continues to be besieged by distortions and simplistic exaggerations. In some circles, brain orientation is threatening to replace astrological signs as the personality label of choice.

THE RIGHT STUFF—AND THE LEFT STUFF

What exactly do we know about the two hemispheres of the brain? At this point, according to the experts, it can be said with confidence that the left hemisphere has a distinct advantage in dealing with the various aspects of language—speaking, understanding grammatical rules, and deciphering the meaning of words. It seems to play the dominant role in classifying objects into standard linguistic categories.

The right hemisphere appears to be more involved in spatial tasks, such as mentally manipulating an image or finding one's way around a maze or an unfamiliar location. It also seems to be more sensitive to emotions, in enabling us both to express them and to recognize them in others. And it plays a relatively more important role than the left hemisphere in making fine sensory discriminations, such as recognizing faces.

In addition, there is some evidence that, in the words of Sally Springer and George Deutsch, authors of *Left Brain, Right Brain*, "The left hemisphere tends to deal with rapid changes in time and to analyze stimuli in terms of details and features, while the right hemisphere deals with simultaneous relationships and with the more global properties of patterns." This distinction, which is not universally accepted, is often interpreted by assigning to the left hemisphere the labels "sequential" or "linear" and to the right hemisphere the terms "simultaneous," "holistic," or "nonlinear."

That much is well documented. What of the other polarities in the ubiquitous charts found in magazines? (See list on next page.)

These are conjecture, inferences made on the basis of the few undisputed differences between the hemispheres. When consulted, a number of psychologists and brain researchers familiar with the split-brain literature stated without exception—often with considerable exasperation—that most of the dichotomies are grossly oversimplified and that some are flatly incorrect. Richard Davidson, director of the Laboratory for Cognitive Psychology at the State University of New York at Purchase, said that calling intuition a right-brain function is "utterly simplistic and inaccurate, an attempt to find an easy answer to what is in all likelihood a fantastically complicated function."

It is easy to understand, however, why intuition was placed in the right hemisphere. Some of the qualities associated with it sound very much like right-brain specialties. Intuitive knowledge can be

Left Hemisphere	*Right Hemisphere*
Western	Eastern
objective	subjective
intellect	feelings
deductive	inductive
convergent	divergent
timebound	timeless
realistic	imaginative
scientific	artistic
conscious	unconscious
waking	dreaming
mind	heart
logic	intuition
rational	intuitive

diffuse and without linguistic content, whereas knowledge arrived at through reason is usually packaged in words and dependent on precise categorization of symbols and concepts. Intuition is an instantaneous, global experience bringing together patterns of meaning, and the right brain seems to process information in simultaneous or parallel fashion. We think of intuition as the faculty that gives us knowledge of other people's hidden intentions and true feelings, and the right brain seems to be more adept at discerning and expressing emotions.

But all we can safely say at this point is that intuitive experiences involve cognitive qualities that now seem to be associated with the right hemisphere, which is not quite the same as saying it is a *function* of the right hemisphere or that it *resides* in it. For one thing, we use intuition in dealing with supposedly left-brain activities; for example, we intuitively grasp the meaning of a verbal phrase or a linguistic concept. Similarly, as we saw in Chapter 4, an intuition can be perceived in words.

Also, while the sequential functioning of the left hemisphere is portrayed as antithetical to intuition, that side of the brain must, at the very least, play an important role in processing the information that later comes together as the hunch or insight. We think of intuition as a nonlinear, holistic cognition, but that is a description of the actual experience. Surely the left hemisphere is involved in the synthesizing and processing activities that precede it, if not in the intuitive moment itself.

In addition, the right brain can't be entirely nonlogical. The spatial tasks in which it excels—negotiating maps and mazes, mentally manipulating geometric forms, pattern recognition—are often used when we engage in the supposedly left-brain act of reasoning. Mathematicians play visual-spatial games in their heads when thinking through a problem; travelers reason out their routes visually; managers will imagine spatially the production sequence of workers and machines. Even dreams and fantasies, which some people have ascribed to the right hemisphere, have been shown to have a logic and sequentiality of their own. And deciphering emotions, which has been called a right-brain job, can entail rigorous analysis and logic, as any clinical psychologist will confirm.

Split-brain studies use either spatial or linguistic tests, and usually find that these tasks are processed in the right and left hemispheres respectively. But it does not necessarily follow that the visual task will be dealt with intuitively and the verbal task rationally. If, for example, a subject is presented with a picture of a complex geometric form and asked to figure out how many edges it has, he might very well analyze the problem either verbally or by mentally manipulating forms. Similarly, if a problem is presented verbally (for example, "John is taller than Paul; John is smaller than Sam; who is tallest?"), the subject might reason it out pictorially by mentally rearranging the three men, or he might get the answer in an intuitive flash.

STUDYING THE STUDIES

In examining the nature of lateralization research we have to wonder how justifiable it is to generalize at all. Much of what we know about the split brain has come from studies with surgical patients whose brains were quite literally split. Some were epilepsy victims who had commissurotomies, in which fibers connecting the two hemispheres are severed. Other subjects had had an entire hemisphere removed, and some brains had been damaged by tumors, wounds, or strokes. When these subjects are unable to perform certain functions, it is assumed that the damaged brain regions are responsible for the defective behavior. We then infer that the damaged areas would carry out the functions in normal brains.

But brain-damaged subjects are hardly typical people. Can we confidently extrapolate to the population at large? Most neuroscientists think not. Springer and Deutsch, whose book is probably the best source on brain lateralization for the lay reader, note "the striking adaptability of the brain," and conclude that "it is not possible to draw firm conclusions about the workings of the normal brain from what we have learned in the brain-damage clinic alone."

Studies of normal persons have employed a variety of ingenious methods for isolating the behavior of each hemisphere to see which plays a more dominant role in a particular activity. Information is presented selectively to either of the two ears, or either of the two eyes, since each transmits to the opposite side of the brain only. Other methods include observing the movement of the eyes or the tilt of the head when a subject engages in different tasks. Various electroencephalographic (EEG) and other processes are used to see which parts of the brain are more active at various times.

In general, these studies have supported the language and spatial distinctions uncovered in studies with brain-damaged subjects. However, as Harvard psychologist Howard Gardner points out, some of the methods "present stimuli in unfamiliar ways, and inferences drawn from them about normal processing are quite possibly erroneous." Like some of his colleagues, Gardner is also concerned that many experiments have not been replicated. Springer and Deutsch write that studies comparing the same subjects' results in different tests thought to study the same function seldom show a high degree of correlation. This suggests that the tests don't measure the same thing after all. The authors also point out that "repeated testing of the same subjects does not always produce the same results."

While considered potentially important, EEG studies have so far yielded confusing and often conflicting results. Like studies measuring blood flow, they analyze the level of activity in the brain's cortex. The idea is that the more active regions of the brain are those most responsible for the kind of operation being performed at the time. However, differences in hemispheric activity levels, when found, are usually small. Neither hemisphere is all on or all off during any particular task. All such studies demonstrate the simultaneous involvement of many areas of the brain, even in simple endeavors. Besides, a lot more may be going on in the less active areas than we now comprehend. Given the complexity of the brain and the vast sea of uncharted regions in it, the EEG is probably only scratching the surface, figuratively as well as literally.

We also have to wonder how valid it is to link actual intuitive experiences with what goes on in laboratory studies on lateralization.

In most experiments the subject is given a stimulus and asked to respond to it. Usually, nothing more complex than simple perception is involved, and the response is immediate. The tests study how the hemispheres respond to incoming information. Needless to say, a lot more is going on when you have a hunch about an unsolved problem, or a strong feeling to take a certain action, or the answer to a nagging problem hits you by surprise. The information processed by the intuitive mind is usually drawn from a history of previous experience and perhaps from extrasensory or other avenues that will be discussed in Chapter 7. What comes together in the intuitive moment may have been contributed by both cortical hemispheres, and probably by areas of the brain outside the cortex as well.

In fact, it might be incorrect to ascribe any rigid division of labor to the hemispheres. We do not even know for sure how strictly we can apply the verbal/nonverbal labels. It turns out that the right hemisphere has a fair amount of linguistic competence, although it cannot direct speech. Evidently, patients with right-brain damage retain their use of language because the left hemisphere is intact, but they lose something—the ability to understand metaphor, subtle nuances of implicit meaning, emotional undertones. We also know that the left hemisphere is involved in certain behaviors that are nonverbal and spatial, such as motor activity. Alan Gevins of the University of California at San Francisco not long ago observed the brain waves of subjects engaged in pattern recognition. According to an article by Gary Selden in the October 1981 *Science Digest*, Gevins found that "very simple numeric or spatial judgments actually involve many areas on both sides of the brain. Complex patterns of brain electricity associated with these judgments changed very rapidly; each sixth of a second, a totally different set of complex patterns was seen."

The analytic/holistic dichotomy, which was probably the original impetus for assigning intuition to the right hemisphere, has also come into question. Justine Sergent of McGill University has found evidence that hemispheric differences may be related to the size and amount of detail of the stimuli, with the right hemisphere favoring larger, nondetailed information. As quoted in *Brain/Mind Bulletin*, Sergent said the earlier studies that suggested an analytic/holistic division "may not have addressed the right questions and may have reached conclusions that are not warranted." She found that both hemispheres recognize faces and both can read; the differences have to do with the size of the letters and degree of similarity between faces. Sergent's study suggests that both hemispheres analyze and both perceive wholes, but that the right interprets vague input while the left processes finely detailed information. This is further evidence that hemispheric differences may have more to do with how each hemisphere handles incoming information than with the complex restructuring that leads to intuition.

Finally, it must be emphasized that all discovered differences between the hemispheres are a matter of degree; they are *average* differences. Neither side of the cortex ever functions to the exclusion of the other. Jerre Levy, whose work with the pioneering Roger Sperry is responsible for much of what we know about the two hemispheres, emphasizes that the functional distinctions are not as rigid or absolute as they are often made out to be. "In the normal individual the two hemispheres are in constant active integration and intimate collaboration," said Dr. Levy. "There is almost nothing a normal person could do that depends only on one hemisphere. Possibly, if you used an exceedingly simple task, repetitive, habitual, and boring, a normal brain might show asymmetric processing, but the instant you increase the task difficulty, it would instigate bilateral hemispheric engagement."

Although blown out of proportion with respect to intuition, the split-brain fad has legitimized nonverbal, nonsequential modes of knowing, and that will no doubt lead to a clearer understanding of the neurobiology of intuition. Perhaps future research will go beyond the current work with perception to situations more closely resembling real-life intuition. It would be interesting to use tests like those devised by Malcolm Westcott to see which hemisphere is dominant at which points in the process and whether there are significant brain differences among intuitive and nonintuitive subjects. We might also study the brain patterns of intuitive and systematic styles, and of people in the various Jungian categories.

To many scientists, the similarities and replication of functions between the hemispheres is more striking than the specializations. As we acquire more data, it is quite likely we will find that complex functions such as intuition and reason involve both hemispheres. Any specialization may turn out to be related to the subject matter, the type of intuition involved, and individual differences in training, strategy, and preference. Split-brain studies have already found differences among subjects, some of whom are better able to use either hemisphere interchangeably. Despite the hyperbole about the "two personalities" of the hemispheres, we still have one brain.

In the meantime, we should be wary of commentary on intuition that blithely places it in the right hemisphere. One danger is thinking that any trait associated with that side of the brain also applies to intuition. The larger concern is questionable self-help procedures. Well-meaning people have assumed that stimulating the right hemisphere will improve every intuitive function, from "getting in touch with your body" to realizing God. Even if we knew for sure that intuition was a right-hemisphere specialty, it would be stretching the point to promise that by "tuning into the right hemisphere," whatever that means, we could improve our intuition.

For example, one adviser presents the following procedure for making decisions: quiet the left brain through meditation or hypnosis (any old thing will do, he implies); "ask your right-half intuition what course you should follow"; then "ask your left brain what should be done." If you get conflicting answers from each of your hemispheres—by the writer's reasoning, one answer that is derived rationally and one derived intuitively—you delay the decision and, when pressed, go with the hemisphere that has been more successful in the past. How you are supposed to know that the message "What should I do?" is going to one hemisphere and not the other is beyond me, and how you can be sure which hemisphere is answering is also a mystery.

At this point, most "right-brain" techniques are based on wild extrapolations from brain research; to promote them in the name of improving intuition seems irresponsible. To my knowledge, we don't even know if they correlate with studies on brain function, let alone intuition.

TOWARD AN INTEGRATED VIEW

A neurological theory of intuition will no doubt have to take into account the vast organizational complexity of the brain. It will also have to take a lesson from systems theory and seek its explanations not just in terms of the specializations of brain regions but in the ways in which they interact. (Figure 2 depicts relevant brain regions.) Researchers are now getting a more integrated picture of the brain as a whole. Even the relatively simple task of seeing seems to activate brain cells in areas of the brain far removed from what had been considered the visual center. And neurons in the visual center turn out to be affected by sound and touch as well.

The integration of the two hemispheres might be more significant in complex intuition than each specialty taken separately. Nature being as economical as it is, the amazing setup it created for transmitting information from one hemisphere to the other is no doubt meant to be used. The corpus callosum, which binds the cortical hemispheres, contains about 200 million fibers. According to psychologist Bernard Baars, each fiber can fire on an average of forty times per second and up to almost a thousand times per second when very active. As many as 2 billion information events travel across the corpus callosum every second, Baars says, which suggests a degree of cooperation between the hemispheres that we haven't begun to appreciate. Research on Transcendental Meditation, for example, has found a high degree of brain-wave coherence—waves recorded from different areas moving in orderly patterns over time—between the two hemispheres. We will discuss the implications of this in the next chapter.

Further, the cerebral cortex, which covers the rest of the brain like a cap and constitutes one quarter of its volume, has many functional divisions, not just the left and right hemispheres. In the kind of tasks used in brain-lateralization studies, it would make sense to look for different activation patterns in various parts of each hemisphere. For example, the frontal area of the left hemisphere might be activated at the same time the posterior regions show right-hemisphere activation. Such patterns are, in fact, being discovered. Possibly the front of the brain is lateralized differently from the rear part of the brain. This would make sense, since front and back are known to have different functions.

The frontal lobe, which straddles the two hemispheres roughly behind the forehead and temples, is especially interesting, given its apparent role in determining our sense of the future. This area is evidently where planning is done. People with damaged frontal lobes are, in a sense, tied to the past; their actions are mainly confined to behavior they have already learned. They can't make projections and carry out forward-looking strategies. There is also evidence that when a person is in an anticipatory state, certain brain waves—called "expectancy waves"—increase in the frontal lobe. Perhaps the frontal region contributes significantly to intuition, particularly its predictive function.

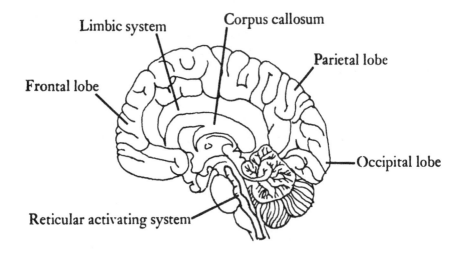

Figure 2. Cross Section of the Right Hemisphere.

We must also consider noncortical areas, such as the reticular activating system (RAS) and the limbic system. The RAS is a network of nerves that runs up through the brain stem as far as the midbrain, from where its fibers spread out, connecting with many areas of the brain. Often called the "alarm bell of the brain," the RAS arouses the cortex so that it can receive incoming information. With experience, the RAS learns to be selective; it adapts to individual requirements, alerting the cortex only to what it deems relevant. Once it rings its alarm, the RAS continues to function, maintaining alertness as long as it is appropriate. To the degree that intuition depends on incoming information of a subtle, perhaps subliminal nature, the RAS might be involved in the early stages. It might also play a role in activating the appropriate areas when confronted with an environmental stimulus that can spark intuitive connections. Also, the RAS helps determine the nervous system's level of arousal, which is significant insofar as a low-arousal/high-alertness condition is favorable for intuition.

Shaped like an ornate illuminated C in a medieval text, the limbic system wraps around the top of the brain stem. This so-called old or primitive brain consists of an interconnected group of structures, and appears to be the seat of the emotions. It seems to have what

Charles Hampden-Turner, in *Maps of the Mind,* called "intelligence of feeling." Quite possibly, the emotional and esthetic components of intuition—the exhilaration of discovery, the sense of pleasure, the wholeness and beauty that accompany knowing—are tied up with the limbic system. The system might also play a role in shifts of mood, motivation, and attentiveness; since confidence, commitment, and receptivity are important variables in intuitive thinking, that function could be significant. Finally, the location of the limbic system—just beneath the thinking cortex and straddling both hemispheres—suggests that it might in some way interact with, or coordinate, different regions that participate in intuition.

University of Pennsylvania psychiatrist/philosopher Eugene d'Aquili has proposed a theory of transcendence based on the interaction of the limbic system and the two hemispheres. He feels it can help explain a variety of intuitive mystical experiences. In the commonly accepted model, one side of the brain communicates with the other via the corpus callosum. D'Aquili believes that in elevated states of consciousness messages begin in the right hemisphere—whose "holistic perceptions" he takes to include the revelation of Absolute unity —and travel through the right parietal lobe (located toward the rear of the head, where the skull curves) and then down into the limbic system.

"Most messages from the right are broken down by the left into its own verbal, analytical language," d'Aquili told *Science Digest* in August 1982. "But when the limbic system gets involved, the thought travels from right to left brain uncensored, because emotions drive it home. In effect, gestalt perception and a simultaneous surge of emotion convince the left that the perception is true." Hence the vivid, revelatory quality of "cosmic" or "oceanic" consciousness and the unshakable conviction that usually accompanies experiences of oneness.

To my mind d'Aquili's conjectures are slightly farfetched; they rely too much on the kind of inflexible division of labor that has afflicted other interpretations of split-brain findings, portraying the hemispheres as argumentative and slightly competitive monarchs. He appears to make the common mistake of assuming that the holism of transcendence must be a right-brain phenomenon because that hemisphere appears to process information nonsequentially. But transcendence does not involve information processing in the usual sense. Further, it seems preposterous to localize what is essentially an experience of boundlessness; the TM research mentioned earlier indicates that interhemispheric coherence is highest during transcendence. Nevertheless, by opening up the two-hemisphere model to other parts of the brain, d'Aquili is probably on the right track.

The frontal lobes, the reticular activating system, and the limbic system are only some of the subsections of the brain that might interact with the cerebral hemispheres in the complex process of intuition. I mention them purely by way of conjecture in hopes of stimulating researchers interested in intuition.

THE AMAZING MICROSTRUCTURE

When asked if there was anything different about the brain of a genius, neurosurgeon Irving S. Cooper once said, "I'm certain there is. . . . I'm using 'genius' in a very restricted sense. I'm thinking of Newton or Einstein—someone who intuitively knows the answer to a problem long before he knows why. Their brains work more rapidly, for one thing. There are billions of connections being made . . . and they are being made chemically, as well as electrophysiologically."

Intuitive people do seem to make connections faster and better. For that reason, any satisfactory theory might have to dig deeper than the usual functional organization of brain regions and take cognizance of the magnificent microstructure where the connections are made. The brain contains about 100 billion cells, a tenth of which are the *neurons* we think of as the nerve cells. Each neuron has itself been likened to a small computer, and can communicate with thousands of others via 100,000 miles of branches called *dendrites*, forming a network so vast it makes the telephone system seem like a series of smoke signals. When the dendrites of one cell approach those of another, chemicals called *neurotransmitters* send messages across the gaps, or *synapses*. Computers can make connections with incredible speed, but they make them one at a time. The brain can manage many independent processes simultaneously, and a change within one cell can, according to Nobel laureate John Eccles, spread to hundreds of thousands of others within twenty milliseconds.

For a long time, scientists interested in this labyrinthine microstructure focused on the structure of the neuronal cells. Now other components are looming as far more important than anyone had realized. Neurotransmitters and various brain hormones, for example, appear to play a significant role in cognitive behavior, causing some investigators to wonder if the brain isn't more like an endocrine gland than a computer. Neurotransmitters also seem to be involved in feelings, because emotional experiences stimulate the release of some of these chemicals. Scientists who are sorting out this finding say it is amazingly complex. The same chemical, for example, will relay different messages depending on what part of the brain it goes to.

On each dendrite are hundreds or even thousands of knobby projections called *dendritic spines*. Francis Crick, codiscoverer with James Watson of DNA's double-helix shape, believes that these innumerable spines may be instrumental in learning. Another previously overlooked substructure that might one day help us understand cognitive events like intuition is the *glial cell*, 100 billion of which surround and encase the neurons. Until recently researchers thought these branchless cells acted only as protection for the information-conducting neurons. Now scientists realize that glial cells are themselves electrically sensitive, and that they are more integrally involved in cognitive activity than previously suspected. Their precise function is unknown at this time. Some researchers believe that glial cells might amplify faint electrical signals or perhaps enhance the chemical interchange at the synaptic junctions.

The old image of an electrochemical relay system composed of neurons may be in for modification as the true complexity of the brain is revealed. I have touched on only a few elements of the microstructure that might someday reveal a great deal about how the mind, with such astonishing speed, can bring together bits of information only remotely related in time and meaning to form the sudden hunch or whispered feeling that we call intuition. Those billions of cells and myriad chemicals certainly have enough to work with: the brain might be capable of storing up to one quadrillion bits of information.

Since we don't really know how the brain works in even the most rudimentary sensory-motor activities, it will be a while before we know what goes on when we do something as routine as recall a telephone number, and longer still before we sort out the neurophysiology of intuition. Brain research has proceeded on the assumption that the mind can be understood by finding out which part of the brain does what, as if it were a small factory with specialized tasks allocated to different sections of a protoplasmic assembly line. That mechanistic view has been supplemented by the traditional reductionist attitude, which holds that we will someday understand the brain by reducing everything it does to elementary electrical and chemical events.

To some people that prospect represents triumph, to others defeat. Is all that we call mind, and all we call knowing, doomed to the same "nothing but" fate that has already, according to some theories, reduced life itself to biochemistry? I think materialists and romantics alike are in for a surprise. As Wilder Penfield concluded after an illustrious career in brain research, "It will always be quite impossible to explain the mind on the basis of neuronal action within the brain."

Reductionism—the notion that we can understand things by discovering the properties of their constituent parts—is based on a drearily mechanistic conception of the universe and matter. But, oddly enough, reductionism inevitably reaches a point at which it leaves mechanism hanging in the lurch. Science has not, in fact, reduced life and matter to biochemistry; it has gone far beyond that concept. So unexpectedly that they themselves have not quite grasped its significance, scientists reduced and reduced until they reduced so far that they left the physical, material realm far behind. Matter is not solid little molecules of solid little atoms; it is an intricate web of an abstract, vibrating, nonphysical something that we have so far called energy.

The same course will no doubt be charted by brain researchers. When science is satisfied that it comprehends the underlying biochemistry of the brain, it will plunge into the atomic level, and then to the bizarre subatomic world of quantum mechanics, where what we think is solid is mostly empty space all abuzz with subatomic particles, which are not really particles but waves. Already theorists are postulating quantum-mechanical models of consciousness. Physicist Lawrence Domash, for example, has suggested that in higher states of awareness the nervous system might behave analogously to a superconductive metal, which has remarkable properties—for example, an electric current can run perpetually without resistance—due to the perfect coherence of its atoms. Domash believes that similar coherence in the atoms of nerve cells might account for transcendence and higher consciousness.

Ultimately, just as the universe, in James Jeans's words, looks more like a thought than a machine, our thinking apparatus will look less like a machine, less like a computer, and more like a mind. Then we will be a step closer to understanding intuition.

THE HERETICAL HOLOGRAPHIC BRAIN

The state of knowledge about the brain is provocative and promising, but to explain intuition we have to reach beyond the demonstrable and proven to the speculative. Let's begin with one of the most stimulating bits of conjecture that neuroscience (and, by implication, physics and metaphysics as well) has encountered in some time: the holographic theory of Karl Pribram.

For many years, scientists searched for the place in the brain where information was stored. The assumption was that each bit of information would leave a memory trace, a discernible, localized pathway that was given the name *engram*. It turns out, however, that there probably is no engram and that memory is diffused, not a localized event. Pioneering researcher Karl Lashley first noticed this when he trained rats to run a maze and then systematically destroyed parts of their brains. The rats' performance was affected adversely, of course, but the changes were related to the amount of tissue removed, not the location. As Lashley wrote in 1950, "It is not possible to demonstrate the isolated localization of a memory trace anywhere within the nervous system. Limited regions may be essential for learning or retention of a particular activity, but within such regions the parts are functionally equivalent."

We cannot take apart living human brains, of course, but the scientific world has had access to people whose brains have been damaged by accidents. It turns out that while behavior is selectively altered by the destruction of brain tissue, memory is not. If the brain worked exactly like a computer, we would not expect such a finding; destroy a connection in a computer and its memory is altered, perhaps lost entirely. Nonlocalized memory is an anomaly, the sort of thing that throws into question conventional assumptions.

Fascinated by memory distribution and related phenomena—for example, how we manage to recognize objects even when distance or perspective alters their images, or how we transfer skills from one limb to another—Stanford neuropsychologist Karl Pribram proposed a theory that blew up a gale of speculation and may have permanently changed our image of the brain. The metaphoric spark in Pribram's thinking occurred when he linked the brain and the hologram, the process invented by Denis Gabor in which three-dimensional images are produced by the interaction of light waves and a photographic plate. Just as we see and hear by processing light waves and sound waves, so might we know, intuitively or otherwise, as a result of the brain's resonating with waves of information.

To understand holograms and the holographic brain, we have to understand something about wave mechanics, and the simplest way to do so is with this frequently used example. If three pebbles are dropped into a pan of water, three sets of ripples begin to traverse the pan. The waves interact with one another. Some peaks line up with other peaks and some troughs line up with other troughs, amplifying each other; this is called *constructive interference. Destructive interference* occurs when peaks meet troughs and the two cancel each other out. The total of all the constructive and destructive interference is an *interference pattern*, which is essentially a record of everything that happens once the pebbles hit the water.

If we were able to flash-freeze the water, the jumble of apparently random squiggles on the ice would enable us to trace each wave backward and determine where the pebbles hit the water. Furthermore, if that sheet of ice were to shatter, we would be able to analyze just about any fragment and reconstruct the precise pattern of the waves. In essence, each small part of the interference pattern contains all the information needed to reconstruct the whole.

With holograms the wave patterns are formed by light. The process begins with laser light, which propagates in coherent waves—all the peaks and valleys line up with one another like spoons in a silverware drawer (see Figure 3). This is different from the light of an ordinary bulb, in which the light waves are incoherent.

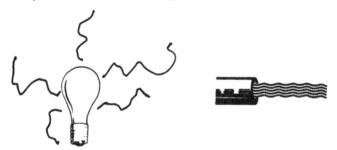

Figure 3. Incoherent waves of a light bulb (left) and coherent waves of a laser.

In the construction of a hologram, the laser beam is split in half. One half, called the *reference beam*, is aimed directly at a photographic plate, while the other half—the *control beam*—reaches the plate after reflecting off an object. What is impressed on the plate is an interference pattern, a swirl of ripples that Peter Russell, in *The Brain Book*, compared to a zebra's coat. The pattern is comparable to the ripples on the sheet of ice in the earlier analogy. When the interference pattern on the plate is illumined by a laser beam whose properties are identical to the original, a three-dimensional image of the object appears in space. This is an exact re-creation of the light field of the object, and is possible only because of the coherent waves of the laser. (In ordinary light, we see just a chaos of lines.) And the image can be reconstructed from just a small section of the plate, because the whole is somehow contained in each part. The only loss is of detail and clarity, and only if the part is very small.

The holographic model is to our previous conception of the brain as a hologram is to an ordinary photograph. There is no point-to-point correspondence between the objects "out there" and the image on the plate, and there is no one-to-one correspondence between human experience and points on the brain. Somehow, according to the holographic theory, the brain absorbs information from the outside in wave form and stores it in some way analogous to the way a photographic plate stores a holographic image. The findings of recent research show that the brain does indeed receive information in wave form: all sensory coding is a form of wave analysis.

By changing the angle of the photographic plate and the frequency of the laser beam, thousands of images can be recorded and then re-created as holograms. Perhaps the brain, with its tremendous capacity for bringing in and storing information, does something similar, in a sense creating an array of interference patterns. When learning or remembering, we might decode and reencode waves, much as television transmission converts images to waves and back again to images. Perhaps our attention, a desire, a need, or an unanswered question acts as the equivalent of the "reconstruction beam" that generates the holographic image when it is aimed at the interference pattern. The result in the mind might be the re-creation of an image or idea, as in memory, or—going beyond the present capabilities of holograms—an entirely new image or thought that combines elements from the stored array of interference patterns.

Our instrument of cognition—whether it is called brain or mind —begins to resemble an oscillating resonator that collects, processes, and transmits vibrations. While this in itself might be difficult to imagine, holographic theory makes it a bit easier to comprehend how several patterns with no obvious connection can simultaneously mesh together into a new unit of knowledge, without a linear series of steps.

If the brain works like a hologram, storing information in such a way that any bit of information is accessible in every part, then knowledge may not depend entirely on a sequence of neuronal connections over time and across physical space. This could help account for the amazing rapidity of intuition. Perhaps the mind decodes and simplifies experience the way scientists mathematically reduce complex wave patterns to simple composite waves. If so, then, as Pribram put it, "all that is needed is to store a few rules rather than vast amounts of detail." Perhaps this would help explain how the mind, outside awareness, apprehends principles, laws, single truths, or forthcoming events from a constellation of impressions or from many sets of constellations. Holography is a very efficient method of encoding; its principles might well apply to something as efficient as the intuitive mind.

Predictably, Pribram's theory has stimulated extreme reactions. It runs counter to the mechanistic image of reality that has dominated Western thought for the past few centuries. Many conservative scientists have rejected the theory outright, taking exception to what they believe is overgeneralizing on Pribram's part. But Pribram notes that physicists and others accustomed to interpreting the physical world in terms of waves don't find the idea all that outlandish. The world of quantum physics is precisely that: a universe of interlocking waves that congeal in an infinite number of ways to create what we perceive as matter and separate objects.

At the same time, there are people who have enthusiastically embraced the holographic model. Some accept it as fact, not hypothesis, and take it literally rather than metaphorically. While the model may, in fact, turn out to be much more than a provocative analogy, at this point it is probably best to think of it as simply that. It is possible that the theory will soon be modified, or even replaced by a new one, which will no doubt represent yet another step toward a less mechanical, more metaphysical understanding of how mind interacts with the world in order to know what it knows.

Neurobiologist Oliver Sacks extended the subject still further in this almost mystical statement: "Our consciousness is like a flame or a fountain, rising up from infinite depths. We transmit, but we are not the first cause. We are vessels or funnels for what lies beyond us.

Ultimately we mirror the nature which made us." In the final analysis, any theory of intuition will have to connect the mind with "what lies beyond us." Some thinkers have taken the first step with the holographic model.

David Bohm, a former colleague of Einstein's and a professor of theoretical physics at the University of London, maintains that the familiar world of cause and effect, of separate objects and forms—what he calls the *explicate order*—derives from a deeper realm that exists outside space and time. Beyond the reach of sense perception and the apparatus of science, Bohm's *implicate order* is "enfolded" in the explicate and constitutes a unified, integral whole. As in a hologram, each part of the implicate realm would contain everything in the whole, and the human mind would have access to that information. Perhaps we might think of the universe as a vast interference pattern, with every event and every thought contributing to it, like pebbles dropped into a pond. If the analogy holds, each mind would contain within it all the information that ever was in all the universe. We would be, in effect, pieces of an all-pervading holographic plate.

It is that kind of thinking that promises to explain how the intuitive mind knows what it knows. Let's carry the notion with us into the next chapter, where we will attempt to tie together many of the threads we have gathered so far.

7

The Intuitive Mind

Knowledge is a function of being. When there is a change
in the being of the knower, there is a corresponding
change in the nature and amount of knowledge.
                                                        —Aldous Huxley

Huxley's statement captures a most important practical message:
the nature and quality of intuition vary with the knower's state of
consciousness. In expanding on this basic theme, we will attempt to
explain how intuition does what it does. This chapter brings together
material from a variety of sources, but its basic framework comes
from what Huxley termed the "perennial philosophy," the common
core of wisdom in the world's mystical traditions. Often viewed
merely as mythology or religious speculation, these venerable texts
are better understood as ancient journal articles penned by researchers who explored consciousness the way modern scientists gather information about material reality. To my mind they actually demystify
questions that have eluded us in the West. At the very least they
suggest hypotheses and theoretical models. My principal source is the
Vedic tradition of India, and in particular the interpretations of Maharishi Mahesh Yogi, whose media image has unfortunately obscured
his important contributions to the study of consciousness.

In the *Rig Veda*, the basic theme of this chapter is expressed,
with characteristic economy, as "Knowledge is structured in consciousness." This statement can be understood on many levels, and
we will return to it several times. One interpretation is that we have
knowledge just by virtue of the fact that we are conscious. In that
respect, when Descartes issued his famous dictum, "I think therefore

I am," he put the cart before the horse—or, as a friend of mine once said, "He put Descartes before the source." The correct order should have been "I am, therefore I think" or "I am, therefore I know."

Whatever we know is known only within our individual consciousness. Even what we call sense perception is the mind's becoming aware of the end result of waves that had been coded and recoded within the organism. And what is known varies with different knowers. A botanist will see a flower one way, a lover will see it another way, a misanthrope another, and a poet like William Blake might see "a heaven in a wild flower."

But what we know, and how well we know, varies not only from person to person but with changes in individual awareness. When we awaken in the morning, the nature and quality of our knowledge changes dramatically from what it had been in sleep or dream states of consciousness, and it continues to change. As we gradually shake the cobwebs, the accuracy and intelligibility of our thoughts increase. During the course of any day we experience fluctuations of awareness, and therefore of our ability to perceive and know. The differences depend on a configuration of conditions that form our state of consciousness.

These simple points apply to knowing of any kind, but perhaps especially to intuition, since it is less protected by the conventions that govern reason. The form that intuition takes, the clarity of the experience, and the degree to which it reflects reality vary as consciousness varies. Certainly one's past experience, preferences, and habits of thought all affect the quality of an intuition. In general, however, the key variable is the knower's state of consciousness, and that is determined by the overall condition of the nervous system. Because the physiology of consciousness is a relatively new field, we don't know precisely what constitutes a conducive state for intuition. But, putting together the known data and the intuitive experience as it is commonly described, we can postulate, as suggested in Chapter 4, that intuition would be favored by a combination of low arousal and high alertness—a calm, wakeful, receptive state with relatively little extraneous mental noise to interfere with the input of the intuitive mind.

Based on the Transcendental Meditation research of R. K. Wallace, David Orme-Johnson, and others, we can further postulate that EEG coherence—a correlation between brain waves from separate regions of the brain—might be an important defining variable. I say this for several reasons: there appears to be a relationship between coherence and the experience of transcendence, which is the epitome of silent alertness; coherence has been associated with creativity, cognitive flexibility, and other performance measures that probably involve intuition; and anecdotal evidence suggests that people who have transcendent experiences are likely to be intuitive in the usual sense of the word. Quite possibly, coherence is an indication of a certain orderly interaction among different areas of the brain, and its exact nature varies depending on which regions are called into play by the particular intuition. Combined with measures of basic physiological stability, such as galvanic skin response, EEG coherence might be the key to an empirical description of the ideal state for intuition. The same parameters, if found, might also apply to the physiology of incubation.

Perhaps, if Lawrence Domash's superconductor analogy is correct, a coherent nervous system would conduct information without resistance, both from the environment and within. Coherence is an especially tempting criterion because of the holographic model of the mind. Perhaps, just as holography depends on the coherence of the laser beam, intuition depends on the coherence of the nervous system. We will come back to this idea as we explore "knowledge is structured in consciousness" metaphorically.

DEEP THOUGHT

Intuition can be understood as the mind turning in on itself and apprehending the result of processes that have taken place outside awareness. A coherent nervous system might process material more appropriately, forming configurations that are in line with the desires and needs of the individual. A more orderly system would also draw the knower's attention to the right place within the mind at the right time, and it would have access to a broader base of information. Ordinarily we think of intuitive knowing as the product of information gathered in by the senses and somehow recombined like ingredients in a soup and served up to the conscious mind. We are going to expand that view and bring into play a richer fund of raw materials.

Picture the mind as an ocean (see Figure 4). The ripples on the surface represent ordinary active awareness, turbulent and ever-changing. We experience this layer as a constant flow of thoughts and sensations, each with a distinct and unique character. Beneath that is a range of deeper levels, which would encompass all nonconscious processes and structures. Underlying and permeating it all is absolute pure consciousness, the changeless, boundless, universal Self. In the diagram, pure consciousness is separated by the straight line at bottom, but that is a shortcoming of illustrations. In fact, all mental events at every level are perturbations within that infinite field, just as waves and currents are individual expressions of the boundless ocean.

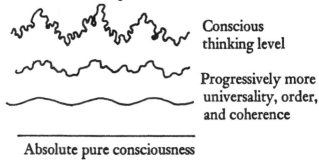

Conscious
thinking level

Progressively more
universality, order,
and coherence

Absolute pure consciousness

Figure 4. Hierarchical model of the mind.

Within the mind, each progressively deeper layer more closely resembles pure consciousness; it would partake more of its qualities, just as objects closer to a fire become progressively hotter and brighter. Each deeper level would be more stable, more universal, less restricted by space and time, and closer to the truth, since pure consciousness is silent, all-pervading, beyond time and space, and eternal. Each level encompasses the levels above it, supporting, ordering, and directing them, just as in the physical realm molecular structures are more inclusive than the material objects they comprise, atoms are more universal than molecules, and so forth. Hence at deeper levels the mind has more in common with other minds; it is less individuated.

At the end of the preceding chapter we presented the possibility that individual minds were analogous to pieces of a universal holographic plate. We each have access to something like a cosmic interference pattern, or perhaps many interference patterns, consisting of information waves. Every event, even every thought, would create a wave that would spread out infinitely and leave a trace at every point in the universe, including each human mind. The surface levels of the mind would contain information pertaining to the individual's unique experience; at deeper levels, waves contributing to the interference pattern would be increasingly more universal, culminating in the all-encompassing Absolute.

We can postulate that the quality of intuition is related to the degree of access our awareness has to deep levels of the mind. Because that would depend on our state of consciousness, there would be a direct relationship between qualities of the nervous system—which we will summarize with the word *coherence*—and access to the depths of the mind, where universal impulses of information can be tapped. We will return to the nature of this information shortly.

To evoke a hologram from what is essentially a chaotic jumble of waves on a plate, the coherent beam of a laser must be focused on it. This elicits the appropriate information and structures it in a meaningful way. The angle and frequency of the reconstruction beam determine the nature of the image projected. Imagine that attention is like a submarine capable of diving within the oceanlike mind and directing a beam of awareness at any point above it or around it, but not below. A person's state of consciousness is equivalent to the depth the submarine of attention is capable of attaining, and this depth is related to coherence. In higher states of consciousness, attention is capable of hovering at deeper levels of the mind, and from there it can aim coherent beams at a wider range of the cosmic fund of information.

We could postulate that when the appropriate configuration of knowledge has been assembled, attention is drawn to the right point in the mind by some kind of resonance effect. If it is capable of the necessary depth and coherence, the mind will dip into itself and have what we experience as an intuition.

Now we have our original point—that the quality of intuition depends on the state of consciousness—expressed in terms of layers of the mind and the holographic metaphor. An intuitive experience would consist of beaming the attention onto some portion of the constantly changing holographic plate we call the mind. What it comes up with depends on the angle and frequency of the beam, which is determined by desire, intention, and need. The deeper one is capable of diving, the more coherent the beam, the wider the range of information available, and the more accuracy and clarity the intuition will have. At maximum coherence, the full range of the ocean could be traversed and the illumination of transcendence would occur.

We will discuss the implications of this model after examining more closely what the deeper levels of the mind might contain.

THE UNCHARTED DEPTHS OF THE MIND

A variety of elements are recombined beneath conscious awareness to give rise to the patterns that become intuitions when attention is drawn to them. Close to the surface, we might assume, are deposits of past impressions—singular memories of physical and mental events. There also would be encoded inferences and conclusions that are abstracted from the concepts, categories, and classes we form and modify as we grow, and that enable us to make sense of subsequent experience. Such stored elements would be part of the information that is combined with acquired data about a particular situation or problem.

We should also leave room for the Freudian subconscious, that repository of repressed emotions whose influence on thought and behavior we have come to take for granted. Some psychologists, notably Eric Berne in a series of papers written some thirty years ago, have linked the subconscious directly to intuition, particularly as it relates to judgments about other people. In this view, primal instincts and early experience shape what we perceive and think. A strict Freudian interpretation of intuition, however, has severe limitations, and invariably turns into a pre/trans fallacy in which all nonrational processes are reduced to a *subrational* level. Freudians have a way of linking divine revelation and artistic inspiration with neurosis, hallucination, and infantile regression. Sages get confused with schizophrenics, transcendence with trance, enlightenment with self-delusion. Nevertheless, the Freudian subconscious has to be included in any consideration of nonconscious processes; and the basic Freudian notion that defense mechanisms and repressed needs influence our thoughts in ways of which we are unaware has to be kept in mind when evaluating intuitive experiences.

But we need to go beyond individual experience and provide the intuitive mind with a broader base of material. The holographic model, in which each mind has access to the whole of a universal pattern, provides a concrete image and makes it easier to conceive of shared information. Such phenomena as telepathy and clairvoyance, for example, become a bit more plausible, since they would no longer depend on particles or energy forms having to traverse space and time. Instead, anything that happens in the universe, including thought, is simultaneously encoded everywhere else. The concept is consistent with the tenets of the "perennial philosophy," and is not far removed from modern physics. Indeed, David Bohm's "implicate order," which postulates a holographlike structure for the universe, was derived from his work in quantum mechanics.

The world according to quantum field theory and relativity is not our familiar world of separate forms and structures. Rather, material reality is viewed as a web of interconnected fluctuations of energy. In the words of Fritjof Capra, in *The Tao of Physics*, subatomic particles "are dynamic patterns which do not exist as isolated entities, but as integral parts of an inseparable network of interactions. These interactions involve a ceaseless flow of energy manifesting itself as the exchange of particles. . . . The particle interactions give rise to the stable structures which build up the material world, which again do not remain static, but oscillate in rhythmic movements. The whole universe is thus engaged in endless motion and activity, in a continual cosmic dance of energy."

The deep levels of material creation, then, are all interconnected, and since the brain is made up of the same stuff as rocks and stars, it does not take much to enlarge that vision to include human consciousness. Most scientists are reluctant to do so, but in traditional non-Western philosophies it is taken for granted that mind and material reality are connected. Indeed—a point we will explore further—they are considered different manifestations of the same basic essence, which is consciousness.

The astounding phenomena associated with subatomic reality make the contention that mind has access to unusual sources of information seem more plausible: particles go backward in time; electrons show up in more than one place at a time; electrons "tunnel" across insulating barriers by dissolving into an unmanifest "vacuum state" and resurrecting on the other side. Perhaps the most curious phenomenon is the EPR effect, named for Einstein and two colleagues, Podolsky and Rosen, in which two subatomic particles that once interacted can instantaneously respond to changes in each other even when they have been separated in space and time by light years.

Enigmas like the EPR effect (since formalized by John S. Bell as Bell's Theorem and confirmed experimentally) have touched off provocative speculation among physicists and armchair philosophers.

Some have suggested that perhaps thought is faster than the speed of light. A small step from that heresy, and in many ways more satisfying, is to suppose that the two particles in Bell's Theorem are somehow connected even though they are far removed from one another. This premise is acceptable in a holographic universe, in which the multiplicity of ordinary reality melts into a seamless, unbroken whole —in Bohm's words, a "single structure of indivisible links." In such a universe, everything is connected, and time and space are not barriers. Human consciousness would be part of that web, and when properly tuned could resonate with any portion of it.

Given such a universe, it is conceivable that the intuitive mind can draw on sources that are not available to the senses and are not confined to individuals. Western thought is sparse in this regard, but a few significant voices have postulated a link between individual mind and a larger, more encompassing field of information and intelligence. The Jesuit philosopher Teilhard de Chardin, for example, conceived of a region called the *noosphere*, which he said is "composed of particles of human consciousness . . . formed by the inner experiences of mankind." But perhaps the most respected figure in modern Western thought to connect the mind with something more universal was Carl Gustav Jung.

THE COLLECTIVE UNCONSCIOUS OF CARL JUNG

In his celebrated break from Freud, Jung gave us a more positive and expanded vision of the mind's depths. The unconscious was no "mere depository of the past," he maintained, "but is also full of future psychic situations and ideas." The unconscious, in Jung's view, is a self-contained entity with its own reality that stands in "compensatory relation" to ego-consciousness. New contents of which the individual has never been aware can arise from the depths of the unconscious, not just in the dream state but in all experiences. Motivated by the basic urge toward self-realization, the unconscious both responds to conscious events and takes the lead.

In Jung's schema, there are two layers of the unconscious: the personal and the collective. The former contains all the psychic material stored beneath the threshold of individual conciousness, including forgotten and repressed experiences and impressions gathered through both sensory and subliminal means. Jung then delocalized the concept with his "collective unconscious," which includes the "inherited powers of human imagination as it was from time immemorial." Here are the universal, primordial images he called "archetypes," which express themselves in the myths and legends of all cultures.

The collective unconscious refers to those contents that are common to everyone, the ancient and universal thought forms of humanity. Jung saw the archetypes as a kind of cognitive instinctual apparatus, as much like feelings as thoughts, that exert a powerful influence, not just symbolically but as spurs to action and original thinking. They are not, in his words, "inherited in the sense that a person consciously remembers or has images that his ancestors had. Rather they are predispositions or potentialities for experiencing and responding to the world."

To Jung, creativity and intuition implied a direct link between the conscious mind and deep archetypal structures. The archetypes have the power to confer meaningful interpretations to experience and to interject into a given situation their own impulses and thought formations. Intuitive people, said Jung, can perceive the inner processes and "supply certain data which may be of the utmost importance for understanding what is going on in the world." They can also prognosticate, foreseeing "new possibilities in more or less clear outline, as well as events which later actually do happen." In Jung's writings there are references to a variety of intuitive experiences, all attributed to the stirring of the collective unconscious.

THE FORMATIVE CAUSATION OF RUPERT SHELDRAKE

With Jung's collective unconscious, individual minds partake of an information base that is not limited by the restrictions of ordinary memory, sense perception, time, or space. Now a provocative and controversial hypothesis has been proposed by British biologist Rupert Sheldrake that links mental and physical phenomena in a single theory of change. Sheldrake's "formative causation" further adds to the source material with which the intuitive mind might work.

According to Sheldrake, all systems are regulated by invisible organizing fields that serve as blueprints for form and behavior. Whenever a member of a species learns something new, the causative field, or blueprint, is altered. If the new behavior is repeated often enough, says Sheldrake, a "morphic resonance" is created, which will affect every member of the species the way violin strings resonate when a related one is plucked. The "morphogenetic field" is outside time and space; action at a distance is central to the theory.

Certain phenomena, previously unexplained, start to make sense with formative causation. For example, when a number of rats learn to perform a new task, subsequent generations acquire the behavior much more quickly. This is not just learning handed down genetically; rats that are not biologically related to the original learners also learn more quickly.

A celebrated variation of this phenomenon was observed in a colony of monkeys on a Japanese island. The monkeys had been unable to figure out how to deal with sweet potatoes covered with sand. Then a young female named Imo had the equivalent of a Eureka! experience: she carried her potatoes to a stream and washed them. This simian Archimedes proceeded to teach the procedure to her family and playmates, who showed it to others. Soon the idea spread like a trendy new diet, and large numbers of monkeys were washing their potatoes. Then a critical mass was reached—what came to be called the "hundredth monkey"—and washing potatoes went from fad to universal norm. Every monkey in the colony was doing it. Not long thereafter it was noted that monkeys on nearby islands and on the mainland had spontaneously acquired Imo's insight.

By extending the theory to human memory and learning, Sheldrake has linked the individual mind to a field shared with others. If the theory is correct, events in the past can create patterns that influence similar configurations in the present, however distant in space and time. "Organisms tune in to similar organisms in the past," says Sheldrake, "and the more similar they are, the more specific is this tuning. In general, the most specific morphic resonance affecting an organism in the present will be that from its *own* past states. Thus its memories need not be stored as traces or impressions within its nervous system, but rather may be given directly from its own past states by morphic resonance."

Perhaps some intuitions flash into our minds because other humans have had identical or related thoughts and deposited them in a morphogenetic field, where they mix with our own previous contributions. We might resonate with those elements of the field that are closest to us biologically and closely related to our desires, interests, and needs. In holographic terms, we might postulate that aspects of the cosmic interference pattern nearest to the individual's heritage and concerns would be most likely to draw attention. They would also respond to the particular frequency of his attention, or reconstruction beam.

Sheldrake's theory helps explain why the same ideas seem to crop up among people who have had no contact with one another, a phenomenon readily observable in the history of art and science. In the early twentieth century, for example, painting and sculpture were becoming less representational, poetry and fiction were breaking out of traditional forms, and science was penetrating the inner structure of matter. It was as if everyone had had the idea to move beyond boundaries and delve beneath the surface of things and had discovered pure abstraction.

Human experience is so diverse, and the human mind so complex, that relating Sheldrake's theory to intuition requires some speculation. Too much of what we intuit is unique to particular individuals, not universally applicable. Perhaps morphic resonance pertains to principles, concepts, and cognitive rules, not just to specific facts or precise behaviors such as washing potatoes. Quite possibly our own past thoughts and those of others with whom we are harmonically related combine with new experiences to form unique configurations. We might experience these as intuitions with specific and unique applications. Something like that could also help explain the creative spark that initiates a morphogenetic field, something now missing from Sheldrake's theory.

PLATO'S FORMS: ANCIENT INSIGHTS INTO MIND

Both Jung's archetypes and Sheldrake's morphogenetic fields are reminiscent of Plato's forms, except that Plato went a bit further. He explicitly linked his archetypal forms to the material sphere as well as to the unconscious mind. Plato held that material objects are merely imperfect, transient copies of transcendental, eternal patterns—the forms. Whereas material structures are relative, changeable, individuated, localized, and defective, the forms are universal, absolute, omnipresent, and perfect models. There are cosmological forms such as the One and the Many, mathematical forms such as the straight line and the circle, forms pertaining to such human qualities as courage, and to principles, concepts, and material shapes. In Plato's account of creation, the forms of the elements—fire, earth, air, and water—are the earliest manifestations, and they resonate in a mathematically lawful manner to generate the world of objects.

The mind, said Plato, has latent, inborn impressions of these abstract forms, which make all sensory experience and all knowledge possible. To Plato, knowing was actually remembering; when we perceive and think, the mind recalls those deep, innate structures that in various combinations and permutations are the prototypes of all that is knowable. We are unaware of the forms, but they make intelligible our variegated experience. The concept was borrowed by the rationalist philosophers of Europe, who held that the mind was not a blank slate at birth, but entered life with certain innate predispositions that shape how we perceive and know—a priori orientations such as cause and effect, time and space, or the axioms of Euclidean geometry. Whether such innate structures actually exist is still a philosophical conundrum, but recent research indicates that infants are capable of far more sophisticated cognitive behavior than previously suspected, much of which cannot be explained by learning.

For example, babies can imitate facial expressions before they ever see themselves in a mirror or know that they have faces like the ones staring at them in their cribs. Also, a study by Barbara Landau and two colleagues at the University of Pennsylvania found that blindfolded children and adults—and, significantly, a two-and-a-half-year-old child blind from birth—were able to set a correct course between two objects along a route they had not previously followed, after moving to each object from a third point. Reporting in *Science* (September 11, 1981), the researchers concluded that "this blind child, and sighted controls, know about some of the metric properties of space, probably Euclidean properties" and can somehow derive new angles and distances. The psychologists suggested that innate knowledge is one possible explanation for these capacities.

Plato's forms add a permanent, unchanging aspect to the universal interference pattern. Sheldrake's morphogenetic fields are derived from previous events, the result more of habit than of timeless properties. They are in constant flux and are modified by new experience. The two positions are easily reconciled: why not both changing *and* nonchanging? Perhaps Sheldrake's fields are created through repeated interspecies experience, but deeper structures—eternal archetypes—are permanently embedded in the matrix of nature. They might constitute, in part, the rules and principles that govern the formation of the more transient components of the hologram. It would make no sense to have changeable, evolutionary fields without reference to still deeper, more fundamental laws that guide their creation and development.

Like Jung, Plato suggested that when the individual mind is in tune with the archetypes, knowledge and action will be more effective. Plato went a step further, and a step closer to Vedic philosophy, when he added that the forms themselves were knowable. This would, in itself, constitute a high level of intuition, since the knower would directly apprehend fundamental properties of nature. Further, Plato stated that knowing the forms constituted the only true basis for knowledge of any kind. Most philosophers either underplay this aspect of Plato's thought or assume that he meant the forms could be reasoned about with the process known as the "dialectic." But, according to philosopher Jonathan Shear, Plato himself held that the forms could *not* be known through ordinary sense perception or reason.

"He emphatically distinguished the dialectic from discursive reasoning as we know it," says Shear, "and specifically from the types of reasoning used in mathematics, physics, and philosophical discourse." Shear points to phrases such as "turning the mind in the opposite direction" and "employing a different faculty" as indications that Plato was alluding to a process similar to Eastern meditation techniques. The purpose was to produce a direct intuitive experience of the transcendental forms.

If Shear is correct, Plato was close indeed to the perennial philosophy. The highest form is what Plato termed the Good, which "imparts truth to the things that are known and the power of knowing to the knower. . . . It is the cause of knowledge and truth." Plato's description of the Good is so reminiscent of traditional Eastern descriptions of the eternal unchanging Absolute—the Tao, or Brahman—that some feel he was talking about exactly that. Hence Plato's direct experience of the Good might be what we termed illumination, *samadhi* in Indian texts. And his suggestion that such an experience "imparts . . . the power of knowing to the knower" is in line with the idea that transcendence opens up channels to other intuitive experience.

ONE STEP DEEPER:
THE VIEW FROM THE EAST

Central to our theme is a universe in which mind and matter, subject and object, knower and known are not separated, as they are in classical scientism. To fully understand how we can turn our attention within and come out with knowledge that pertains to the outside world, we have to assume a certain isomorphism between mind and matter. This is central to the perennial philosophy, and is particularly explicit in its Eastern manifestations. As the *Upanishads* so succinctly express it, "What is within is also without. What is without is also within."

The oceanlike model we used for the mind can portray all of creation. On the surface are all the forms and objects of the familiar, tangible world. Underlying and pervading them, as we know from science, are increasingly universal and nonmaterial levels of reality, which encompass the more individuated manifestations—molecules, atoms, subatomic particles, fields, each more abstract and all-pervasive. The basis of it all is undifferentiated Being, the Absolute, which is the source and substance of existence. Every form and every structure is a manifestation of the Absolute, a perturbation in an infinite field directed by cosmic intelligence. And so is the mind.

Much has been made of the parallels between modern science and Eastern cosmology, and with good reason. But it must be emphasized that, at least in a few crucial respects, the twain have not yet met. One difference is the absence in the West of an unchanging, absolute foundation to the phenomenal world. Also, because of the unpredictable, uncertain nature of subatomic phenomena, physics views the fundamental patterns of reality as indeterminate and probabalistic. By extension, knowledge is held to be inevitably uncertain and approximate. The East is more optimistic. In Indian cosmology, for example, there are still deeper, more subtle layers of reality, which we might call tendencies, or laws of nature—not laws in the scientific sense, derived by the human mind, but nature's eternal regulatory mechanisms. These tendencies, which are knowable to the developed intuition, might be thought of as a hierarchy of ordering principles that structure and guide the evolutionary flow of creation, organizing and ordering the cosmos.

The other step not yet taken in the West is to link the seamless web of interrelated energy events that constitute reality to human consciousness. We have already stated that when a person transcends, he comes to know the Self, which is also the basis of all creation. It is also true that the same intelligence which flows through the material realm is flowing through us; the patterns and principles that govern the ebb and flow of the "outside" are also at work "inside." The universe is made of consciousness. This adds another dimension to the holographic model and explains why mystics and yogis have been able to turn within themselves and come out knowing how the universe works. They simply perceived their own nature, which is, so to speak, nature's nature.

The ancient texts were not written by philosophers reasoning with knitted brow or collecting objective data in particle accelerators along the Ganges. Wisdom was intuited directly, and the fact that each day science moves a step closer to the perennial philosophy attests to the potential power of the developed intuitive mind. The yogis and sages intuited directly the dynamics of consciousness. They expressed their insights in terms we now consider religious or mystical, but we are gaining new respect for those ancient voices, and are coming to understand that the sages may have intuited eternal principles. Creation myths, for example, may have been direct intuitions, expressed in a variety of ways, of how the unmanifest One becomes the manifest Many, an event that is said to be repeated with the creation of every thought and that can be cognized directly in higher states of consciousness. "How do I know the ways of all things at the Beginning?" asked the Taoist sage Lao Tzu. "By what is within me."

Perhaps the parallel structure of the objective and subjective realms explains how poets, in Wordsworth's words, "see into the heart of things" and how scientists are able to penetrate hidden secrets of nature. One of philosophy's great conundrums has been what is referred to as the "unreasonable effectiveness of mathematics." Somehow mathematicians are able—by purely mental procedures, a central element of which is intuition—to derive information that is applicable to aspects of physical reality which have never been observed and that predict consequences which were previously unsuspected. The isomorphism of inner and outer might also explain why minds like Einstein's can do what they do. As Jeremy Bernstein said of Einstein, "He arrived at results by a phenomenal intuition of what they should be by a deep inner contact with nature." Perhaps "deep inner contact with nature" is actually deep inner contact with one's self.

Patanjali's *Yoga Sutras*, the most authoritative of the ancient yogic texts, spells out how knowledge of the outer world can be obtained by turning within. This explanation relates to an earlier assertion—that transcendence opens other intuitive channels. An entire chapter of Patanjali is given over to an explication of *siddhis*, or supernormal powers. Among them are many having to do with direct intuitive knowledge. According to Patanjali, by directing his attention within in certain ways the yogi can know "the past and the future," "other minds," "foreknowledge of death," "objects at a great distance," "the cosmic regions," "the arrangements of the stars," "the bodily system," "the distinction between absolute and relative," and more. It is also said that "everything can be known."

What is most interesting in our context is that the prerequisite for these powers is said to be *samyama*, a complex term that boils down to the ability of the mind to remain absorbed in the transcendent and also think. This seems to be a contradiction, since transcendence is perfect, nonlocalized unity, consciousness without thought. But it is said that an expanded mind can linger at the level where the changeless Absolute meets the transient relative—on our diagram, the straight line at bottom. It is as if the mind has one foot on either side and can operate willfully without losing the universality of awareness associated with pure consciousness. This state of awareness is called *ritam bhara pragya*, which translates as "full of unalloyed truth."

To use an earlier image, this would be a case of the submarine of attention gaining the ability to station itself at the very deepest level of the mind. Theoretically, with attention so situated, the mind can know anything, because it commands the entire territory. At that level there would be no restrictions of time or space; consciousness in its pure state is said to be infinitely correlated with everything in creation. Polarities dissolve, enabling the knower to apprehend the unity that underlies the apparent diversity; this might also elicit fruitful analogies that contribute to intuitive insight. And intuitions from that level would be experienced with great clarity, since the nervous system would be at maximum coherence. There would be no "static" to interfere with the apprehension of the impulse, which would be perceived in its purest, least adulterated state.

Patanjali also describes what we called the "intimacy" of intuitive experience, that sense of entering into the object of knowledge and knowing its essence. According to one commentary, Patanjali states that for someone operating from the level of *samadhi*, or transcendence, "the mind can achieve identity with a gross object so that the object alone remains without the thought waves of our own reactions." An alternative way of describing this is to say that the thought waves of the knower resonate perfectly with the fundamental vibrations of the object. This would provide what Immanuel Kant called knowledge of the "thing-in-itself," which he contended was impossible to obtain through reason or sense perception, as they are always filtered through subjective awareness.

In theory, a person whose awareness is situated at the junction of the unmanifest and manifest would be operating in harmony with cosmic law. He might be able to intuit directly nature's eternal organizing principles. More important, his intuitive mind would be guided and directed by those principles, whether he was consciously aware of them or not. We don't have to understand the laws of gravitation in order to sit, lift, or avoid falling out of windows. Similarly, we don't have to understand all of nature's laws in order to act in accord with them. In a high state of consciousness, actions are said to be spontaneously right. The intuitive impulses that inform and guide the enlightened mind would be appropriate for both the individual and the environment, since the mind would be resonating with the deepest impulses of nature. We would know what nature intends us to know. In religious terms this has been called living in accord with divine will. But regardless of their spiritual orientation, those happy people who seem to do everything right—in Patanjali's terms, those who "avoid the danger that has not yet come"—are probably functioning much of the time from some deep level of the mind.

These descriptions of higher states of consciousness might sound remote and farfetched, but they are worth contemplating seriously, and perhaps they can serve as an ideal toward which to strive. They can be seen as prototypes of what the intuitive mind can attain, and they epitomize the essential message of this chapter: knowledge is structured in consciousness. We have introduced a loftier interpretation of the aphorism: Consciousness contains within it all possible knowledge.

THE PRACTICAL IMPLICATIONS

We began by stating that the quality of intuition depends mainly on our state of consciousness. Higher consciousness is defined metaphorically as the ability to station attention at deeper levels of the mind. It should now be clear why pursuing illumination is not only a lofty goal in its own right but a way of cultivating all functions of intuition: each added degree of illumination is synonymous with purity of consciousness, which means functioning with greater frequency and consistency from the deepest levels of the mind. Physiologically, we postulate that higher consciousness would be associated with a high degree of stability, order, and alertness in the nervous system. In everyday terms, this would be experienced as mental clarity, inner calm, and the relative absence of extraneous mental noise.

If this analysis is accurate, it would follow that the most important thing anyone can do to develop intuition is to cultivate a higher state of consciousness. While individual states of awareness vary, each of us can be said to operate at some basic level around which we fluctuate, depending on a variety of physical, mental, and environmental factors. With diligence, we can increase the rate by which consciousness expands.

Our way of life is not exactly conducive to establishing the core of silence that provides the best background for intuition. Serenity has been considered a luxury, not a practical virtue. The constant bombardment of the senses, the often overbearing pressure and pace of modern life, the linking of happiness with outer achievement and material acquisition, and the short-circuiting of our connection to nature—all these conditions have created a kind of chronic arousal and a low signal-to-noise ratio. At the same time, additional leisure time and relief from drudgery have created more opportunities for us to attend to the condition of our minds and bodies. Americans have seized these opportunities to alleviate the buildup of tension and stress, and such efforts can only improve the physiological conditions for intuition, whatever their primary intent.

In this context, we ought to increase our efforts to understand the physiology of consciousness. Each new finding helps us isolate the behaviors that contribute to higher states of awareness. There are, of course, a multitude of ways to cultivate consciousness, because literally everything we do, think, or come into contact with affects our nervous system. The array of practices advocated by various consciousness disciplines, both ancient and modern—all of which aim for the same paradoxical condition of inner silence and maximum alertness—attest to the many ways the task can be approached. But few activities are universally appropriate. Everyone is different and everyone is changing, and with those variations come changes in what each nervous system needs in order to sustain a coherent state. Those who assiduously follow a path of consciousness development might change their eating, exercise, and other habits as their needs change. If they make the right choices for themselves, they will gradually become more intuitive, whether or not that is a conscious goal. In cultivating a coherent nervous system, we should find that intuition becomes more consistently fertile and truth-producing.

With respect to lifestyle, each of us should experiment to discover the conditions that bring about a consistent level of inner silence and heightened clarity—the hallmarks of a consciousness conducive to quality intuition. Certain procedures can be recommended without hesitation, including yoga exercises and meditation, the main constituents of respected paths for expanding consciousness (we will discuss these further in Chapter 9). Equally important is to discover which activities, substances, and environments detract from the desired state, and then to avoid them.

In the remaining chapters we will focus exclusively on practical considerations, discussing ways by which we can get the most out of our intuitive capacity. This is like learning to draw water from a well. Raising our level of consciousness is like digging the well deeper.

8

Getting Ready for Intuition

If it be now, 'tis not to come; if it be not to come, it will
be now; if it be not now, yet it will come: the readiness is
all.

—Shakespeare (*Hamlet*)

Intuition can't be ordered, commanded, implored, or contrived.
We simply have to be ready for it. As discussed in the preceding
chapter, the central factor in determining readiness is our state of consciousness. In addition, we program the intuitive mind with our goals,
perceptions, beliefs, and the way we approach problems and decisions. Certain attitudes and behavior will encourage intuition, and
these are worth cultivating as long as we remain true to ourselves.

In subtle ways we tell the intuitive mind what we expect of it,
and we get what we expect. If we doubt its capacities or mistrust its
contributions, we make intuition, in effect, hesitant. Its appearances
will be erratic and its input ambiguous. On the other hand, acceptance
and confidence create receptivity. If we issue an open invitation and
make intuition feel that visits are welcomed at any time, it can become a perfect guest, showing up on all the right occasions, dressed
properly and bearing felicitous gifts.

SETTING THE STAGE

We can't fool the intuitive mind with postive-thinking mumbo-
jumbo. Artificial enthusiasm, cajolery, suggestion, or evangelical pep

talks about how intuitive you really are if only you believe are of limited and temporary value. The mind knows what you really believe, and it responds accordingly. The chief factor in determining your attitude is your own experience. It would be absurd to contrive a mood of unlimited confidence or try to fool yourself into thinking that your intuition is infallible. But as you notice its contributions to your life, your faith will grow, naturally and spontaneously.

Nevertheless, it is a good idea to examine how you feel about intuition and to ferret out negative programming. It is possible to believe in something intellectually and yet harbor mistrust on an emotional level. And the impact of the emotions will be stronger. Some honest introspection about your degree of acceptance and confidence in intuition can be educational. It is also useful to watch yourself respond to the arguments and anecdotes presented here, to discussions of the subject with friends, and to your own internal dialogue when you are confronted with intuitive messages. You might catch yourself reacting with skepticism and other forms of resistance that you may not have realized you had.

Anti-intuitive behavior may be rooted in deeper psychological factors. Low self-esteem, for example, can translate into a mistrust of anything coming from within ourselves; a need to fail can program the intuitive mind for mistakes or turn us away from correct intuitions. It is no coincidence that intuitive people tend to be confident and independent; such traits are needed in order to be open to an unpredictable, surprising, often unconventional source of knowledge that comes from within ourselves. Excessive security needs, fear of change, and intolerance of uncertainty can also stifle intuition, causing us to seek control and predictability through rigid adherence to rules and standardized procedures. Problems are thus defined simplistically, and only the most obvious information and alternatives are considered. With such an attitude, intuition is programmed for safety, not innovation.

Deep-seated defense mechanisms can't be uprooted by exhortations in a book or a seminar in self-esteem. But many attitudinal barriers to intuition are just bad habits and negative thought patterns that we acquire by emulating our parents and other models. They can be overcome, in part at least, through diligent self-awareness. We can catch ourselves picking on our mistakes instead of congratulating ourselves for our successes; anticipating disasters instead of miracles; reaching out too often for security and predictability instead of freshness and creativity. At such moments it takes little more than a gentle shift of attention to replace negative input with a positive equivalent. Over time, the habits might change.

"I can't solve that problem" or "I'll never find the answer" tell the intuitive mind not to bother. Confident thoughts, along with the conviction that you deserve and expect not only an answer but the *best* answer, stirs intuition to positive action. The same holds for other forms of resistance. By simply adjusting our attitudes we can tell our intuitive minds that we are open to nonobvious, innovative answers, that we expect the unexpected.

We can also replace fear of change and disorder with what John Keats called "negative capability," the quality of "being in uncertainties, mysteries, doubts, without any irritable reaching after facts and reason." Someone who feels he can manage unpredictable, changeable, or ambiguous situations is giving intuition a vote of confidence, since it is needed under such conditions. We can even create those conditions intentionally, in order to stimulate intuition (some of the procedures discussed in this chapter do just that). Accompanied by effective methods of personal growth, such attitudinal adjustments can, in time, reprogram the intuitive mind, instilling encouragement and confidence.

We also work against intuition by taking ourselves, our work, our dilemmas, and our problems too seriously. A certain playfulness and an appreciation of whimsy and absurdity seem to favor intuition. As was mentioned earlier, humor and intuition have in common wild, illogical leaps that can often be as practical as they are entertaining. Of course, work and personal problems are serious in the sense that they are important, but too often that translates into an excessively sober, even somber attitude, often a misguided attempt to appear earnest and weighty to other people. The connection between intuition and playfulness is easy to see in sports or art, but it applies as well to any field. The most creative and innovative people are those who revel in unsolved problems and play with their imaginations like children do with toys.

In a similar vein, relaxing some of the constraints of analytic procedures in favor of a degree of informality can make the mind more hospitable to intuition. Decision making and problem solving are usually portrayed as a straight line made up of formal, rational steps, each one taken after we are certain of the previous step: define the problem, set objectives, gather information, identify alternatives, project consequences, choose the most propitious option. Even when the role of intuition is acknowledged, the preparation stage is depicted as strictly rational and well ordered. Unfortunately, when followed too mechanically, formal methods can lead to what anthropologist Ashley Montagu has called "psychosclerosis," the kind of mental rigidity that can stifle intuition, particularly in its creative function.

I am not suggesting that professionals disregard their formal training or that anyone ignore data collection and analysis, even in everyday, informal situations. Well-structured, orderly work can't be blithely skipped in favor of a hoped-for revelation. Rigorous rational-empirical procedures and carefully acquired factual knowledge feed the intuitive mind and add precision and conviction to its products. As Henri Poincaré said of the conscious work that preceded his intuitive insights, "These efforts then have not been as sterile as one thinks; they have set agoing the unconscious machine and without them it would not have moved and would have produced nothing."

What I am suggesting is a certain flexibility of style and a readiness, when appropriate, to give up some predictability and control for the sake of providing the intuitive mind with room to maneuver. The looseness of a less-structured, intuitive style may seem disorderly, but it might be guided by an imperceptible goal-oriented sense of direction and it might adhere to a pattern that the conscious mind can't decipher. Of course there are times when analytic rigor and procedural discipline are perfectly desirable, but rigidly insisting on them just to satisfy a psychological need for security can jeopardize intuition.

Frequently we get off on the wrong foot in this regard. In our education and training we have taken "look before you leap" to absurd extremes. We are told to formally plan and outline each step from problem to solution. But in reality problems are often ill defined, causes are unidentifiable, goals are abstract, and the routes to them are fogbound. Imposing a predetermined or arbitrary structure can often prevent the intuitive mind from operating freely and finding a better way. The result is either mediocrity or paralysis, as with the fabled jackass that starved to death because it could not decide which of two equal-sized haystacks to choose from.

We might take a lesson from writers and artists in this regard. A study by J. W. Getzels of the University of Chicago found that the most successful artists seemed not to know what they were doing until a form emerged relatively late in the process. "The artists' actions reveal that they are working in a goal-directed way but without full conscious awareness of what the goal is," Getzels said. "They cannot tell what the drawing will be, but their behavior shows that at some level the goal is quite clear." In the early stages of any enterprise, it sometimes pays to temporarily set aside the demand for order, the compulsion to do things by the book, and the need for quick resolution.

Conceptual flexibility can be as important as behavioral flexibility. The best attitude is one that combines passion for truth with detachment and a certain willingness to question assumptions. A protectionist attitude tells the intuitive mind to find ways to support already established beliefs rather than the truest or most creative ideas. A dogmatic mind will both reject contrary intuitions and steer away from information and experiences that might call entrenched beliefs into question.

We see what we expect to see, even on the level of ordinary sense perception, as a number of experiments have proven. One study, for example, mixed into a normal deck of playing cards a few anomalies such as red spades and black hearts. A significant percentage of the subjects did not notice the altered cards, reporting, say, a red ace of spades as the ace of hearts and a black six of hearts as the six of spades. Then the experimenters dropped the casual suggestion that just because spades are customarily black it does not logically follow that they will *always* be black. That was enough to make a significant number of subjects see the unusual cards for what they really were. If we want to receive innovative and unconventional knowledge, we should drop such a casual suggestion to our intuitive mind, letting it know that we expect the unexpected and are prepared to question our assumptions and beliefs.

Finally, it is important to look for, encourage, and expect intuitive input at any stage in the process of solving problems or making decisions. As we have noted, even the most technical, rulebound, rational procedures can be stimulated and advised by intuition. If, in your thoughts and attitudes, you divide the labor too rigidly you will restrict the range of intuition. Let's turn to some specific ways to stimulate the intuitive mind in the early stages of solving a problem or making a decision. These methods can supplement rational-empirical procedures.

GIVING DIRECTION TO YOUR INTUITION

Goals and problems form a feedback loop: the things we want program the mind to look for ways to get them; that leads to the identification of problems (by which is meant both obstacles and opportunities), and the problems in turn create objectives (solutions to the problems) for the intuitive mind to work on. For example, a broad goal might be to improve your marriage. Intuition may provide you with opportunities to do that—anything from an idea for an imaginative gift to new ways of handling disagreements. It might also provide insights into serious problem areas—for example, you realize that your spouse's hostile resistance to your suggestions are rooted in a deep-seated fear of being controlled. That might lead to the objective of finding less threatening ways to express suggestions and criticism or building up your spouse's self-esteem. Intuition might then help you meet those objectives.

The more precise we are about what we want, the better equipped intuition is to move us directly to the target. An excess of precision can backfire, however, as intuition will be programmed so narrowly it might overlook unusual or unanticipated opportunities. For example, if your goal is to make a lot of money this year, that doesn't give your intuition much to work on. Defining the goal as making $50,000 this year provides a more explicit set of instructions. Making the money in the commodities market is an even more specific goal, and trading soybeans still more so. However, if you set your goal that narrowly, you might place blinders on your intuition; it might not recognize or create opportunities outside soybeans. In some cases, the narrow focus might be exactly what you want. Each goal should be evaluated carefully and the parameters delineated.

Even before attacking specific problems, it is a good idea to write a clear description of your important life goals, those deeply felt desires and intentions that impel your actions and thoughts. Be as specific as possible, indicating exactly what you want to accomplish, and if possible how and when. These general goals usually suggest short-range or localized objectives that structure day-to-day choices. Here the intuitive mind should be told when the objectives are specific and when there is room for change. Goals and objectives should also be reevaluated frequently; this keeps your intuition up-to-date, so to speak, and the process of revision might also stimulate an intuitive insight into the nature of your goals.

By writing down goals and objectives in this manner, a balance of commitment and openness can be programmed into the intuitive mind. Among other things, this combination can make you more receptive to the intuitive recognition of opportunity, a key element in discovery and creativity.

WHAT IS THE PROBLEM?

On the outskirts of Thebes, a sphinx blocked access to the city, presenting wayfarers a riddle. If they answered correctly, they could enter; if they failed, they were devoured by the sphinx. Everyone had failed until Oedipus arrived and was asked: "What creature walks on four legs in the morning, two legs at noontime, and three legs in the evening?" Oedipus answered, "Man. He crawls on all fours in infancy, stands upright in maturity, and leans upon a stick in old age."

Of course, Oedipus was not so intuitive as to realize the identity of the woman he later married. What he did with the riddle, though, was to expand the boundaries and question the assumptions that conventional thinking would bring to it. His unfortunate predecessors took the riddle at face value, and limited the range of operations of their intuition. The limitations were in their minds, not in the problem itself. We can restrict intuition's ability to provide the best solutions by oversimplifying problems, not looking beyond the obvious parameters, or failing to question our own assumptions. For that reason, we should always look for fresh ways to define and redefine the situations in which we find ourselves.

Edward de Bono, whose teaching and many books on "lateral thinking" have made an important contribution to creativity, tells of a skyscraper that was built with too few elevators. Those who worked in the building were livid about the long delays at rush hours, and many threatened to quit. Solutions were suggested, including constructing additional elevators outside the building, staggering work hours, and replacing the elevators with faster ones. All proposals were expensive and potentially disruptive. Finally someone suggested a simple solution: hang mirrors near the elevator doors. "In hindsight the answer is obvious," says de Bono. "The problem was not so much a lack of elevators as the impatience of the staff." The employees became so occupied with adjusting their hair and clothing and watching each other perform before the mirrors that the annoyance of waiting was alleviated.

I had a similar experience recently when I ran out of file space and spent a good deal of time trying to figure out how to rearrange a crowded office to accommodate an additional file cabinet. My wife took one look and suggested hanging plastic baskets under the shelves of my bookcase, as there were several inches of space between each shelf and the books beneath it. I had defined the problem as lack of file drawers; she saw it as "How can we add some storage space for papers?"

We often place blinders on intuition by oversimplifying problems because we are intolerant of complexity. This is caused in part by the neat problems we learn from in school, which tend to convince us that everything has a single identifiable cause. In real life, important problems are usually multifaceted. Peter Senge of MIT's Systems Dynamics Group says that one consistent finding of his organization's research is that "problems never come in isolation, whether in business, society, or individual lives." As Senge points out, we tend to assume that cause and effect are closely related in space and time. Usually, he says, they are not.

Restrictive problem definition can have serious consequences. During the 1973 oil crisis, for example, almost everyone identified the problem as the Arab embargo. It took a long time for people to go beyond that simple view of causation to ask such questions as "Why are we dependent on Middle East oil?" Similarly, businesses confronted with decreased sales might look only at the obvious places —the sales staff or the marketing department—instead of confronting basic issues about their product or management policies. Or a couple with a deteriorating sex life might look at superficial aspects of the problem, such as performance in bed, rather than at deeper emotional factors. As Senge notes, the problems and solutions are seldom in the obvious places, and creative ideas come to the intuitive person who can face up to the insecurity of looking beyond the obvious.

EXPRESS IT IN WRITING

Particularly when you find problems difficult to pinpoint or have a feeling that the right approach or solution is just barely evading your grasp, it is a good idea to set down on paper whatever comes to mind about the situation. By writing out your thoughts, however disconnected, tangential, and ungrammatical, you can start to unleash your intuition. Much of what comes up will be irrelevant or ridiculous, but by writing down the story without evaluating or judging the product (no one need see it but you), any of three things can be accomplished: you might find intuitive answers to intractable questions, or insights into your true feelings about the situation, or you may see a pattern emerging from the process that helps you zero in on the real problem and structure it properly for subsequent analysis.

Here are two procedures for getting started when spontaneous writing is sluggish. The first involves sentence completion. Just add whatever comes to mind to any or all of the following fragments and then keep going.

What I know about this situation is . . .
What I don't know is . . .
The thing that bothers me is . . .
Some of the things I'm unsure about are . . .
Some of the things that might happen are . . .
If I had my way . . .
Other people involved think . . .
Under no circumstances will I . . .
I have a feeling that . . .
If push comes to shove I . . .

Another practical way to get started is a variation of Gabriele Lusser Rico's strategy in *Writing the Natural Way*. Rico has developed a procedure called "clustering," in which a key word is used as a nucleus to evoke clusters of associations. "As you spill out seemingly random words and phrases around a center," says Rico, "you will be surprised to see patterns forming until a moment comes—characterized by an 'aha!' feeling—when you suddenly sense a focus for writing." When applied to real problems or decisions, the cluster might lead to a precise ordering of your thoughts or even a crucial insight into the situation itself.

To cluster, you begin with a "nucleus word" in a circle. It can be any word, really, but it might be best to use the first one that comes to mind when you consider the situation you're dealing with. "Now you simply let go," says Rico, "and begin to flow with any current of connections that come into your head. Write these down rapidly, each in its own circle, radiating outward from the center in any direction they want to go. Connect each new word or phrase with a line to the preceding circle. When something new and different strikes you, begin again at the central nucleus and radiate outward until those associations are exhausted."

Each word should be entered without evaluation or analysis, and the entire process should take only a few minutes. At some point, a focus or pattern is likely to emerge, and you might feel a definite sense of change—a physical sensation, perhaps, or a sense of wholeness or relief. At that point, writing can begin, or something even more significant might have emerged by way of insight. Figure 5 depicts a clustering sample from one of Rico's students.

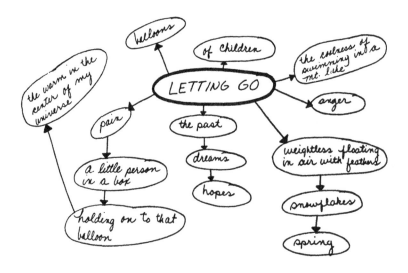

Figure 5. Example of clustering, using "letting go"
as the nucleus word.

The idea of expressing your thoughts and feelings about a situation can be extended a bit further. Since language is a linear medium, a strictly verbal statement might not be enough to stimulate all the faculties that feed the intuitive mind. Also, nonverbal modes can elicit emotional content, unfiltered by the logical demands of language, so your feelings about the situation or the people involved may emerge. We can bring other senses and thought patterns into play by expressing problems, tasks, and goals in several different media. Here are some suggestions:

Draw or paint the situation, preferably in color, as both an abstract and a representational picture.
Play it on a musical instrument, or sing it.

Express it physically as a charade, a dance, or a mime.
Sculpt it in clay or wood.
Create a symbol for it.

With serious problems and important decisions, use as many media as possible. Pay no attention to the quality or form of your expression; let it pour forth without censorship or deliberation. The purpose is to prepare and stimulate your intuition, not to display your artistic skills. Most important, don't look for anything or expect a bolt of lightning. No significant insight may burst forth during the process itself, but raw material and patterns of organization are being supplied to the factory of intuition. The end products may surprise you at any time.

NOT JUST THE FACTS, MA'AM

Anyone who wants to become more intuitive would do well to follow the advice Henry James gave to writers: "Be one of those on whom nothing is wasted." Conventional decision-making and problem-solving strategies emphasize hard data—well-documented facts and statistics that can be analyzed and used as the basis of logical inferences. This is, of course, indispensable, and modern technology has made possible an astonishing degree of speed, accuracy, and breadth of analysis. However, relying too heavily on this kind of input can deny the intuitive mind the kind of raw material it relies upon. For one thing, hard data deal with the past, since anything that can be measured or analyzed has to have already happened. Further, a great deal that is relevant to a situation and useful to the intuitive faculties is outside the range of analytic apparatus.

Successful decision makers recognize these limitations and rely far less on hard data than their image and training would suggest. According to management scientist Henry Mintzberg, executives lean toward "soft" data—rumors, hearsay, gossip, body language, casual conversation, speculation. Mintzberg discovered, for example, that high-ranking managers favor face-to-face meetings over written reports and documents so they can read expressions, gestures, and voice tones. One advertising executive expressed it this way: "I think my hunches pay off because I take in things that other people disregard, either because they are not very perceptive or because they've bought the idea that the only worthwhile input is what you can convert to logic or numbers, which is what you need to defend your decisions."

A first step in absorbing soft information is simply to expose yourself to a wider range of input, to indirect and subtle sources that have no apparent rationale and no immediate payoff. For example, a corporate vice president named Virginia Hathaway often eschews executive lunches to eat in the employee cafeteria. She plants herself near crowds of workers, makes several trips to the vending machines and food lines, and takes in chitchat and visual impressions. Sometimes she also rides up and down the elevators at the end of the day. This exposure doesn't always provide Hathaway with information that applies directly to her decisions about marketing office equipment, but she learns a lot about people and her company, and she is convinced it is a good use of her time.

Another executive goes a step further. An officer of a large food-processing company, he occasionally disguises himself as an unskilled laborer at one of his firm's plants or offices. He also makes a point of frequenting supermarkets and diners in different communities. He says he got the idea from his wife, a novelist who researches her books much the same way. Like Virginia Hathaway, he feels such exposure improves his on-the-job intuition.

Studies show that brain waves change when subjects are fed subliminal stimuli of which they are unaware. The intuitive mind makes use of that material, creating analogies and drawing bits and pieces from areas unrelated to the subject at hand. Indeed, it can be hypothesized that one trait characteristic of exceptionally intuitive people is a high level of receptivity to this kind of information. They might also have a wide range of interests and exposure to an unusual variety of life experiences.

The executives cited in the preceding examples intentionally gathered soft data; they were looking for material that related to their responsibilities, however remotely. There is also something to be said for expanding the breadth of your experience for no reason other than to supply material for the intuitive mind to use, perhaps in ways you will never know about. Traveling, wandering around a strange part of your city, going to clubs and restaurants you normally avoid, reading a wider range of books and magazines, taking courses that have nothing to do with your profession, talking to people you think you have nothing in common with—such adventures are not a waste of time and are not mere entertainment; they can enrich the knowledge base on which intuition rests.

An excellent way to soak up a large spectrum of impressions is to venture out on "absorption sessions," in which you intend to accomplish or discover nothing in particular but simply act like a sponge. The proper attitude is summed up in the motto of the Zen swordsman: "Expect nothing, be prepared for anything." You should have no preset ideas about what is being sought or perhaps even where to go, nor should you try to judge or evaluate what you perceive. A random selection of locales is often a good way to start, using a map, a list of bus or train routes, or the yellow pages to generate choices. Once out, a useful policy, whenever a choice presents itself, is to select an area that strikes you as unusual or even irrelevant, or one you've never experienced before.

The primary purpose of absorption sessions is, as noted, to absorb new information, both consciously and subliminally, but a bonus might be the unexpected appearance of an important intuition. For that reason, it is a good idea to take along a pad or tape recorder, not to record what you see—that would force you to filter impressions through the logical arrangement of words and concepts—but to note significant intuitions that might be triggered by some experience.

The possibility of attracting an enlightening intuition is another reason not to deliberate or analyze when deciding where to go or what to do during an absorption session. The more you follow your impulses and lean toward the unusual, the more you allow the operative function of intuition to take over. It might guide you toward those uncanny concurrences that Carl Jung described in his concept of *synchronicity*, coincidences that are not causally related but that contain substantive meaning. Jung proposed that some undiscovered interaction between the environment, the unconcious, and the conscious mind was responsible. Perhaps in some way the intuitive mind resonates with a pattern of information waves and quietly directs what seems to be random behavior.

The following examples of intuitions occurred because the intuiters followed impulses to do something out of the ordinary. The first involved a stage director who was bothered by his propensity for fighting with actors: "I had an urge to go to the zoo, of all places, and I did it even though I was busy and I'm not particularly fond of animals. As I walked past the bear cage, I saw two cubs scrapping with each other. Like the other spectators, I got alarmed, but a zookeeper explained that the bears were only playing. Suddenly I realized that I had this need to spar with other men. It's like some atavistic form of play, but everyone takes me seriously and I get into trouble. The intuition helped me change my behavior. Now whenever I flare up, I remind myself of the bears and tell my sparring mate not to take me seriously."

The other incident was related by a historian: "I had to meet my husband on a street corner, and I was early. There were two shops from which I could see the corner—a bookshop and a men's clothing store. I love bookstores and have no interest in men's clothing, but on a whim I walked into the latter. Inside, some guy was blabbing about his trip to Jerusalem. I was about to leave and go to the bookstore, where I belonged, when something he said—I don't even remember what—made me realize that my current research topic might bear some resemblance to the Crusades. That led to a fruitful line of investigation."

BRAINSTORMING WITH YOURSELF

One of intuition's chief functions in problem solving and decision making is generating alternatives. In straightforward situations, alternatives can be inferred more or less routinely from the facts. But intuition allows us to go beyond the obvious to fresh, innovative possibilities; if it is fertile, intuition might generate a large quantity of alternatives, many of which will be absolutely useless but may nevertheless stimulate other, more practical ideas.

Too often, this generative function is impeded by our tendency to step in and evaluate as soon as an intuition appears. Our schools and institutions encourage this; we are rewarded for right answers and for pointing out what is wrong with ideas. This process creates one of the biggest psychological obstacles to intuition: the onus of having to be right. The fear of being wrong is so deeply ingrained that our minds become geared to not making mistakes as opposed to finding something that will work. As MIT's Peter Senge has noted, "Creative intellects are at peace with what they don't know. They are willing to not understand. You can't be intuitive if you're trying to be right."

Certainly the ability to analyze and judge the products of our intuition is of crucial importance. But we tend to do it too quickly and peremptorily, forcing premature closure and killing fragile intuitive ideas before they have a chance to develop and reproduce. In order to make the most of intuition, we must slow down the rush to judgment. Whenever possible, an intuition should be regarded as a windblown seed and left alone to see if it takes root.

Under ordinary circumstances, the mind will naturally think

about the intuition, analyze it, and test it against the facts; the heart will respond in its way, letting you know how it feels about the intuition. Sometimes it is impossible, and unwise, to battle these tendencies, but as a rule they should be delayed as long as possible. At the very least, final judgment should be postponed, and criticism should be balanced with the recognition that *part* of the intuition might be valuable—if not in its own right, then possibly as a catalyst that can spark a chain reaction culminating in a breakthrough. For example, a couple I know was pondering what to do with a three-day weekend. The husband suggested hiking in the Himalayas, an unlikely weekend outing for Americans. But it set off something in his wife that led her to suggest a yoga retreat, an activity they might not have thought of but which they enjoyed a great deal.

To counteract the critical urge, it is a good idea to set aside a judgment-free period for generating solutions to specific problems. *Brainstorming*, created by Alex Osborn in 1948, is a formal method widely used by organizations, principally in groups, where the collective interaction yields extra power because each person's thoughts spark the others'. The rules are easily enforced, and the principles can be adapted to individual use. There are essentially four rules:

1. There is to be no criticism or judgment of any ideas presented. Evaluation is done in a subsequent session.
2. Quantity is desirable; the more ideas the better. As the Chinese proverb states, "The best way to catch a fish is to have many lines."
3. No idea is too bizarre, too wild, or too irrelevant. The purpose is not to be correct but to fuel the process of generating imaginative alternatives.
4. Combinations, modifications, and improvements on previously mentioned ideas are encouraged.

In group brainstorming (which can be very fruitful, particularly among friends who are committed to improving their intuition) a leader formulates the problem, enforces the rules, and determines when to end the session. Another person is designated as notetaker. If you're alone, you'll have to act as leader, notetaker, and group. Since the act of writing can interfere with the flow of ideas, however, you might want to use a tape recorder. After a period of time—at least a day, if possible—examine the list of ideas, employing all the rational-empirical methods at your disposal. Pare down the list, combine similar ideas, and eliminate the truly absurd and implausible. Then schedule an evaluation session, where the strengths and weaknesses of the remaining ideas are analyzed. A final decision may be reached, but new ideas might pop up or new problems be recognized.

Generally, one of three criteria is used for deciding when to terminate a brainstorming session. Some people advocate stopping when the group loses enthusiasm or when the time between ideas begins to lag. Others, however, feel that this could cut off the session at just the wrong time. Evidently the most fruitful period comes after the inevitable letdown, when the initial excitement wanes and the obvious ideas have been used up. Another possibility is not to stop before a certain number of alternatives have been generated. Particularly when brainstorming solo, this prevents you from quitting when frustration builds or an appealing solution is found (it may be attractive, but not the best). Perhaps the best policy when working alone is to set a time limit of, say, fifteen to twenty minutes. This not only prevents premature closure but it is useful for training the intuitive mind to work under time presure, which in many situations will be imposed by circumstances.

When working with a group, of course, the responsibility for generating ideas is spread out, and each person has time for brief incubations. To compensate when working alone, it is often a good idea to take relaxation breaks during the sessions (see Chapter 9 for suggested methods), particularly when a spree of writing or recording ideas has taken your attention too far in the outward direction. Also, a second brainstorming period before the evaluation session can help compensate for the absence of group interaction, in which fertility is often geometrically increased.

The value of a brainstorming session is precisely its formality. The overall impact of the rules is to create an atmosphere in which logic can be intentionally violated, which breaks down hackneyed thought processes and gives the intuitive mind unconditional license to express itself. In a group, people who start to evaluate and judge are reminded of the rules. When the meeting takes place in one person's mind, however, it is not as easy to keep out the judgmental thoughts that pop up spontaneously. The challenge is to enforce the rules without defeating the purpose of brainstorming. If you are too rigorous about stifling judgmental thoughts, that effort in itself can prevent the generation of ideas. The important thing is to quiet the critical input without strain, and to disallow extended analysis and final acceptance or rejection.

During formal brainstorming, or at any other time, intuition can be stimulated to generate ideas through the deliberate use of analogies. This can help break brittle thought patterns by revealing hidden relationships between objects or events. Important discoveries or new ways of viewing a problem can result when the mind brings together items that have no apparent relationship. Niels Bohr said that the original impetus to his theory of complementarity—that the wave and particle descriptions of electrons were aspects of a single reality— was a thought he once had about relationships: you can't know another person simultaneously in the light of love and the light of justice. In a commercial vein, Fred Smith created Federal Express when he linked the need for overnight package delivery to banking, where all canceled checks go to one place and then back to the individual branches.

To use analogies deliberately, you simply take an object, a concept, or an event and look for qualities, functions, or processes to associate with the problem under consideration. The purpose is not to find accurate analogies, but to stimulate the machinery of the intuitive mind. Let the analogies come, whether they are obvious or absurd, and pay no attention to logic, facts, or common sense.

Another way to prod the generative function of intuition is to use random stimuli, a favorite method of Edward de Bono. You choose a criterion for producing a random word or object and then let the selection trigger a chain of associations. These associations are allowed to connect with aspects of your problem, and the ideas produced are treated with the nonevaluative rules of brainstorming. The idea is to deliberately insert a piece of information that is unrelated to the problem in order to shake up the mind and produce a restructuring of thought.

Following are two ways of randomly selecting a stimulus:

1. Establish a predetermined criterion for choosing an object from the environment—the second blue object you see, the first object other than a person to pass a certain spot on a street, and so forth.

2. Find random words in a dictionary. Use dice or a mechanical random-number generator to produce two numbers, one for a page, the other to locate a word on that page.

The object or word is then used to generate ideas during a timed period, usually brief. De Bono emphasizes that there is no single correct way to use the stimulus; anything about it—functional properties, physical characteristics, its opposite, variations in spelling—can be used to get things going. Here is an example of a session from de Bono's book, *Lateral Thinking*. The word selected from a dictionary was "noose," and the problem was "the housing shortage."

> Noose—tightening noose—execution—what are the difficulties in executing a housing program—what is the bottleneck, is it capital, labor, or land? Noose tightens—things are going to get worse with the present rate of population increase. Noose—rope—suspension construction system—tentlike houses but made of permanent materials—easily packed and erected—or on a large scale with several houses suspended from one framework—much lighter materials possible if walls did not have to support themselves and the roof. Noose—loop—adjustable loop—what about adjustable round houses which could be expanded as required—just uncoil the walls—no point in having houses too large to begin with—but facility for slow stepwise expansion as need arises . . .

Such chains of association can stimulate the intuitive mind to find accurate or useful ideas. In addition, you can use brainstorming principles to generate alternative causes of problems when causation is unclear, or alternative predictions for future events.

So far we have looked at some ways to stimulate the intuitive mind and provide it with good conditions under which to operate in the early stages of decision making and problem solving. But perhaps even more important than how to approach problems is knowing how and when to get away from them. That is the subject of the next chapter.

9

Turning Off to Tune In

The seed of mystery lies in muddy water.
How can I perceive this mystery?
Water becomes still through stillness.
How can I become still?
By flowing with the stream.

—Lao Tzu

The composer ran into a creative block and could not complete a commissioned work. As the frustration mounted, he labored harder and harder, but the pieces would not come together. Friends urged him to get away, but he continued to jeopardize his health and sanity by toiling long hours in vain. Finally his doctor ordered the composer to take a holiday, and the orchestra that had commissioned his work threatened to fire him if he did not take off. Reluctantly, he went to a remote village in Italy. On his first morning there, after a sound sleep, he heard the church bells ringing and in an instant all the pieces fell together and the composition completed itself.

He should have taken a lesson from another composer who was known to say, at the start of a day's work, "Nothing comes to me today; we shall try another time." Since this other composer was Beethoven, we can assume he was not being lazy. He understood the importance of incubation, a lesson that anyone who wants to improve his intuition should learn.

Incubation seems to be a universal principle. It can be found not only in contemporary theories of creativity and problem solving, but also in the folklore of cultures throughout time. In *The Hero with a Thousand Faces*, Joseph Campbell traces the standard heroic path: separation, initiation, return. At a critical juncture, the hero turns away from the mundane world and, usually with the aid of some higher power, acquires wisdom and strength. Thus empowered, he returns to fulfill his mission. The pattern can be found in ancient mythology (Prometheus and Jason are examples from Greece), in various fairy tales and fables, in *Hamlet* and other literary classics, and most prominently in the lore of the great spiritual traditions: Moses, Jesus, and Buddha all withdrew to commune with the divine before completing their work. In the *Bhagavad Gita*, Arjuna leaves the battlefield to confer with Lord Krishna before returning to vanquish the forces of evil.

When wrestling with comparatively trivial problems and decisions, an incubation break is worth considering. Yet it seems that when we stand to benefit most from this process we often do the opposite. As pressure mounts and desperation grows, we press on, often greeting the urge to get away with guilt and self-loathing. We rearrange the pieces of our puzzle yet again and repeat the same lines of reason, hoping to find a hidden gem in the junk pile of facts we have already sorted through a hundred times. A common problem, it is most pronounced in business and professional communities.

The anti-incubation mentality stems from a lack of understanding of intuition and the conditions under which it works best. A desire to shift gears may be a message from the intuitive mind telling you to withdraw; it needs a rested, coherent nervous system and a little solitude. Knowing the difference between that need and laziness or escapism is a key factor in developing one's intuition.

Typical signs of a strong need to incubate include fatigue, mental dullness, irritability, despair, and physical signs of stress. But if those symptoms appear you have probably waited too long. It is far more efficient, not to mention healthy, to catch earlier signals such as loss of clarity, repetitious thought patterns, lack of concentration, and mild frustration. You could jump the gun, of course, and lose out on the value of additional analysis or fact-finding, but more common is waiting too long to incubate. There are, unfortunately, no formulas for knowing when to incubate; it is an individual matter, acquired through self-observation and experience.

Equally individual, but perhaps less difficult, is knowing *how* to incubate. Technically, incubation covers any activity that isn't related to the particular problem under consideration, but various activities will have greater or lesser value in nourishing intuition. Through self-awareness and trial and error, you can come to know when to have vigorous exercise and when to sleep in, when to get away for the afternoon and when to take a long vacation, when some mindless activity will work best and when to engage the mind full throttle on some different project. With the use of the intuition journal we will describe in the next chapter, you might find a pattern linking certain physical and mental signs with specific forms of incubation to see which combinations lead to successful intuitions.

As a rule, the best forms of incubation for the intuitive mind are those that produce the coherent state of restful alertness discussed in Chapter 7. Many forms of rest and recreation will take your mind off your work and help you blow off steam, but the aftermath might be fatigue and dullness. The procedures described in this chapter were selected for their efficacy in establishing the right state of consciousness, along with their ease of practice and universality of application. They are mainly brief forms of incubation that can be worked into a regular routine or used when you are under pressure and want to establish suitable conditions for intuition. We will also discuss what to do when you hear the footsteps of intuition in the distance and want to be sure it doesn't get away. But first, let's look at the oldest and most ubiquitous form of incubation.

TO SLEEP, PERCHANCE TO DREAM

"What if you slept?" wrote Samuel Taylor Coleridge. "And what if in your sleep, you dreamed? And what if in your dream you went to heaven and there plucked a strange and beautiful flower? And what if, when you woke, you had the flower in your hand? Ah! What then?"

Coleridge once awakened with a flower in his hand—the poem "Kubla Khan," which he proceeded to set down as he had perceived it during sleep. Sadly, he was interrupted by the infamous "visitor from Porlock," and when Coleridge returned to his room he found that all but eight or ten lines "had passed away like the images on the surface of a stream into which a stone has been cast."

Who can say how much art and how many great ideas have been denied us by other kinds of visitors from Porlock? Sleep is a great healer ("nature's soft nurse," in Shakespeare's words) and a terrific incubator ("dear mother of fresh thoughts," according to Wordsworth). Once regarded as a time when all bodily functions shut down, sleep is now understood to be a rather busy, cyclical process in which a great deal of work takes place, physically and psychically. The injunction to "sleep on it" is not just a metaphor; in some as yet undiscovered way, a rearrangement and ordering of mental content can take place during sleep, leading to intuitive discoveries either in dreams or on awakening, where they might be waiting like guests at a surprise party.

There are several practical implications to consider in this regard. For one thing, sleep is not the waste of time that many busy people think it is. A good nap during a hectic schedule might at times be more productive than work. Winston Churchill and Thomas Edison are among those who slept comparatively little at night and took catnaps during the day.

That brings up another practical point. Many people have erratic sleeping patterns; they awaken during the night, sometimes more than once, and find it difficult to get back to sleep. The usual response is to blame this on insomnia. Karen, a healthy and well-adjusted research scientist, had tried everything from sleeping pills to psychotherapy to stop her frequent awakenings. Then one night she decided to stop worrying about it and get out of bed. Instead of tossing and turning, she got some work done. To her surprise, she was remarkably creative in those predawn hours. Eventually, she and her employer readjusted her schedule, keeping her mornings free in case she worked during the night and needed the morning to sleep in. She also arranged to have some equipment and a computer terminal installed in her home so she could make the most of her inspired awakenings.

While interruptions of sleep are not to be encouraged, if they do happen it might be a good idea to adjust your attitude toward them. Instead of being annoyed or alarmed, you might look upon them as possible opportunities, calling cards from the intuitive mind. You might keep a pad or tape recorder at your bedside to record your thoughts. This serves two purposes: the act of expressing the contents helps get it out of your mind, so that it is less likely to interrupt your sleep again; and it gives you the opportunity to capture worthwhile intuitions that might otherwise be forgotten by morning. You can analyze and elaborate during the day.

Of course, the same pad or tape recorder can be used to record the contents of dreams, which have been valued by virtually every culture throughout history as sources of prophecy, carriers of practical wisdom, messages from gods or departed souls, or revelations of repressed psychological conflicts. Solutions to problems and creative breakthroughs have frequently arrived in dream form. René Descartes, whose name is virtually synonymous with rationalism, was a soldier undecided about his future when he realized in a dream that he should combine mathematics and philosophy into a new discipline. Robert Louis Stevenson dreamed the plot of *Doctor Jekyll and Mister Hyde.*

My favorite dream anecdote concerns Elias Howe, the inventor of the sewing machine. Howe had labored for several years and was one small detail away from his goal. Then one night he dreamed he had been captured by a tribe of savages whose leader had commanded him to finish his machine or else be executed. In the dream the terrified inventor was surrounded by warriors leading him to his death, when he suddenly noticed that his antagonists' spears had eye-shaped holes near the points. Howe awakened from his dream and whittled a model of a needle with the hole near the point instead of in the middle of the shank. That change was the key to completing a workable sewing machine.

Sometimes dreams forecast the future. A few days before his death, Abraham Lincoln dreamed that he awakened in the night and wandered downstairs in the White House, where he came upon a throng of civilians and military guards surrounding a corpse. When he asked who had died he was told, "The President. He was killed by an assassin."

Some dreams are self-evident; others require extrapolation and interpretation. The dreams of Coleridge and Lincoln were quite literal. Elias Howe's dream, like Kekule's (the dancing snakes biting their own tails, which led to the realization that benzene molecules were closed circles), are examples of dreams that needed some interpretation, but not much. Other dreams are not as obviously connected to waking-state realities. Carl Jung once dreamed that he was addressing appreciative multitudes rather than speaking privately to physicians, which convinced him on waking to write *Man and His Symbols* for the general public, a task he had been reluctant to undertake.

Because dreams—particularly recurring motifs that carry insistent messages—can be sources of intuitive information, it might be a good idea to do as many psychologists suggest and write down your dreams upon awakening. However, it is important not to get carried away by dream content or to bestow upon dreams the responsibility for decisions that should be managed by the waking state. There is, as yet, no evidence that every remembered dream is revelatory. True, in the hands of a competent psychologist any dream can be used as a clue to the psyche's hidden contents, but often what is most important is the patient's response to the dream; the dream itself might be just a catalyst, like ink blots.

The big problem with dreams, of course, is that they are often heavily symbolic, which means that their value depends on interpretation. And interpretation can be risky. In the Bible, the pharaoh dreamed of seven lean cows following seven fat cows. Joseph interpreted the dream and advised the pharaoh to store grain during the next seven years in order to avert famine in the subsequent seven. Sure enough, that strategy saved Egypt from crop failure. But, like the enigmatic messages of astrologers and psychics, dreams can be cryptic, and misinterpretations can be disastrous.

Unless you are using dreams with a trained therapist as the "royal road to the unconscious," as Freud put it, be very careful about looking to them as a source of intuition. There is no reason to take them any more seriously than waking-state intuitions, particularly when the message is not self-evident. No one believed in dreams more than Carl Jung, so it would be prudent to note his attitude. Like most contemporary psychologists, Jung was opposed to applying formulaic interpretations to symbolic dream content, and would certainly cringe at those supermarket pamphlets and slim paperbacks that purport to tell us the symbolic meaning of everything from an abyss to a zoo. "Learn as much as you can about symbolism," Jung told his students; "then forget it all when you are analyzing a dream."

The reason for Jung's attitude was this: "No dream symbol can be separated from the individual who dreams it, and there is no definite or straightforward interpretation of any dream." Jung insisted that the dreamer's individuality and the interpreter's intelligence, empathy, and experience all were important. While noting that an interpreter of dreams can't ignore facts and logic, Jung contended that "intuition is almost indispensable in the interpretation of symbols, and it can often ensure that they are immediately understood by the dreamer."

In short, we have a Catch-22: dreams can be a door to intuitive knowledge, but all too often you need good intuition to open the door.

For those who are particularly interested in dreams and want to increase their recall, some psychologists recommend quietly suggesting to yourself before sleep that you are going to remember your dreams. Apparently the mere decision to remember can enhance actual recall. Research indicates that you can also learn to specify the subject matter of your dreams, just as you phone room service in advance to order the next morning's breakfast. This, evidently, is a skill that some people possess naturally. No strain or force should be used, and it is probably best to explore such procedures under the guidance of a psychologist experienced in dream work.

Research also suggests that we can gain a certain amount of control over our dreams. Some people, for example, have the ability to remain wakeful while dreaming, aware of what is going on. Evidently, motivated people can be trained to accomplish this *lucid dreaming*, as it has been called, and Patricia Garfield gives instructions for it in *Creative Dreaming*. It has been suggested that lucid dreaming might improve dream recall, permit us to take notes during the process, and even allow for directing the content as the dream progresses. Some psychologists believe this can stimulate intuitive input.

I am personally somewhat leery of such dream manipulation. We don't know that much about the basic function of dreams or their psychophysiological underpinnings. Tampering with them might possibly lead to unanticipated side effects. Perhaps the value of the dream state is diminished by too much manipulation, or even by too much attention after the dreams occur.

Some unforced presleep programming can increase your chances of being surprised by intuition on awakening or during dreams. In the shadowy period before dozing off, you might drop your question, your problem, or your dilemma into your mind like a letter into a mailbox. Don't try to articulate it clearly and don't strain to get down the details or to finish your sentence if your mind wanders off to other thoughts or to sleep. A hazy thought, the merest idea, will be better than a precise verbal statement. Drop it in, and let it go. A few gentle repetitions are enough to tell your unconscious what you are looking for.

MEDITATION: THE INNER CORE

I agree with psychologist Frances Vaughan that "the regular practice of meditation is the single most powerful means of increasing intuition." More than a way to incubate when you want to attract intuition, meditation is a technique for expanding consciousness and is most effective when practiced routinely (the usual prescription is twice a day for about twenty minutes). This regularity guarantees effective, regular incubation, and also reduces the likelihood of looking for intuitive answers while meditating, which would detract from its value. Insights do arise during meditation, but so do useless and absurd thoughts. It is *after* meditation, when the mind is quiet and clear, that intuition is likely to be at its best.

Most people think of meditation as a form of relaxation, useful for reducing tension. That alone would recommend it as an aid to intuition, which is hampered by anxiety and high arousal. All forms of relaxation are useful in this regard, meditation all the more so since the rest it produces is exceptionally penetrating. But the real value of meditation—and the reason it is the central component in virtually every spiritual path and consciousness discipline—is in nurturing the state of consciousness we called illumination. Transcendental Meditation (TM), the most popular and widely researched technique, is described as "taking the attention from the conscious thinking level to finer states of thought until the mind arrives at the source of thought, pure consciousness." In terms of the analogy described in Chapter 7, one traverses the ocean of the mind and transcends; at the same time the nervous system achieves an exceptional stability and coherence.

A typical meditation session fluctuates, the physiology becoming more or less orderly, the mind now quiet, then more active. Transcendence is usually instantaneous and hazy at first, becoming clearer and more pronounced as daily practice continues over weeks and months. Overall, the effect is to purify consciousness and activate deeper levels of the mind. This allows the meditator to function from those deeper levels—that is, with a coherent nervous system. Meditators say that they carry into thought and action a restfully alert mind and that their inner core of silence is, over time, less likely to be disturbed by outer events. Not surprisingly, they also report that their intuition becomes more dependable and their decisions become both more spontaneous and more appropriate. Learning ability, creativity, academic performance, and other indices of mental functioning that imply good intuition have been positively correlated with meditation.

Dozens of different meditation techniques are available in books, magazine articles, and countless institutes and seminars. Unfortunately, the field suffers from a shortage of discernment. Commentators have lumped together methods with superficial similarities, a mistake akin to ignoring differences among automobiles because they all have four wheels and transport the driver from one place to another. Virtually every scientific study, for example, has used TM subjects, but the findings have been extrapolated to anything even remotely resembling meditation. The various techniques sound alike, and they usually profess the same goals, but there are acute differences, many of which are not readily apparent on the surface. It is fair to infer that procedures which vary even slightly in practice will also vary in their effects. And any method that is powerful enough to make a difference in our lives should be approached with discrimination.

It is impossible in a short space to describe or evaluate every available meditation technique, but anyone who is unfamiliar with the subject or not committed to a particular program can keep in mind the following considerations.

Simple relaxation procedures—soothing mood shifts such as imagining you are on a secluded beach or the sequential unwinding of muscle groups—are useful when you are particularly tense or when you're trying to settle down during a crisis. But they won't necessarily induce illumination or produce the mental coherence that is favored by intuition.

Be wary of techniques that require intense mental manipulation or strenuous control. Meditation should be natural and effortless. A technique that calls for concentration—focusing the awareness on a single object, idea, or concept and preventing the attention from wandering—is likely to keep the mind localized and active. So might contemplation practices—that is, thinking *about* something, such as God or Oneness. Many techniques involve blanking the mind, a misguided attempt to duplicate *samadhi*, which is awareness without thought. But transcendent experience is not just a blank mind; it is a mind illuminated by pure consciousness. This state can't be achieved through trying or control, since the very effort will keep the mind from sinking to quieter, more universal levels. Too much effort can also cause mental strain.

Selection criteria should also include authenticity. In the East, where consciousness has been the main focus of intellectual inquiry, meditative disciplines have developed over the centuries. In the West we are comparative neophytes, and that status should confer a certain humility. But when meditation became respectable, psychologists and physicians began inventing their own imitations of Eastern procedures. In an attempt to make meditation more palatable to Westerners, they often made the mistake of eliminating or altering key elements. For example, many teachers have arbitrarily substituted English words or nonsense syllables for traditional mantras, the sounds whose vibratory qualities are largely reponsible for the effectiveness of many forms of meditation. With all due respect, professional training in Western scientific disciplines might qualify someone to study the effects of meditation, but not necessarily to teach it.

Meditation is a delicate art, ideally transmitted directly by a competent teacher to a willing student so that personal attributes can be considered and questions can be answered. For that reason, techniques taught in books or on tape are, as a rule, less effective. It is not uncommon to misconstrue instructions and thus either get less than optimum results or suffer such unwanted side effects as headaches. Also, the meditation experience varies; it is important to understand those variations and how to deal with them appropriately. The availability of followup is an important consideration; you should have a place to turn for information and guidance.

With these guidelines you should be able to find a meditation procedure that can serve as the hub of a regimen for developing intuition. It will make all other procedures more effective. If I were asked to be more specific, I would recommend TM because it is widely available and its effects have been well documented.

GETTING PHYSICAL

On occasion a decision is needed but there is either no time or no use for further fact-finding or analysis. At such times, feeling a strong desire for intuitive guidance, you might look for the silence that supports intuition, but by force of habit your mind is racing with worry, apprehension, or one more futile turn around the track of reason. You may be tempted to try forcing the thoughts out of your mind, blanking it, or otherwise coercing it into silence, but that is precisely what should be avoided.

Forceful attempts to quiet the mind are a contradiction. Trying is an active condition, maybe even more active than the ratiocination you are trying to eliminate. The thoughts you substitute might be more pleasant, perhaps even a welcome diversion, but the effort will keep the mind aroused. This can be avoided by using physical means to create the coherent calmness that is conducive to intuition. Because of the intimate correspondence between mental and physical states, the mental noise level will lower naturally, and you will avoid the fatigue and tension that often result from making unnatural demands on the mind.

During these procedures, don't look for intuition or try to coax it in any way. As we have said repeatedly, intuition is to be tempted, not pursued. It may be expecting too much not to hope for it, but even too much hoping can get in the way. The recommended procedures are good ways to create restful alertness and will have a positive, intuition-enhancing effect whether or not they lead to an immediate intuitive breakthrough. While following these procedures, let your attention drift to the physical activity but don't try to shut off your thoughts. Whenever you become aware that your attention is gripped by mental noise, gently shift your attention to the physical procedure.

STRETCHING FOR INTUITION

Yoga *asanas*, or postures, are an effective way to decrease tension and quiet the mind; done correctly, they will also increase mental alertness. Yoga classes are available everywhere and, when conducted by a qualified instructor, are the best way to learn. Here I offer a few simple, safe positions I have found useful. They should be performed slowly and with no exertion or strain. The body should not be forced into an uncomfortable or painful position. Never try to bend or stretch beyond your capability. Simply move in the direction of the illustrated posture and hold the position when you begin to feel a strain. Your body will gradually become more flexible. The exercises should be done in loose clothing and on a well-carpeted floor or a padded mat. Customarily done before meditation, yoga postures are an excellent way to incubate daily and will have a cumulative effect on your intuition.

Back Stretch. Sit on the floor with your legs straight ahead. Slowly bend your body forward, sliding your hands along the top of your legs. Grasp your big toes. If this is impossible, hold your ankles or shins—the nearest point to your feet that is comfortable. Without bending your knees, pull your trunk a little lower toward your legs, using your arms rather than your back muscles. This should be a gentle process, with no sudden movements or force. Bend forward as far as possible without strain (see Figure 6). In the prototype position your forehead will touch your knees. Remain in the final pose, relaxing your whole body, for about ten seconds before returning to the starting position. This can be repeated two or three times. Over time, gradually increase the duration.

Figure 6. Back stretch.

Shoulder Stand. Lie flat on your back with your feet together and your arms at your sides. Brace your palms against the floor, stiffen your abdomen, and slowly raise your legs, keeping your knees straight. When your legs are perpendicular to the floor, swing them back so that your hips leave the floor. Brace your palms against your lower back for support. Slowly and carefully, straighten to a modified upright position, with your trunk at a 45-degree angle to the floor as in Figure 7. Your weight should be on your elbows, not on your neck or shoulders. After some practice, you will be able to attain the more upright position (Figure 8), with your trunk and legs at a right angle to the floor and your chin against your chest. Hold the position for twenty to thirty seconds at first, gradually lengthening the duration.

To leave this position, bend your knees and lower them toward your forehead. Place your hands at your sides for support. Roll forward slowly and carefully, and when your buttocks touch the floor, straighten your legs and lower them. Rest briefly.

Figure 7. Modified shoulder stand.
Figure 8. Shoulder stand.

Figure 9. The cobra.

The Cobra. Lie on your stomach with your palms down at chest level and your forehead on the floor. Slowly raise your head and shoulders, as if trying to see behind you as far as you can (see Figure 9). Try to raise your shoulders without using your arms, just your back muscles. Then, using your arms, slowly bend your back. Stop when your navel leaves the floor. Hold about ten seconds at first, and increase as you progress. Slowly reverse, lowering first your trunk and then your shoulders, neck, and head until your forehead is on the floor. This can be repeated once or twice after a brief pause.

Yoga Mudra. Sit in the lotus position (Figure 10) if possible, in a half-lotus position (Figure 11), or simply cross-legged. Hold one wrist behind your back with the other hand, your arms relaxed. Take a deep breath and hold. Slowly bend your trunk forward until your forehead touches or nearly touches the floor, stopping if you feel strain (Figure 12). Hold about ten seconds, then exhale as you return to the starting position. This can be repeated two or three times.

An alternate form is to not hold your breath but to exhale while bending forward and breathe normally while holding the final position as long as is comfortable.

RESPIRATION FOR INSPIRATION

Breathing exercises can have a calming and enlivening effect on the nervous system; it is not coincidental that the word *inspiration* applies both to oxygen intake and creativity. The *alternate-nostril technique* is a traditional yoga practice, customarily done after *asanas* and before meditation. I have found it useful as a brief incubation when under pressure (five minutes is about maximum for anyone who has not been practicing the technique for some time).

Eyes closed, sit erect and comfortably. Close your right nostril with the tip of your right thumb. Breathe in, slowly and deeply, through the left nostril. Without straining, take in a bit more than your normal breath, and hold it for two or three seconds.

Now switch nostrils, releasing your thumb and closing the left nostril with your right middle and ring fingers. Exhale slowly and noiselessly, but don't strain to maintain an uncomfortable pace. After exhaling, hold the breath for a second or two and then breathe in through the right nostril, keeping the left one closed. Hold your breath a few seconds, then switch nostrils again, exhaling through the left, then inhaling through the left. Again, the sequence: out/in/switch nostrils; out/in/switch nostrils, and so forth.

Figure 10. Lotus position.

Figure 11. Half-lotus position.

Figure 12. Yoga mudra.

Even in the most hectic circumstances, you should at least be able to take a few deep abdominal breaths. Doing so can provide a lot of incubation in a very short time. Most of us breathe in short, shallow breaths, particularly when under stress. As a result, stale air is not expelled and the oxidation of tissues is inadequate. This affects not only our tension level but our mental functions; the brain uses 20 percent of all the oxygen we take in. By learning to breathe with the abdomen instead of just expanding the chest, energy distribution can be improved. This should be our normal way of breathing, especially when under stress.

Practice a few times a day in the following manner until *abdominal breathing* becomes natural. Place your hands on your abdomen immediately below the navel, with your middle fingertips touching. Breathe through your nose, inhaling slowly, and push your abdomen out as though it were a balloon expanding. Your fingers should separate. As your abdomen expands, your diaphragm will move downward, allowing fresh air to enter the bottom of your lungs. Keeping your back straight aids the process.

As the breath continues, expand your chest. More air should now enter, filling the middle part of your lungs. Slightly contracting your abdomen, raise your shoulders and collarbones. This will fill your upper lungs. Hold your breath for a few seconds, without strain. Slowly exhale through your nose, drawing in your abdomen. Your expanded rib cage will return to normal position, and your lungs will empty. Exhaling completely will expel all the stale air. Repeat the procedure a few times.

The first few practice sessions may cause slight dizziness. That is normal. Don't strain to retain the breath or go any slower than is comfortable.

MUSCLING UP TO INTUITION

When you want to invite intuition and are inclined to recline, quiet calmness can be achieved with this technique for reducing muscular tension. It is also a good way to help induce sleep when tension interferes with that form of incubation.

Lie on your back, eyes closed, arms at your sides palms down. Don't cross your legs. After taking a few seconds to settle down, stiffen the muscles in your arms and hands, clenching your fists and raising your arms slightly. Hold that position for ten to twenty seconds. Then let your arms go suddenly limp. After about twenty seconds repeat the procedure, but this time relax the muscles gradually.

Now tense your leg muscles, pointing your toes away from you as far as they will go. Hold for ten to twenty seconds and then suddenly release the tension. Repeat, relaxing gradually. Then, tense your leg muscles, pulling your toes toward your knee. Release suddenly, then repeat, releasing gradually.

Take a deep breath, holding it with your chest expanded. Then exhale, letting your chest go suddenly limp. Repeat, relaxing your chest muscles gradually.

Eyes still closed, raise your forehead, hold for about ten seconds, and then suddenly relax. Lower your forehead in a frown, then relax. Repeat, relaxing slowly. Open your mouth as wide as you can. Hold, then relax. Repeat, relaxing gradually.

IMAGINING AND INTUITING

The use of inner visualization has become widespread in therapeutic settings; evidence suggests that it can generate insight into feelings and personality traits and that it can help bring about desired changes in attitude, perception, behavior, and even physiology. Visualization procedures can also be used to evoke spontaneous mental events that may contain significant intuitive input. In this context, imagery should be used judiciously, particularly in the absence of a competent guide. I suggest using it when faced with an important decision or when you feel there is an answer within you eager to reveal itself. The product should be evaluated the same way as any other hunch or spontaneous insight.

There are good reasons for prudence. For one thing, it is difficult enough in everyday life to know the difference between legitimate intuition and fantasy, fear, or desire; it can be even more difficult when you are intentionally creating imaginary scenes. It takes practice and self-awareness to distinguish deliberate visualizations from the spontaneous ones that might be the products of the intuitive mind.

Also, as with dreams, the meaning of conjured-up imagery may not be obvious. Interpretation often requires considerable self-awareness, analysis, and, of course, intuition. The content can be symbolic and obtuse. It can also be deeply personal and emotionally charged, which is why some visualization procedures work best in the presence of a trained counselor or supportive group. Frances Vaughan, who devotes an entire chapter to the subject in *Awakening Intuition*, cautions that interpretation, "in the initial stages of working with imagery, is apt to cause problems. Not only does it interfere with the spontaneous flow of imagery, but it can also lead to premature mistaken assumptions which contribute to self-deception rather than intuitive knowledge."

Another potential problem is taking imagination too literally. Some of the intuition-invoking procedures in magazines and workshops have you imagine, say, being beyond space and time or communicating with the "higher self." This kind of suggestion can be useful, but it can also be dangerous if you assume that by so doing you actually *are* beyond space and time or in touch with the higher self. The real versions of such transcendent experiences come from achieving a higher state of consciousness, not merely from imagination. If you suggest to yourself that you are a king, you might come to feel more powerful and self-assured, but don't expect anyone to kneel before you. Similarly, it would be a big mistake to assume (and I have seen this encouraged) that whatever comes out of majestic imagery should be accepted as the product of cosmic intelligence.

Finally, overuse of imagery as a route to intuition can lead to dependency. You might begin to believe that the only way to connect with the intuitive mind is first to create a certain mood or imagery contrivance. This would, however, interfere with spontaneity and innocence. Intuition is not an appliance that you plug in as needed; it is more like a telephone network into which you should always be connected. That is why I have emphasized such consciousness-expanding techniques as meditation.

With these caveats in mind, we can recommend some visualization procedures for invoking intuitive input in selected situations. They should always be preceded by a period of relaxation or meditation to establish a receptive condition, and they should be approached with as much innocence as possible. It would be unrealistic to expect a major breakthrough every time, and as we have said repeatedly, a sense of urgent expectation can be counterproductive. Even if nothing specific comes of the visualization, the time has been well spent; the intuitive mind has been primed and will respond when it is ready.

Besides, even no answer is an answer of sorts; your intuition might be telling you that more information, analysis, or time is needed.

A MENTAL JOURNEY

As a relaxing and inspiring way to make a direct request of intuition, a mental journey is best facilitated by means of step-by-step instructions from another person so that you can sink entirely into the imagery without having to think about what comes next. I suggest that you create your own process and either memorize it or make a tape recording you can play to yourself. Soothing, unobtrusive music (instrumental, since lyrics might start you thinking about the meaning of the words and thus interfere) makes an excellent background. Here are the basic steps:

1. Sit or lie down in a comfortable position, eyes closed. Take deep breaths and relax completely.

2. Imagine yourself getting up from your present location and embarking on a journey. You will have decided in advance on your mode of travel—flying (in a vehicle or on your own), on foot, in a boat, or in any kind of craft you may devise—and on a route, whether across desert, through forests, over mountains, in the air or in outer space, and so forth. Evoke the feeling of actually moving, observing such details as the wind on your face, the smell of the air, the sights around you. It should be a pleasant journey, not an arduous adventure.

3. Arrive at the destination you have chosen in advance—an oasis, a clearing, a mountaintop, an island, a planet. It should be a place with special meaning to you.

4. Make your way to a sanctuary of some kind—a cabin, a cave, a shrine, or something fantastic and unique. The spot is yours alone, and it has sacred meaning to you. It should be a sanctuary you would really like to have, a place to go to whenever you need guidance.

5. Within the sanctuary is a source of wisdom. This too should be something with personal relevance—a disembodied voice, a symbol, an altar, a machine or device, a person. This source is really part of yourself; you can trust it and be perfectly honest with it.

6. Ask this source your question, or present it with your problem. Then let it respond. Don't force anything or impose

ánything. Just see what happens. When something is evoked—
and it may be mundane, absurd, nebulous, ambiguous, or
even a nonresponse—accept it without judgment or analysis.
7. Leave your sanctuary with gratitude and return slowly to
your starting point, retracing your journey.

INTUITION ON THE SPOT

In this process, you close your eyes, relax, and imagine yourself
in a situation where you must act on the decision or problem that
concerns you. Conjure up a no-exit situation, making the scenario as
realistic as possible, and sink into it with your senses and emotions. Imagine what you would actually see and hear and how you
would feel inside. If there are other people involved, have them do
what you think they would do under the circumstances. Don't jump
right to the climax. Set up the scene slowly and deliberately, like a
dramatist, letting the events and characters take on a life of their own.
Set the play in motion and then become a spectator, as if you were
watching the action on a screen. At the appropriate moment, confront your own character with a question or decision. The response
may be the answer you have been looking for.

The procedure can be used for any kind of situation. If it is a
business decision, for example, you might imagine yourself in a meeting with colleagues or your boss; you might be asked to vote or to de-
clare your position on the issue. If you are deciding whether to
marry, you might see yourself at the wedding ceremony having to
say "I do." If you are deciding whether to go to law school, you can
put yourself in the registrar's office about to pay your tuition. If the
problem is interpersonal, you might seat yourself across from the
other person at dinner and see how you express your feelings on a
troublesome issue. If you are seeking an answer to a professional
problem, you might imagine yourself addressing a gathering of peers
who eagerly await your solution. If it is a choice between alternatives,
picture yourself at a crossroads with no way of turning back. If it is
a prediction you need, project yourself into the future where the
event is taking place.

What appears on the screen of your mind may be the product
of your intuition, but it may also be a projection of your wishes or
fears. With time, you should become more sensitive to the difference.
It should be remembered, however, that any strong indication of
your own feelings can be revealing. An editor who tried this tech-

nique imagined herself seated across the desk from a literary agent who asked for a yes-or-no answer about a proposed book. The editor found herself sweating profusely and shaking in fear when her imagined self was about to say yes, and she had an equally strong sense of relief when she saw herself answer no. That told her to turn down the book.

You may also find out something about the other people involved. In your scenarios, you can force others to act as well as yourself, and their on-screen responses may reveal information about their strategies, feelings, or secrets that you were unconsciously aware of. As was suggested earlier, there can be a problem with interpretation, but no more so than with any other intuitive input. Afterward, the products should be evaluated carefully before action is taken.

THE HERALD ARRIVES

Like a royal personage, intuition is often preceded by a herald, only in this case the announcement is discreet, perhaps hardly a whisper. Most often it is a barely perceptible shift of feeling. "I call intuition cosmic fishing," wrote Buckminster Fuller. "You feel a nibble, then you've got to hook the fish." It might arrive during the exercises outlined earlier, or it might appear when least expected. Learning to recognize and respond to the intimation of intuition is important, and is best approached with this philosophy from *Huckleberry Finn*: "There warn't nothing to do but just hold still, and try and be ready to stand from under when the lightning struck."

The precursor can be so wispy, so ephemeral, that it might pass by unnoticed, and so might the intuition itself. If you are attentive, you will sense the herald early. You will find yourself momentarily diverted by something in the corner of your mind, like a shadow on a street or a bird flying past the periphery of your vision. It might be just a subtle corona on the fringes of awareness. You don't want to ignore the herald, but you don't want to pounce, either. As Huck suggested, you have to hold still but also be ready.

Your tendency at such times might be to grab for the intuition or become anxious about losing it. The more accommodating attitude is one of surrender. You should become a spectator and adopt a receptive, witnesslike stance, preferably relaxing and closing your eyes. If the mind were an automobile, you would shift to neutral at such a time, neither churning it into drive nor shutting off the engine. It is important not to try and render the amorphous presence more concrete, as that will engage and activate your mind, making it less receptive. Let the message assume its own form, or let it remain formless; if you impose structure, you will change it, and then it will become something other than the intuitive impulse that was announced.

The best strategy is to let your attention rest on your body. This will help prevent manipulation. If particular sensations draw your attention, follow the body's lead. More than likely, one area or another will come to be associated with the herald. At some point a sense of meaning will emerge, like a whisper in the dark. It might assume any of the languages of intuition—a word, an image, an emotion. Attend to it, but don't analyze or evaluate.

See how your body responds to the initial apprehension of meaning. Is there a change in the sensations you were experiencing earlier? What about the sense of anticipation that alerted you in the first place? Is that gone, replaced by a sense of completion or equilibrium? If so, the meaning that came to you was probably the message that had been intended. If there is still a sense of discomfort or incompleteness, further elaboration or an alternative meaning may be forthcoming. Remain in neutral, letting your attention shift to bodily sensations as before, until some new sense of meaning emerges. (Eugene Gendlin's book, *Focusing*, is about a well-researched process much like this.)

A feeling of wholeness, balance, or completion is a good guide to whether the intuition has run its course. With experience, you will come to know when it is futile to wait for more. If, after a minute or two, nothing satisfactory seems to be arriving, it is best to resume activity. It might have been a false alarm, or more incubation time might be needed. If you remain in that expectant state too long you may become impatient, start to look for something, or implore it to hurry up. This can only create tension, which will do no good for your health or your intuition. It is always best to let intuition play the role of predator.

We have been concerned with the etiquette of inviting intuition to our home. But nothing we have said, in this section or elsewhere in the chapter, guarantees that whatever shows up will be the real thing not an imposter. That is the subject of the next chapter.

10

Forgo It, or Go for It?

One night in 1893 James Couzens, a humble clerk in a Detroit coal company, saw someone rolling down a street in a noisy contraption that had been put together in a tool house from salvaged parts and bicycle wheels. As bystanders laughed, Couzens sensed that the bizarre vehicle and the eccentric behind the wheel represented more than entertainment. He took the thousand dollars he had saved and made a down payment on stock in the inventor's company. He also made a commitment to raise another $9,000 to bring his investment up to a hundred shares. In 1919 Couzens sold his stock in Henry Ford's company for $35 million.

A thousand dollars was a lot of money for a clerk in the Gay Nineties, so Couzens was taking quite a risk by acting on his hunch. Fortunately for him, it worked out well. It doesn't always, as most of us have found out. There are times when you might feel absolutely sure of an intuition, only to discover that you have been deceived, and other times when the intuition is not so convincing and you turn your back on it, only to regret it later. One of the big questions, therefore, is what to do with an intuition once it pops up. We will be addressing that issue in this chapter, beginning with some of the reasons we reject valid intuitions and accept misguided ones.

WHY WE PASS ON IT

In the original manuscript describing his sun-centered cosmos, Copernicus mentioned the possibility that planetary motion might be elliptical rather than circular. He crossed it out. History credits the discovery to Johannes Kepler, who also had turned his back on the idea for three years before accepting it. "Why should I mince my words?" Kepler wrote. "The truth of Nature, which I had rejected and chased away, returned by stealth through the back door, disguising itself to be accepted. Ah, what a foolish bird I have been!" Kepler finally opened the door to elliptical motion, but, in turn, he closed it to universal gravitation, leaving that gem for Newton.

When you find yourself leaning away from an intuitive idea, you may be acting like a "foolish bird." When the situation arises, you might consider the following possibilities before making your final decision.

Is the intuition something you don't want to know? Intuition sometimes functions as an early warning system. Unfortunately, we don't always want to hear the news, preferring safe untruth to an uncomfortable truth. For example, a nagging inner voice tells you that certain problems in a relationship are irreconcilable, but you reject the message, rationalizing it away, because you don't want to face the responsibility of ending the relationship and being alone. Or your intuition keeps telling you that the pains in your chest ought to be examined, but you chalk it up to heartburn because you can't handle the thought of serious illness. Or your intuition tells you that you ought to cut your losses on a business decision, but you fight it off because you can't own up to having made a mistake.

Are you afraid of censure? Particularly in organizations, people fight off intuitive ideas—especially unorthodox ones—because they have a need to be accepted as a member of the group or because they don't want to offend a particular person. When asked what single characteristic he has observed in intuitive executives, one corporate president replied, "They don't give a damn what anyone thinks." In addition to not wanting to rock the boat, many of us feel we have to project an image of cool rationality, so we go overboard to appear precise, sensible, and realistic. Hence when the facts and figures don't support an intuition, the fear of ridicule or rejection is magnified.

Are you yielding blindly to authority? When intuition is contradicted by authority or convention, it becomes that much harder to accept. Yet, as history repeatedly demonstrates, one of intuition's main functions is to generate ideas and discoveries that do not conform to accepted views. For example, according to legend, Edwin Land was strolling on a beach with his daughter when he stopped to take a photograph of her. "Why can't I see the picture now?" the little girl asked. Reportedly, Land turned the innocent remark into something more than a paternal anecdote: the world's first instant camera. The idea was rejected by the Eastman Kodak Company, forcing Land to create Polaroid.

The list is long of scientists whose ideas were scorned or even "disproven" by irrefutable evidence. To Simon Newcomb, vice president of the National Academy of Sciences in 1903, the impossibility of flying machines was "as complete as it is possible for the demonstration of any physical fact to be." To the great physicist Lord Kelvin, Darwin's theory was impossible because the earth could not have been in existence long enough. Systems theory was rejected in the 1940s as "trivial, false, misleading, and unsound." What intuition does best is go beyond what is known; but at times it is difficult not to be dissuaded by authorities, since they achieve that stature by being right more often than not.

Are you being self-critical? You might reject an intuitive message because you don't like yourself for having thought it or suspect the thought has come from a part of yourself that you disapprove of. For example, you have a strong feeling that your spouse is keeping something from you, but instead of taking the intuition seriously, you scold yourself for being suspicious or judgmental. In fact, you might have been too suspicious of yourself.

Here are two actual examples. Steve Roach, a musician who composes with sophisticated synthesizers, had just finished programming some important material into a computer and was about to take a break. The thought "Copy that material onto a cassette" flashed in his mind. His immediate reaction was "That's dumb—you're just being paranoid." A power surge destroyed his work. The other example was related by attorney Julia Mackey: "I parked my car on a side street in New York City, and as I locked the door my eye caught a black man looking in my direction. Something inside said, 'Get the suitcase out of the back seat and take it with you.' I immediately chastised myself for what I suspected was latent racism. The suitcase was gone when I returned an hour later."

Are you afraid of the new? Psychologist Rollo May, in *The Courage to Create*, says of a breakthrough of his own that "it not only broke down my previous hypothesis, it shook my self-world relationship. At such a time I find myself having to seek a new foundation, the existence of which I as yet don't know. This is the source of the anxious feeling that comes at the moment of the breakthrough; it is not possible that there be a genuinely new idea without this shake-up occurring to some degree."

When intuition throws a cherished belief or comfortable assumption into question, it can be unsettling. If we have difficulty dealing with the period between the destruction of the old and the stabilization of the new, we might battle the intuition in an effort to maintain our psychic equilibrium.

Are you being too demanding? We often reject intuitions because they don't meet all of our standards of precision, proof, or completeness, not realizing that intuition often provides a global pattern, a direction, or a new perspective, the details of which have to be filled in later. Also, we might misinterpret the somewhat amorphous message, filling it in with erroneous details.

For example, you might have an idea to open an art gallery but immediately drop it because answers to such questions as "Where would it be located?" or "How will I raise the money?" are not immediately answerable. Or you might have a strong feeling that your firm ought not to sign a contract for a particular deal. But you can't immediately come up with sufficient reasons to justify the notion, so you drop it. You might also abandon an intuitive impulse because you can't structure it into a verbal statement or explain how you came to know it. Be reassured by psychologist Eric Berne: "To understand intuition it seems necessary to avoid the belief that in order to know something the individual must be able to put into words what he knows and how he knows it."

Sometimes our initial interpretation of an intuition is off the mark. Discovering that, we might abandon the entire message instead of trying to reinterpret it. Here we might take a lesson from Saint Francis of Assisi, who once heard an inner voice say, "Go and restore my church." At first he thought it was the voice of God telling him to repair a ruined chapel; later he realized that his mission was to restore the institution of the church itself.

Here is a poignant example of the interpretation problem from a Chicago woman:

> One night I sensed there was something wrong with my husband. Then, just before I fell asleep, I realized he was having an affair with his assistant. The conviction grew over the next few days: When I called his office, the assistant's voice seemed weird. Then, one night when my husband said he was having dinner with a friend, I followed him, convinced he was having a rendezvous with the as-

sistant. When he ended up in a restaurant with another man, I concluded that I was just an insecure, jealous wife, and dropped the whole thing. I soon found out that my intuition was working on a different level. My husband *was* troubled, and the assistant had something to do with it: she had embezzled funds, and when my husband found out, her lover, an officer of the company, threatened to fire him if he didn't keep quiet.

Are you selling yourself short? Many of our examples have been of intuition as a protective device, dispensing unpleasant information as a warning. Intuition is just as likely to provide the opposite: good news, encouraging information, opportunities, and the like. Such input—an insight into your own virtues, a strong positive feeling about a relationship, a hunch about a business opportunity—might be rejected because of an inclination toward pessimism or because you feel yourself incapable or undeserving. Your intuition might be pushing you toward a love affair that is likely to be a challenge or toward an enterprise whose success would represent quite an accomplishment. You might reject such intuitions as "unrealistic" or mere fantasy, when the real problem is an unconscious feeling of inadequacy or a deep-seated lack of confidence. Your intuition might know better than your conscious mind what your true capabilities are.

Are you afraid of the risk? Following through on an innovative or unusual intuition might carry with it considerable risk. The financial losses on a business hunch can be great or a scientific hypothesis might cost a great deal of time and money only to be disproven. And in both instances there is a loss of prestige as well. Other intuitions carry interpersonal risks, as in the case of the suspicious wife. In fact, to some people the risk of simply being wrong is intolerable, and the risk of looking foolish can be the biggest risk of all.

Is it lack of faith? Perhaps the most ubiquitous form of resistance, and probably the easiest to overcome, is disbelief in intuition. Given our cultural reverence for rationality and provable data, it is easy to understand why we might respond to intuition with, essentially, "Oh, come on!" This is especially true, of course, if the intuition is not supported by facts or logic or we can't figure out how we could possibly have arrived at the knowledge. Often the biggest barrier to accepting intuitive inspiration is an ideological conviction, perhaps unconscious, that such things just don't happen.

MISTAKING THE CHAFF FOR WHEAT

Of course, the opposite problem also occurs. In *The Act of Creation*, Arthur Koestler notes that Faraday, Darwin, Huxley, Planck, and other great scientists confessed to having been misled by false inspirations on more than one occasion. Einstein told of having lost "two hard years of work" because of one. Let's look at some questions that might save you from getting caught in the embrace of what only *seems* to be a good intuition.

Do you want it to be true? It is quite easy to confuse desire with intuition. You feel very strongly that Diane in the sales department is attracted to you. Is it intuition or wishful thinking? You have a strong gut feeling that the real estate market is about to soar: is it a powerful hunch or a powerful hope? It is probably a good idea to be extra diligent about substantiating any intuitive idea that you find yourself wanting to believe.

Is it intuition or impulsiveness? As Italian psychologist Roberto Assagioli points out, the concept of will has fallen into such disrepute that reaction has "swung to the other extreme: a tendency to refuse any kind of control and discipline of drives, urges, wishes, whims—a cult of unbridled 'spontaneity.' " What seems to be intuitive might actually be reactive behavior, perhaps rooted in an ideology that disdains self-control.

Is it intuition or image-making? Some people—autocratic executives, for example—have such a strong need to appear decisive, confident, and self-assured that they will deny ever feeling confused or doubtful. They are so intent on maintaining an image of infallibility that they adamantly defend any point of view that comes to mind in the name of superior intuition (although in many circles they will use the term "judgment" or "savvy"). Similarly, people on a spiritual path often take intuitive experiences as a sign of progress and will find ways to display their prowess to fellow seekers.

Is it intuition or rebelliousness? An excessive need to be different, to fight authority, or to resist the appearance of knuckling under can cause many people to cling to an unorthodox intuitive notion. In such cases, the more outrageous the idea the more vigorously it is embraced, even in the face of contradictory evidence.

Is it intuition or intellectual laziness? People who are predisposed to accept intuition can use it as justification for taking the easy way out. Instead of analyzing a problem or going after facts, they acquiesce to the first plausible intuition that comes along, without submitting it to verification.

Is it intuition or fear of uncertainty? We have argued that an intolerance of uncertainty can restrain the intuitive mind; it sometimes works the other way around. You might unconditionally accept a solution because it provides relief from indecision or ambiguity. Owning up to the true complexity of a situation might require suspending judgment on early intuitions in order to gather information and generate alternatives.

Is it intuition or emotion? The ordinary emotions of human interaction can distort the intuitive mind. You might be angry with someone and "intuit" that he is doing something evil. You might be intimidated by an employer and "intuit" that he is going to fire you (that kind of mistake can easily become a self-fulfilling prophecy). You might have a strong "intuition" that something horrible is about to happen, but you may really be expressing a need to feel victimized.

I know of one lawyer who was absolutely convinced that friends of his would not win a contested inheritance that would set them up for life. How did he know? "Intuitively," he said, with great authority. He turned out to be wrong, and later admitted to an extreme case of envy. Fortunately, the friends had employed a different attorney.

VALIDATING INTUITION

The best way to prevent either type of error—rejecting valid or useful intuitions or accepting fallacious ones—is to raise your level of consciousness so that your mind makes fewer mistakes. That might seem a facile way out, but it is indeed the best approach, just as strengthening the body is the best safeguard against disease. But we have said all that can be said about the importance of expanding consciousness to develop intuitive capacity.

As the questions in the two previous sections suggest, self-deception is a notorious deterrent to the effective use of intuition. It follows that self-awareness would be a prime asset. Understanding your strengths, weaknesses, tendencies, habits, vulnerabilities, and minor neuroses is the best way to keep psychological nuisances from contaminating intuition. Space does not permit a detailed discussion of this area, but the reader is encouraged to be honestly introspective and to take whatever steps are necessary to increase self-understand-ing. If you are observant, you will gradually acquire sensitivity to your patterns of interaction with intuition, and if any psychological factors are standing in the way, they will be revealed.

The nuances of the intuitive experience itself are important in deciding whether to heed an intuitive idea. The strength of certitude and the intensity of feeling might be markedly different with correct intuitions as opposed to erroneous ones. This can be misleading, how-ever, since emotions such as those discussed in the preceding section can be equally powerful. Two important considerations, as we saw with the Kepler anecdote, are persistence and repetition. If a feeling or idea does not relent and its nagging voice keeps coming back at unexpected times, the intuitive mind probably feels strongly about it. Observation and keeping a journal (described later in this chapter) will help you determine the mental and physical correlates of your good intuitions as well as the difference between intuitions and de-sires, fears, or other emotions.

Whenever possible, you should submit an intuition to all the analytic and quantitative tests at your disposal. When it comes to verification and evaluation, the rational-empirical methods of sci-entism are at their best. Indeed, it can be argued that they were de-signed for that purpose. If, as in many personal situations, sophisti-cated procedures are neither feasible nor desirable, the essential tools of science can be emulated and its objective attitude can be adopted. Objectivity is especially important when evaluating an intuition you want to believe, or when you're resisting one because it is risky. In such cases, it helps to stand aside and ask yourself how you would feel if the intuition belonged to someone else and had nothing to do with you.

Particularly in important situations, rationality should be brought to bear before you commit to an intuitive idea. Force yourself to defend it logically, even if the jury consists only of yourself. Analyze available facts and figures dispassionately to see if they support the intuition. Reason through all the possible consequences of being right or wrong with rigor. Consult the experts and weigh all potential fac-tors influencing the outcome. Whenever possible, conduct a safe test of the intuition before making a larger commitment.

Keep in mind, however, that rational-empirical procedures are not flawless, particularly when time and resources are limited. In addi-tion to weaknesses inherent in the information itself—its validity and reliability, the soundness of the premises on which it is based—we may still be overly subjective in our interpretation of the data. This is especially true, of course, when we have to deal with nebulous personal problems and when unpredictable human beings are involved.

Many of our intuitions—and our evaluations *of* intuitions—are based on preconceptions about such concepts as causality and probability. Yet research indicates that most of us have a quite limited grasp of these variables and that we frequently err when dealing with them. About our judgments of causality, for example, Yale psychologist Robert Sternberg has found that "people are more inclined to ascribe their own failings as due to external factors (for example, bad luck), but to ascribe the failings of others to internal factors (for example, the other's incompetence)."

Another common error is to confuse correlation with causation; when two things happen concurrently we tend to assume one caused the other. You may take the cold tone in someone's voice as proof of your intuition that he disagrees with you, when in fact he approves of what you say but is fuming inside because your remarks remind him of an argument he had with his wife. Here is an example, related by a manager named Hal Morrison: "I hired Ted because I had a hunch he had strong leadership qualities. But when I saw him at our Tuesday-morning staff meetings he seemed inarticulate and indecisive, so I figured my intuition was wrong. I reasoned that groups of people intimidated him. It turned out that he *was* a good leader, but Monday-night football made him tired on Tuesday mornings."

In the absence of formal training we also tend to incorrectly estimate probability, an important consideration since so many of our intuitive judgments are based on the likelihood of something occurring. A common error has to do with availability. In *Human Inference*, social psychologists Richard Nisbett and Lee Ross point out that "objects or events are judged as frequent or probable, or infrequent or improbable, depending on the readiness with which they come to the judge's mind." So people from, say, Pennsylvania are always astounded by the number of Pennsylvanians in prominent positions, failing to realize that they are simply more likely to take notice of Pennsylvanians. Hence if they have an intuition that a particular person will succeed, they might take the fact that he is from Pennsylvania as substantiation.

We also tend to selectively seek out information that confirms our beliefs and ignore, forget, or rationalize evidence to the contrary.

The woman who thought her husband was having an affair might take as proof every nice word he said about his assistant. She might either ignore the negative things he said or take them as proof of a coverup attempt. Similarly, if an intuition appeals to us, or if we *want* it to be true, we will unconsciously look for facts that prove it. Psychologist Leon Festinger found that when people have *cognitive dissonance*—the tension created by holding two contradictory ideas—they adopt strategies such as rationalization to reduce it. For example, cults that believe the world is going to end on a certain date do not give up their vision when the predicted doomsday passes. They draw closer together, find a way to explain the miscalculation, and make a new prediction. We would do well to emulate scientists, who design experiments to *disprove* hypotheses.

In analyzing our intuitions, we are often peering into the future darkly. Formal analytic tools can help us identify trends and apply the lessons of the past. However, we must remember the prognostic limitations of hard data. They yield probabilities and approximations, which don't tell us unequivocally what will happen in a specific instance. Furthermore, statistics are gathered and interpreted by experts with personal assumptions and vested interests. Not only do expert predictions contradict one another all the time, but studies have shown that the manner in which data are presented will determine the way people respond to them; the same statistics packaged in two different ways are likely to elicit two different reactions.

Also, according to J. Scott Armstrong of the Wharton School at the University of Pennsylvania, "Dozens of carefully constructed studies have demonstrated that expertise beyond a minimal level is of little value in forecasting change." Armstrong claims that research in psychology, economics, medicine, sports, sociology, and the stock market has borne out this conclusion.

Naturally, specialized knowledge and experience are an advantage in forecasting, but Armstrong and others believe that decision makers often exaggerate the importance of expertise. History provides no shortage of expert predictions whose real value turned out to be entertainment: the music moguls who told the Beatles that groups with guitars were on the way out; the man who sold half the Coca-Cola Company because he thought the name was "unappealing"; the scientists polled in 1948 who predicted that if we made it a national priority we might land a man on the moon by 2148; the experts who predicted in 1899 that the horseless carriage in which James Couzens invested his savings would never be as popular as the bicycle.

The failure of expert forecasts is not always funny, of course. In 1973 Golda Meir, then prime minister of Israel, was talked out of her conviction that war was imminent. Soon thereafter, Syria and Egypt attacked, and her unprepared army suffered heavy casualties. Meir later revealed that she had contemplated suicide at the time. "I couldn't forgive myself," she said, "for not following my feeling and fears and accepting the opinion of the experts."

INTUITION EVALUATING INTUITION

These caveats about rational-empirical methods are not meant to discredit them but to point out the folly of assigning to them full responsibility for verifying intuition. As we have noted frequently, intuition does more than feed us discoveries and creative ideas. It also works with our rational faculties to evaluate those very contributions. And, just as analysis provides feedback about intuition, so does intuition provide feedback about analytic procedures. We should look for it in these final phases of problem solving and decision making.

When a scientist formulates a hypothesis, he thinks, "If the hypothesis is true, when X occurs, Y should follow." He then devises an experiment, creating X under controlled conditions and seeing if Y follows. Business leaders do the same thing with their ideas; they run market tests or conduct limited sales campaigns to see if a product or advertising concept produces the predicted results. Often we can do the same with our intuitions. The jealous wife mentioned earlier, for example, tested her intuition by reasoning, "If my husband says he is not coming home for dinner, he is meeting his assistant." In following him she was conducting an experiment.

When feasible, that empirical approach should be used to validate intuitions. However, we often fail to appreciate the role of intuition in the design of experiments. Benjamin Franklin wanted desperately to make contact with a thundercloud, but no tall tower was available. For some time, his ideas were predictable—spires, long iron rods—and also futile. Then, while relaxing one day, he drifted into a daydream and the memory of kite-flying crossed his mind. The rest of the story we all learned in grade school.

Similarly, in 1903 Otto Loewi conceived a theory about the role of chemicals in transmitting nerve impulses but could think of no way to test it empirically. He forgot about it until one night in 1920, when, in his words:

> I awoke, turned on the light, and jotted down a few notes on a tiny slip of thin paper. Then I fell asleep again. It occurred to me at six o'clock in the morning that during the night I had written down something most important but I was unable to decipher the scrawl. The next night, at three o'clock, the idea returned. It was the design of an experiment to test whether or not the hypothesis of chemical transmission that I had uttered seventeen years ago was correct. I got up immediately, went to the laboratory, and performed a simple experiment on a frog heart according to the nocturnal dream.

Loewi's discovery of inhibitory and excitatory impulses at nerve terminals earned him a Nobel Prize, and the experimental design was called by physiologist Walter B. Cannon "one of the neatest, simplest, and most definite experiments in the history of biology."

Interestingly, Loewi said that if he had stopped to analyze the design instead of acting immediately, he would have rejected it. There is an important lesson in that: rationality may overrule intuition, but it may not be right. Even with sophisticated procedures, the numbers may be incomplete or ambiguous, the experts may disagree, the projections may point in several directions. Intuition helps us spot flaws in the analysis, uncover prejudices, reinterpret data, and so forth. And, in the end, when intuition and analysis have each had their say and it is time to act one way or the other, it is usually the evaluative function of intuition that we look to. Even when we think we are being perfectly rational, it might really be our intuition telling us that the analysis is okay. Robert P. Jensen, chairman of General Cable Corporation, told *Fortune* magazine of the time he was faced with five decisions involving $300 million: "On each decision, the mathematical analysis only got me to the point where my intuition had to take over." That is a typical experience.

With the procedures discussed in Chapter 9 you can use intuitive input to help evaluate an intuition. Essentially, the judgment process boils down to predicting the outcome of each alternative, which is seldom as straightforward as it sounds. In relatively complex situations, outside events over which you have little or no control will affect the outcome. Thus you have to figure out what will happen if you follow your hunch *and* X, Y, and Z occurs and compare that to what will happen if you reject the intuition. The more complex it gets, the more you will need your intuition.

Suppose, for example, you are a latter-day James Couzens and have a hunch that the odd young man with the personal helicopter is going to alter the future of transportation. Deciding whether or not to invest your savings means considering all the significant variables that can affect the outcome. You might use the brainstorming process to generate a list: solar power for the vehicle becomes feasible, General Motors buys a minority share in the company, a new alloy cuts down the weight, the prototype is completed on schedule, the government bans personal helicopters, the auto companies sabotage the invention, the cost of production exceeds current estimates, the inventor absconds with the capital, and whatever else your imagination can come up with.

You can then use the spontaneous-writing method to project the consequences of each contingent event. One way of stimulating the process is to begin with an incomplete sentence, such as, "If I invest my savings and X happens, then . . ." or "If I don't invest and Y happens, then . . ." Of course, these outside variables can occur in combination, and there are many possible permutations. If you acknowledge the true complexity of a decision, your writing will be convoluted, and that is fine for the purposes of the procedure. You are using it to give your intuition the opportunity to contribute to the evaluation process; feelings about the decision and new insights into the entire situation may emerge.

Naturally, your decision will be based not only on what *can* occur but on how *likely* it is to occur. Expert analysis and quantitative data will help determine the probabilities, but they may not be enough, which is why management is often called "the art of making decisions on insufficient information." You might want to use visualization to add an intuitive estimate to the process. For example, you can imagine yourself a contestant on a quiz show. The announcer says, "For the grand prize, on a scale of one to ten, what is the probability that the government will prohibit personal helicopters?" Give yourself no more than a few seconds to answer.

One reason why intuitive predictions are important is that the theories on which formal decision making is based assume that the decision maker does not influence the outcome. But, in many cases, what you *want* to happen or *believe* will happen has a great impact on the actual results. If, for example, you become an active participant in the helicopter venture, you can influence the future. If you are deciding whether to obey an intuition to propose marriage, your desires and intentions should count more than divorce statistics. (The role of belief and personal influence recalls the importance of one's level of consciousness; theoretically, as awareness expands, desires correspond more closely to reality, and what we believe will happen is more likely actually to occur.)

Of course, you won't always have enough time to properly employ rational-analytic methods or even to use procedures for stimulating intuitive input. And even if you *do* have the time, you may still end up ambivalent or unsure. You might then turn to visualization—journeying to your sanctuary or putting yourself in a no-exit situation—and call on the evaluative function of intuition for the final verdict.

As we have said many times, becoming familiar with the nuances of your own intuition, along with the way you react to it, is one of the key ingredients in using the faculty effectively. The intuition journal is a useful device for acquiring that sensitivity.

THE INTUITION JOURNAL

During the night before he was to sign the papers on a major construction project, George Naddaff awoke and told his wife, "I'm not going through with it." The next morning he changed his mind and went ahead with the deal. It was a disaster. "To this day," George says, "whenever I have those vibrations I back off." George can't be more specific about his "vibrations," but he knows clearly enough what they felt like, and he knows how to respond when he feels them again.

Such feedback teaches you how to respond to your intuition. Keeping a journal will enable you to discover which constellation of factors correspond with successful intuitions and which are associated with faulty ones. By keeping the journal diligently, you should become more aware of the signals that indicate when your intuitive voice is leading you in the right direction. This in turn should increase your confidence in and awareness of your intuition, making it more effective.

In an 8½-by-11-inch notebook, maintaining the same numbering system throughout for easy reference, record the following information:

1. The date and time.
2. The content of the intuition. What was the basic message?
3. The subject area: Professional? Another person? Yourself? Politics? Philosophy? Other?
4. Was it: A warning? An opportunity? An affirmation? A contradiction of a belief? Positive information? Negative? Other?
5. The function of the intuition (as noted in Chapter 3): discovery, creative, predictive, operational, evaluative, illuminative. Keep in mind that these can occur in combinations.
6. Structure: Was the intuition primarily verbal, visual, kinesthetic, symbolic, just a faint idea? Describe it as well as you can.
7. Was it a quick flash or a prolonged experience?
8. Was it: Very vivid? Clear? Somewhat unclear? Very hazy?
9. Was the message obvious or did it require interpretation? How did you interpret it?
10. What were you doing immediately prior to the intuition? Was your activity related to the intuition? Had you intentionally incubated?
11. Was there an intimation, or herald, just before the intuition? If so, describe what it felt like and how you responded to it.
12. How did you feel immediately afterward? Was there a sense of exhilaration? Relief? Happiness? Wholeness? Peace?
13. What level of certitude did it carry? Indubitable? Quite certain? Somewhat certain? Doubtful?
14. What was your initial reaction? Skepticism? Rejection? Reserved judgment? Criticism? Hesitation? Unequivocal affirmation?

The previous items can be noted at the time of the intuition. Later, add to your journal the following:

15. Did it represent a departure from custom or authority?
16. Did it go against facts or logic?

17. Was it something you wanted to hear?
18. Was it something you didn't want to hear?
19. Did it return to you at various times? When? How often? How insistently?
20. Did you analyze it? Did you gather information to support and refute it?
21. Did you try to be objective in your evaluation?
22. Did you seek out other opinions?
23. Did your feeling about its veracity change over time? If so, what caused it to change?
24. Was the situation or subject matter: Extremely important? Very important? Moderately important? Not very important? Trivial?
25. Were you under pressure to make a decision or come up with an answer?
26. Did acting on the intuition represent: A great risk? A moderately high risk? Some risk? Not much risk? What exactly was the risk?
27. Were you ever afraid of following up on it? If so, what were you afraid of?
28. Did you ultimately accept the intuition? If so, can you say why?
29. Did you reject it? Can you say why?
30. How did it work out in the end? Was the intuition verified by experience or was it refuted?
31. If you turned down a good intuition, do you understand what caused the error?
32. If you went with an intuition that turned out to be wrong, do you understand why you did? (In answering 31 and 32, refer back to the beginning of this chapter.)
33. In retrospect, would you do anything differently?
34. What is the main lesson to be learned from this experience?

When evaluating your intuition, keep in mind that it might be speaking on several levels. Part of it—or your subsequent interpretation—may be wrong, but on another level it may be working for you. Consider this experience. Jane was walking around a shopping area and was drawn irresistibly to a store that sold dance and exercise outfits. She had no need for anything in the shop, but the feeling persisted, so she retraced her steps. Her interpretation was that her intuition was alerting her to a sale or a unique item. She was wrong, but she enjoyed her conversation with Sherri, the saleswoman, enough to arrange a lunch meeting. Two days later Jane lost her job. Depressed, she called her new friend to cancel lunch. Sherri said she was quitting her job, and Jane took it.

You should also leave room in your journal for random observations and items of importance to you that are not included in the format. Ideally, the entries should be reviewed periodically, perhaps once a month. Record your observations at the time, noting any patterns you come across, such as "My intuition seems to be more accurate at work than with relationships." If your review leads to a resolution—for example, "The next time I feel that sensation in my stomach, I will follow my hunch"—record it in the journal. Also mark any progress you notice in the quality of your intuition. If you use the journal effectively, there should be ample opportunity to do that.

PRACTICE MAKES PERFECT

The following practice ideas are pleasant opportunities to learn about your own thinking patterns and the nuances of your intuition. In most cases, you will be stating answers or making decisions with insufficient time and information to reason adequately. Where appropriate, use the intuition journal to record your experiences.

1. Practice making quick decisions on minor matters. Give yourself a ten-second limit when, for example: ordering from a menu, deciding what to wear, selecting a driving route, choosing a movie or restaurant, buying a clothing accessory.
2. Practice making predictions, going with the first thought that comes to mind. For example, predict who is calling when the phone rings; the outcomes of sporting events; the subject of the next morning's main newspaper headline; the performance of certain stocks; what a colleague will wear to work the next day; which line will get to the teller's window first; what will be in the morning mail; the winners of various awards.

3. Cover the captions on newspaper photographs and quickly state what is going on. Alternatively, cover the captions on cartoons and come up with your own. These can be approached in two ways: trying to be correct or trying to be inventive.

4. Turn off the sound on the television and, after five minutes of watching, describe the story. Alternatively, turn off the sound during a commercial and, assuming you haven't seen it before, guess the product. This is best done with a partner who can verify by listening in with earphones.

5. After brief meetings with strangers, try to describe them in detail: family background; what kind of students they were; what their hobbies are; what their relationships are like; what they think of themselves; their personal habits and tastes in reading, entertainment, clothing, furniture, food, and so on. For verification, use a mutual acquaintance or the people themselves, if they are willing.

6. Working with a friend, use photographs or sketchy information (names, professions, and ages) and have one person describe the other's acquaintances.

7. Read mysteries and predict the solution.

8. Practice brainstorming with the following problems: lost pets; carrying packages in the rain; stolen cars; reading road maps while driving; flat tires; unemployment; dripping faucets; humidity; dirty streets; the budget deficit; students who can't read; cleaning skyscraper windows; day care.

9. Use the same list to practice redefining problems.

Some of these exercises can be done in a group, which is not only more fun but provides the opportunity for inventing new practice methods. Indeed, a regularly scheduled support group composed of people who share an interest in developing their intuition is an excellent idea. The group can discuss each person's experiences, share the insights that come from keeping an intuition journal, and even provide intuitive input for one anothers' problems and decisions. It might also tackle larger problems, such as what we as a society can do to improve the intuition of our leaders and citizens, an area that we will examine next.

11

Making the World Safe for Intuition

If ever an age cried out for intuitive wisdom it is ours. Yet the educational institutions that teach us how to use our minds, and the organizations in which we use them, have not been structured to nurture intuition. We need to change this and to make a high priority of understanding how the intuitive mind works. Such a venture has implications beyond personal success and happiness. By developing knowers whose subjective skills match the precision and reliability of our objective methods, we can harness a vital resource for humankind.

If the experts agree on anything, it is that the coming decades will be more complex and unpredictable than ever and that the information we will have to process will be not only vast but volatile. In such an atmosphere, split-second decisions have to be made with limited information, and mistakes are not only more probable but potentially more catastrophic. This is of special concern, of course, in the centers of power. In his recent memoirs, former national security adviser Zbigniew Brzezinski wrote, "The external world's vision of internal decision making in the Government assumes too much cohesion and expects too much systematic planning. The fact of the matter is that, increasingly, policy makers are overwhelmed by events and information."

Computers will help immeasurably, but human intuition has to guide their use and fill in the pieces that logical machines can't supply. In both the public and private spheres, we need innovative thinkers unfettered by "psychosclerosis," leaders with nimble minds tuned to high ideals and cosmic intelligence. Plato, I believe, had that in mind when he sought to empower "philosophers," a word that had different meaning then: "Those who are capable of apprehending that which is eternal and unchanging . . . fix their eyes on the absolute truth, and always with reference to that ideal and in the greatest possible contemplation of it establish in this world also the laws of the beautiful, the just, and the good."

But it is not just among the powerful that we need quality intuition. Sometimes we forget that each of us is a cell in the collective brain. The way we think and what we know fashion our behavior, and whether that behavior is noble or vile has a major impact on social conditions. It is not enough merely to implore individuals to act morally and ethically or to accept personal responsibility for social, economic, or ecological conditions. That approach has never worked, even under threat of eternal damnation.

The apparent shifting of values, of which growing respect for intuition is a part, is encouraging. In the past two decades large segments of society have rejected the materialism that had become synonymous with quality of life, and have begun to search for higher meaning and purpose. More recently, seekers of personal fulfillment have begun to learn that their goal is not incompatible with social and planetary responsibility; indeed, true self-realization implies a harmonious synergy between the self and the people and objects that constitute the environment. This complementarity of collective and personal priorities (symbolic perhaps of the 1960s and 1970s, respectively) is a reflection of a world view moving away from mechanism and materialism and incorporating some of the organic, spiritual vision of the East.

We are discovering our symbiotic relationship with nature and with one another and coming to accept the ancient truth that we reap what we sow. The optimistic assumption is that new belief systems will translate into more appropriate and harmonious behavior, and convince us to act as trustworthy citizens of a small planet. To a degree this is true. However, belief alone is not sufficient. If it were, we would all have been behaving like good Christians and Jews and Muslims for centuries. It is not enough just to believe that we are linked inextricably to nature, or that there is a common spiritual core to our being, or that all creatures are one and that everything each of us does affects the whole. But raising the quality of intuition can solidify positive beliefs and translate responsible values into effective action.

Only when abstract concepts are truly *known*, apprehended with direct intuitive intimacy, can they take on the kind of experiential quality that can transform behavior. We protect and nurture that which we perceive as part of ourselves, but the sense of connection with people and nature has to be deeply felt, not just thought about. Furthermore, while certain beliefs can foster a willingness to act responsibly, they don't tell us how to do it or what the consequences of specific actions will be. For this we need intuition.

THE EXPANSION OF SCIENCE

A concerted effort to understand and develop intuition in no way compromises the standards of impartial inquiry and rigorous verification that have made science uniquely powerful. Indeed, it may be just what science needs at this moment in history. We need scholars and scientists with the "deep inner contact with nature" that Jeremy Bernstein attributed to Einstein—not merely to discover solutions to practical problems, but to tackle the great cosmic puzzles that science now stands poised to investigate.

The traditional goal of science has been to formulate a complete, unambiguous system of deductions, derived from unimpeachable laws, that describes the way nature works. At the turn of the century, science's self-confidence had reached its apex and physicists were asserting that their job was just about done. They had penetrated the nucleus of the atom and vaulted our vision light years into the heavens, and now they were ready to unlock the deepest secrets of the universe. But instead of final truths, science found a fairyland of unpredictability.

In a series of shattering events that demonstrated both its limitations and its integrity, science turned its gaze upon itself and found itself wanting. A turning point came in 1927 with the famous uncertainty principle of Werner Heisenberg. Heisenberg demonstrated that it is impossible to obtain prediction and control at those deep subatomic levels where the physical becomes nonphysical. The act of measuring inevitably alters what is being measured, just as inserting a thermometer into water provides the temperature of water with the thermometer in it. The separation of the knower and the known, a basic tenet of scientism, was destroyed, and the dream of certainty gave way to a resigned acceptance of approximation and probability.

Concurrently, mathematicians were trying to establish once and for all an axiomatic system—some formal collection of symbolic statements—that would provide complete, consistent mathematical knowledge. This quest was dealt a death blow in 1931 by Kurt Gödel, whose incompleteness theorem proved that such a system was impossible. No formal system can be both consistent (containing no internal contradictions) and complete. There will always be a true statement, derivable from the system, that the system itself can't prove. Along with Heisenberg and others, the work of Gödel demonstrated that, in Jacob Bronowski's words, "The laws of nature cannot be formulated as an axiomatic, deductive, formal, and unambiguous system which is also complete."

Science now resembles the Cretan who said, "All Cretans are liars." It claims to be the only way to know reality, but the message of modern science is, "What science knows is tentative, incomplete, and uncertain." If both statements are true, then there is no way to know reality except tentatively, incompletely, and uncertainly. The conclusion that science will never fulfill its traditional dream has led to both resignation and despair. But it must be remembered that the limitations discovered by science and mathematics relate to the methods of science and mathematics, not necessarily to reality or human cognition. They did not prove that certainty and completeness cannot be achieved, only that they can't be achieved by science as we know it.

The history of science resembles a Zen novice wrestling with a *koan*, those insoluble puzzles that can't be answered with logic or empirical observation. The fortunate seeker will come to transcend rational thought and surrender to direct intuitive experience. And it is precisely this point to which science has come. It has laid bare the fickle, paradoxical nature of what in India is called *maya*, the familiar world of bounded forms and limitless change that veils absolute reality. It now has to transcend both that realm and its own methods if it is to unravel the cosmic mysteries.

The goal of physics since Einstein has been to find the "unified field" that many feel must underlie and permeate the multiplicity of creation. No doubt this goal will be achieved. But when it is, it will be an inferred truth. Through scientism, no one will experience it directly, just as no one has ever perceived an electron. The real unified field is what we earlier called the Absolute, that which the *Upanishads* describe as "smaller than the smallest, bigger than the biggest." Inferring it alone will be, as science now promises, incomplete, tentative, and always somewhat uncertain. It can be truly apprehended—and the knower sublimely transformed—only through the intimate intuitive experience we called illumination.

On two levels, then, science stands to gain from a technology of intuitive knowing. On one level, it will make possible more of the innovative discoveries and important insights to which intuition has always contributed. On another level, it provides hope that what biologist Edwin Schrodinger called "*the* task of science"—answering the question "Who are we?"—will be adequately fulfilled. It may be argued that such an "expanded" science—one that sanctions intuitive or subjective knowing—would not be science at all. But if by science we mean the enterprise that goes after a collective body of reliable knowledge by submitting premises to controlled experimentation and repeated validation, there is no conflict whatever. I am not suggesting that physicists "turn in their calculators for mantras," as one alarmist put it, only that we recognize the current limits of scientism and the importance of enlarging its methodology to include enlightened subjectivity.

I emphasize the status of science because it is our recognized custodian of knowledge. In our civilization, what each of us knows is largely determined by what science knows. But how we go about knowing is primarily a function of education and other institutions. Let's explore some suggestions for how they can better nurture the intuitive mind.

THE LIBERATION OF INTUITION

Consider these thoughts on education: "The hitch in this was . . . the fact that one had to cram all this stuff into one's mind for the examinations, whether one liked it or not. This coercion had such a deterring effect upon me that, after I had passed the final examination, I found the consideration of any scientific problem distasteful for an entire year."

The person recalling that college experience nevertheless went on to advanced study, where he often had a friend attend lectures in his stead. This, he said, gave him freedom to choose his own pursuits until examination time. He adds: "It is, in fact, nothing short of a miracle that the modern methods of instruction have not yet entirely strangled the holy curiosity of inquiry; for this delicate little plant, aside from stimulation, stands mainly in need of freedom."

That "holy curiosity" is a lightning rod for intuition, and we can be thankful that one irrepressible student, Albert Einstein, didn't lose it. Others do, unfortunately, when pressure and drudgery take the joy out of learning. Combined with a variety of pedagogical foibles, the dampening of natural curiosity inhibits intuition, which works best when highly motivated. One thing we need to do, then, is convey the delight of discovery to students at an early age so that they leap after knowledge for the sheer exhilaration of it.

We might begin by rethinking the way we use rewards and punishments. Brandeis social psychologist Teresa Amabile studied creativity in both children and adults under two sets of conditions: when subjects knew their work would be judged, and when they were doing it for pleasure alone. She found that when creative performance requires going beyond the obvious and commonplace, the imposition of extrinsic motivation results in lower levels of creativity.

Current education uses external motivation almost exclusively; learning is something we do to avoid punishment or obtain rewards. This seriously restrains intuitive thought, particularly its creative function, which works best when the mind is unpressured and genuinely animated by an intrinsic need or desire. From the earliest grades we penalize errors severely, and even reprimand pupils who offer up guesses, half-formed feelings, and vague hunches, the very things that frequently lead to discovery. This behavior tells children that it doesn't pay to take risks. They become mistrustful of thoughts that are not exactly what the teacher expects or that might be construed as "off the subject." They learn to play it safe, which is obviously not the best strategy for intuition.

We should reward the bold idea that is slightly off the mark and the creative alternative that is not quite right, simply for having been conceived. That would help create an adventurous attitude and give intuition license to operate. We should also let students know that guessing can be a useful strategy that, if refined, will serve them well in real life, where remembered facts and mechanical procedures won't always do. Instead, teachers ridicule guessers. But, as psychologist Blythe Clinchy wrote in a 1968 article on intuition and education, "After all, a hypothesis is simply a guess in testable form. . . . A more serious problem than the wild guesser is the child who appears unable to guess, who is afraid to take a chance for fear of being wrong."

We further restrain intuition, Clinchy points out, by demanding that students immediately explain and defend their answers. In so doing, we often reward what psychologist Jerome Bruner calls "articulate idiocy." Students who can manipulate words are praised while their less glib classmates are made to feel foolish, even though the latter may be wiser. This conveys to them the notion that you don't really know something unless you can express it verbally and explain how you arrived at the knowledge. That, of course, is untrue even for adults, and all the more so for children, who frequently know a great deal more than they are able to verbalize. This attitude also discourages nonverbal modes of thinking, which are integral to intuition and which are evidently natural to a child's thought processes.

Along those lines, we should convey to students a greater respect for their innate capacity for fantasy, visualization, and imagination, all of which aid intuition. Biographer Peter Brent notes that, in addition to superior powers of observation and reason, Charles Darwin had a great capacity for reverie. "Such castles in the air are highly advantageous," Darwin said of his daydreams. And where would we be if Einstein, the disobedient student, had not dared to imagine himself riding on beams of light? That fanciful side of great thinkers is rarely portrayed.

We would make great progress toward liberating the child's intuitive abilities if we placed more emphasis on personal discovery rather than rote memorization of facts or the mechanical application of rules for solving problems. In most educational settings, students are given problems rather than being allowed to find their own. Then they are told what form the expected answer is to take and asked to follow prescribed algorithmic procedures to get there. It would be far better if, at least on occasion, they were allowed to experience firsthand what we all have to do in adulthood: identify problems concerning matters we care about and find our own ways of solving them. This would give them the opportunity to develop a flexible, individualized approach to problem solving, and in the process learn to be guided by their intuition. As it is, students learn to look for the "right way" of doing things, which isn't always the best way.

Since we learn by example, an excellent way to start would be to get teachers to display intuitive thinking in the classroom. Let them demonstrate the way an inquisitive, mature mind works as it pursues knowledge and solutions to problems. Right now, teachers tend to recite facts and display the finished products of their after-hours work. If students could see their teachers make guesses and wild stabs, run up blind alleys and chase after fugitive hunches, their own uncertain intuitions and meandering images would gain legitimacy. Of course, this would require teachers who were, in fact, inquisitive and took joy in pursuing knowledge. It would also require teachers who were willing to make mistakes in front of their students. This may be asking a lot, but we nevertheless ought to realize that teachers are not only dispensers of information; they are models for how to use the mind.

At the very least we ought to give students a more inspiring, and more realistic picture of how discoveries are born. Even in higher grades, virtually the entire emphasis is on the products, not the processes, of great minds. As we have seen, scientific principles, mathematical theorems, and important ideas are displayed in their neat final structures, giving students the impression that the logical statements and linear proofs reflect the actual means of discovery. This sets up the inference that their own groping and chaotic speculations are not the stuff of smart minds but aberrations to be discouraged.

Taking this argument a step further, we might make intuition and creativity subjects of study in their own right, thereby eliciting in students greater respect for these functions of the mind. This can be conveyed through direct experience as well as conceptually by giving students more opportunities to *be* creative and intuitive. Traditional learning objectives need not be compromised, as they often are in experimental programs or "free" schools. In this regard, we ought to encourage teaching methods that let children learn about math and science by emulating mathematicians and scientists, actually *doing* everything, from finding problems to solving them. The same can be done with the humanities or any other subject. By discussing intuition and observing it in action, students at an early age can begin acquiring sensitivity to it.

As Einstein's memoirs suggest, the problems we have been discussing do not disappear in higher education. The emphasis on extrinsic motivation and rote learning, the shortage of demonstratively intuitive teachers, continue throughout. In some ways the problems are even compounded.

The growing trend toward pragmatism is, while understandable, somewhat unfortunate. Certainly we need to bring the basic "three Rs" back to education, and we need to produce competent specialists and technicians. But we also need intuitive people who can invent and create, and excessive pragmatism can work against that. Unrelenting pressure to make the grade not only causes intuition-dampening anxiety but it also favors doing things by the book. And by emphasizing professional training, we perpetuate the unfortunate image of school as a kind of supermarket where students stock up on items they will "need" when they get out. The demand for early specialization weakens the impact of an already fragmented curriculum, cutting down the students' exposure to disciplines not directly related to their career goals.

Diversity, interdisciplinary breadth, and substantive exposure to the arts and humanities should be required, not just because they make for more sensitive human beings but because they make for more intuitive and creative professionals in all fields. The intuitive mind is fostered by exposure to the esthetic and emotional undercurrents in human affairs. It needs a rich storehouse of variegated impressions with which to make connections. For example, in *The Medusa and the Snail*, Lewis Thomas attacks the current pre-med curriculum, with its heavy science orientation and competition for grades and test scores. He calls for a core curriculum that "could be used for evaluating the free range of a student's mind, his tenacity and resolve, his innate capacity for understanding human beings, and his affection for the human condition." Such a program would produce not only better physicians but more intuitive professionals of all kinds.

The importance of diversity in higher education and in professional training should extend to life experience as well as to the classroom. Many business leaders, for example, feel that business schools are overemphasizing formal, quantitative methods and arcane theories of decision making. While the skills acquired are vital, it is widely felt that students emerge unprepared for the everyday demands of business. Business schools might do well to follow Stanford's lead and institute courses exclusively geared to improving creativity. Creativity in Business, taught by a marketing professor and an artist, has become a popular addition to the Stanford curriculum and would no doubt enhance intuitive ability. Also, many executives favor more exposure to the real world, in business and other settings, as a way for future leaders to see how decision makers actually function and to acquire the capacity for effective intuition.

Similar criticism has been leveled at other institutions that prepare professionals. A blue-ribbon panel of psychologists, convened in 1958 to discuss the training of researchers, was unanimously opposed to attempts to systematize training procedures. The productive researcher, they concluded, is often rather *unsystematic*, and might be productive *"because* he is illogical and willing to follow his hunches instead of the implications of existing knowledge and methods." The psychologists decided that formalized procedures were actually "ancillary" to training and that exposure to the research process through some form of apprenticeship was the best way to train people without stifling their originality.

An important by-product of diversifying experience might be to reduce the number of people who end up in the wrong occupation. As noted earlier, career choice is largely an intuitive decision, or at least it should be if making a life is as important as making a living. A more complete set of impressions would greatly aid intuition in making the selection. In turn, a suitable occupational choice will be beneficial later on, because the intuitive mind works best where it is fluent and highly motivated. Nothing dampens intuition more than being stuck in a role that fits one's head like a wrong-sized hat. In addition, diversity of experience can add flexibility to the intuitive mind, whatever its focus. This would provide society with an adaptable work force that is better equipped to deal with change.

In the world of work, we need to provide both opportunity and incentive for intuition at all levels of organizational life. We have mentioned several times the need for intuitive policy makers. But the American work force—blue, pink, and white collar—is better educated and more sophisticated than any in history. This represents a rich resource for innovation and productivity that has barely been tapped. Thankfully, intuition may now be getting an indirect boost as the autocratic management methods and elephantine hierarchies that have dominated organizations come under critical scrutiny.

Intuition is covertly stifled when people are overmanaged, tasks are rigidly defined and specialized, and decisions are handed down from the top. Management by imposition—"This is the way we do things around here"—effectively clamps down on innovation by telling people precisely how to work instead of telling them what needs to be accomplished and giving them room to find their own solutions. In this respect, the trend toward Japanese-style management, with its emphasis on communication and participation, is a good sign. Perhaps it will make motivation less exclusively extrinsic and appeal to the inherent pleasures of contributing, meeting challenges, and using our potential. This can give the intuitive mind incentive to discover something more than ways to work less or promote our own self-interest.

The efficacy of liberating intuition by encouraging participation was pointed up by a corporate president who prides himself on his open-door policy with employees. Once someone proposed packaging a product in small, cigar-shaped bottles, an idea that was considered a sure-fire marketing success. However, cost estimates for retooling the production system were astronomical. None of the managers or technicians could think of a solution, and the idea was about to be scrapped when an assembly-line worker saved the day for $175. He bought some hockey pucks, drilled holes in them, and put the tubes in the pucks so that they could stand up on the existing bottling line.

Motivating and liberating intuition can be further accomplished by giving people a stake in the success of the organization and by letting everyone in on the Big Picture—the overall purpose and strategy. In addition, organizations can feed the intuition of their employees by regularly exposing people to other parts of the organization. Varying assignments on occasion can provide the kind of "soft information" that helps the intuitive mind make unusual connections. The trend toward decentralization of authority may also aid intuition by providing people with greater autonomy and flexibility in establishing objectives, schedules, and procedures.

All institutions need to rethink customary definitions of productive behavior. The nose-to-the-grindstone mentality that equates sweat with dedication and toil with productivity has to be reevaluated in the light of what we know about the value of incubation and the deleterious impact of stress. In this regard the intuitive mind might benefit indirectly from the new passion for health and fitness. To combat turnover, health costs, and declining productivity, organizations have heartily endorsed stress-reduction procedures. With meditation, exercise, and sufficient vacation time, employees will become both healthier and more intuitive. Finally, training and development can be enlarged to include liberal arts programs that expand the sensitivity and information base of the employees. And seminars and workshops directly geared to improving intuitive ability can be a useful addition.

These general suggestions are by no means definitive. Much

more can be done, and no doubt will be as we come closer to answering the questions "How do we know what we know?" and "How can we know better?"

RESEARCHING INTUITION

Perhaps our biggest task is to build up a comprehensive body of knowledge about intuition. Because we are now far from having achieved this, much of the material in this and other books has to be considered speculative. We need a thorough research commitment to determine, for example, the degree to which intuitive ability is innate or acquired and whether certain categories of people are predisposed to intuitive thinking. We need to determine the precise range of subjective experiences that fall under the heading of intuition. We need to examine the various functions of intuition to see if different psychological and physiological events characterize each one. We need to find out what is going on in our brain when we have a hunch, when we feel certain as opposed to doubtful, when we turn out to be right instead of wrong.

We also need a tremendous research effort to find out how neurological mechanisms differ during intuition and other mental functions such as analysis, everyday reasoning, and formal logic. We have to investigate the incubation phenomenon to find out why it works and exactly what is going on in the nervous system at the time. We also need to pinpoint when incubation works best and what forms are most productive. We must determine whether we have innate mental structures that frame what we know and how the human mind is connected to more universal sources of information. We also have to explore the role of subliminal and psychic information in the composition of intuitive knowledge. And we have to step up research on the links between the precepts of the perennial philosophy and the findings of modern science, a project that has been undertaken in earnest by a productive but small number of thinkers.

This proposed research, of course, must be directed toward practical application. Everything we have discussed about the need for intuition in various areas of society points up the importance of answering such questions as the following: What makes a person more intuitive? What conditions lend themselves to quality intuition? How can we identify intuitive people?

In terms of style, intuitive people can be identified with some success, and there have been attempts to apply the information. Intuitive students, for example, should be treated differently from their more systematic or analytic counterparts. The Jungian instruments mentioned in Chapter 5 have been used for this purpose, and psychologists have devised different ways to motivate, teach, and evaluate intuitives and other types so that their propensities can be maximized. Similar efforts are being made in terms of hiring people, assigning tasks, and creating work teams. Weston Agor and other management consultants feel we should place intuitive and analytic people where their styles can be most valuable. The former should probably not be asked to do budgeting or purchasing, for example, and the latter should not be placed in roles that call for imaginative leadership.

Greater awareness of these stylistic differences can lead to mutual enhancement. For example, Estée Lauder, founder of the giant cosmetic firm, is known for her intuitive ability to outpredict any market research on which fragrance will sell. She combines her skills with those of her son, Leonard, a business-school graduate. "I can blithely spend millions on a certain investment without asking anyone," says Leonard, "but I wouldn't launch a fragrance without her signed approval."

The composition of the intuitive style as well as its virtues and limits need to be studied with more precision. So, too, should the prized ability to switch hit, using the style most appropriate for the occasion. Such research can immeasurably aid our efforts to develop intuitive thinking skills.

Efforts must also be made to identify people with intuition of exceptional quality. Gifted intuitives might be specialists whose intuition works superbly in specific subject areas or generalists with the ability to tune into areas outside their experience and answer questions with some degree of precision. Teamed with various experts, such people might be able to generate hypotheses that would not otherwise be considered, or perhaps identify facts that would not be ascertained by ordinary methods. To a degree this has been attempted. The Mobius Group in Los Angeles, for example, has reported on the use of gifted intuitives for tracking down sites for archaeological digs. And the Center for Applied Intuition in San Francisco has a program called Intuitive Consensus, in which group intuition is brought to bear on scientific and technological problems.

Identifying intuitive people—and otherwise legitimizing the faculty—might also lead to economic support for the kind of visionary inventors and entrepreneurs who historically contribute so much to progress. Too often such people get lost in the bureaucratic shuffle that funnels grants and venture capital. Current funding procedures favor well-organized people with carefully outlined projects aimed at predictable results. This works against people who might attack problems more circuitously, who tinker and explore and meander about before coming up with an intuitive breakthrough. If we insist on knowing in advance exactly what the findings will be, intuitive people won't have the opportunity or resources to discover the unexpected.

Perhaps the most important avenue of future research is in the area of higher consciousness, since the mind's potential far surpasses its current state of development, even for the brightest among us. If we would allocate to that endeavor a portion of the energy and resources we now devote to researching artificial intelligence, we might surprise ourselves regarding our own natural intuitive capacities. In this context, a vital area of research should be the yogic and meditative disciplines. If, as I have suggested, illumination is both the most exalted state of knowing and a means of opening intuitive channels, then we need more hard data on the practices associated with them. We need to find out the precise physiology of transcendence and higher awareness and the best methods by which they can be cultivated. When we understand the highest expressions of human knowledge, we will better understand how we know anything.

It is hoped that scholars and scientists will step up their efforts to understand the intuitive mind in all its intricacy and depth. They will be among the first beneficiaries of that effort. But, long before we have all the answers, we as parents, educators, policy makers, leaders, and citizens can do a great deal to develop our own intuitive faculties and to make the world safe for intuition. If we succeed, intuition will make the world safe for us.

References

Adams, H. "The Good Judge of Personality." *Journal of Abnormal and Social Psychology*, 1927, 22, pp. 127–181.

Adams, James L. *Conceptual Blockbusting*. San Francisco: W. H. Freeman, 1975.

Agor, Weston. *Intuitive Management*. Englewood Cliffs, N.J.: Prentice-Hall, 1984.

Agor, Weston. "Using Intuition in Public Management." *Public Management*, February 1983, pp. 2–6.

Albrecht, Karl. *Brain Power*. Englewood Cliffs, N.J.: Prentice-Hall, 1980.

Allport, Gordon. "The Study of Personality by the Intuitive Method." *Journal of Abnormal and Social Psychology*, 1929, 24, pp. 14–27.

Amabile, Teresa M. "Effects of External Evaluation on Artistic Creativity." *Journal of Personality and Social Psychology*, 1979, 37, pp. 221–233.

Aranya, Swami Hariharananda. *Yoga Philosophy of Patanjali*. Calcutta, India: Calcutta University Press, 1963.

Asimov, Isaac. *Please Explain*. New York: Dell, 1976.

Assagiologi, Roberto. *The Act of Will*. New York: Viking, 1973.

Barnett, Lincoln. *The Universe and Dr. Einstein*. New York: Bantam, 1968.

Barrett, William. *Irrational Man*. Garden City, N.Y.: Doubleday, 1958.

Barron, Frank. "The Disposition Toward Originality." *Journal of Abnormal and Social Psychology*. April 1953, *48*, pp. 163–172.

Barron, Frank. "Some Personality Correlates of Independence of Judgment." *Journal of Personality*. March 1953, *21*, pp. 287–297.

Baumgardner, Steve R. "The Impact of College Experience on Conventional Career Logic." *Journal of Counseling Psychology*, January 1976, pp. 40–45.

Baumgardner, Steve R. "Vocational Planning: The Great Swindle." *Personnel and Guidance Journal*, 1977, pp. 17–22.

Benbow, Camilla Persson, and Stanley, Julian C. "Sex Differences in Mathematical Ability: Fact or Artifact?" *Science*, December 12, 1980, pp. 1262–1264.

Bentov, Itzhak. *Stalking the Wild Pendulum: On the Mechanics of Consciousness*. New York: Dutton, 1977.

Bergson, Henri. *Creative Evolution*. Westport, Conn.: Greenwood, 1975.

Bergson, Henri. *An Introduction to Metaphysics*. New York: Bobbs-Merrill, 1955.

Berne, Eric. *Intuition and Ego States*. New York: Harper & Row, 1977.

Berne, Eric. "Intuition VI: The Psychodynamics of Intuition." *Psychiatric Quarterly*, 1962, *36*, pp. 294–300.

Berne, Eric. "The Nature of Intuition." *Psychiatric Quarterly*, 1949, *23*, pp. 203–226.

Bernstein, Jeremy. *Einstein*. New York: Viking, 1976.

Beveridge, W. I. B. *Seeds of Discovery*. New York: Norton, 1980.

Black, Meme. "Brain Flash: The Physiology of Inspiration." *Science Digest*, August 1982, p. 85.

Board, Richard. "Intuition in the Methodology of Psychoanalysis." *Psychiatry*, 1985, *21*, pp. 233–239.

Braverman, Jerome D. *Management Decision-Making: A Formal-Intuitive Approach*. New York: Amacom, 1980.

Bronowski, Jacob. "The Creative Process." *Scientific American*, September 1958, pp. 59–65.

Bronowski, Jacob. *The Origins of Knowledge and Imagination.* New Haven: Yale University Press, 1978.

Bruner, Jerome. *Beyond the Information Given.* New York: Norton, 1973.

Bruner, Jerome. *The Process of Education.* Cambridge: Harvard University Press, 1961.

Bruner, Jerome, and Clinchy, Blythe. "Toward a Disciplined Intuition," in Jerome Bruner, *The Relevance of Education.* New York: Norton, 1971.

Bucke, Richard M. *Cosmic Consciousness.* New York: Dutton, 1969.

Bunge, Mario Augusto. *Intuition and Science.* Westport, Conn.: Greenwood, 1975.

Burden, Virginia. *The Process of Intuition.* Wheaton, Ill.: Theosophical Publishing House, 1975.

Buzan, Tony. *Use Both Sides of Your Brain.* New York: Dutton, 1976.

Campbell, Anthony. *Seven States of Consciousness.* New York: Harper & Row, 1974.

Campbell, Joseph. *The Hero with a Thousand Faces.* Princeton: Princeton University Press, 1968.

"Canadian Study Frames New Right/Left Paradigm." *Brain/Mind Bulletin.* March 28, 1983, p. 1.

Capra, Fritjof. *The Tao of Physics.* Berkeley, Calif.: Shambhala, 1975.

Chubb, Jehangir N. "Thought and Intuition." *Aryan Path,* 1949, 20, pp. 109–115.

Clinchy, Blythe. "The Role of Intuition in Learning." *NEA Journal,* February 1968, pp. 33–37.

Combs, Allan L. "Synchronicity: A Synthesis of Western Theories and Eastern Perspectives." *ReVision,* Spring 1982, pp. 20–28.

Connelly, Donald P., and Johnson, Paul E. "The Medical Problem Solving Process." *Human Pathology,* September 1980, pp. 412–419.

Cornford, Francis MacDonald (trans.). *The Republic of Plato.* New York: Oxford University Press, 1941.

"Creativity: Looking for the Right Questions." *Leading Edge Bulletin,* September 28, 1981, pp. 1–2.

Cvetkovich, George. "Cognitive Accommodation, Language, and Social Responsibility." *Social Psychology Quarterly*, June 1978, pp. 149–155.

d'Aquili, Eugene G. "The Neurobiological Basis of Myth and Concepts of Deity." *Zygon*, December 1978, pp. 257–275.

Dean, Douglas, and Mihalasky, John. *Executive ESP*. Englewood Cliffs, N.J.: Prentice-Hall, 1974.

de Bono, Edward. *Lateral Thinking*. New York: Harper & Row, 1970.

de Bono, Edward. *New Think*. New York: Basic Books, 1967.

Dillbeck, Michael C., et al. "Frontal EEG Coherence, H-Reflex Recovery, Concept Learning, and the TM-Sidhi Program." *International Journal of Neuroscience*, 1981, *15*, pp. 151–157.

Dillbeck, Michael C., and Bronson, Edward C. "Short-Term Longitudinal Effects of the Transcendental Meditation Technique on EEG Power and Coherence." *International Journal of Neuroscience*, 1981, *14*, pp. 147–151.

Dreistadt, Roy. "The Use of Analogies and Incubation in Obtaining Insights in Creative Problem Solving." *The Journal of Psychology*, 1969, *71*, pp. 159–175.

Durant, Will. *The Story of Philosophy*. New York: Simon and Schuster/Touchstone, 1961.

Edwards, Betty. *Drawing on the Right Side of the Brain*. Los Angeles: Tarcher, 1979.

Einstein, Albert. *Ideas and Opinions*. New York: Dell, 1973.

Einstein, Albert, and Infeld, Leopold. *The Evolution of Physics*. New York: Simon and Schuster, 1938.

Ferguson, Marilyn. *The Aquarian Conspiracy*. Los Angeles: Tarcher, 1980.

Ferguson, Marilyn. *The Brain Revolution*. New York: Bantam, 1975.

Fischbein, E. (ed.). *The Intuitive Sources of Probabalistic Thinking in Children*. Boston: D. Reidel, 1975.

Fisher, Milton. *Intuition*. New York: Dutton, 1981.

Forem, Jack. *Transcendental Meditation*. New York: Dutton, 1973.

Fuerst, Robert E. "Inference Peddling." *Psychology Today*, March 1979, pp. 92–96.

Gardner, Howard. "Breakaway Minds." (An interview with Howard Gruber.) *Psychology Today*, July 1981, pp. 64–73.

Gardner, Howard. "What We Know (and Don't Know) About the Two Halves of the Brain." *Harvard Magazine*, March/April 1978, pp. 24–27.

Garfield, Patricia. *Creative Dreaming*. New York: Ballantine, 1976.

Gendlin, Eugene. *Focusing*. New York: Bantam, 1981.

Ghiselin, Brewster. *The Creative Process*. New York: New American Library, 1937.

Giannini, James A., et al. "Intellect vs. Intuition—A Dichotomy in the Reception of Nonverbal Communication." *Journal of General Psychology*, July 1978, pp. 19–24.

Gleidman, John. "Mind and Matter." *Science Digest*, March 1983, p. 68.

Goleman, Daniel. "Holographic Memory." (An interview with Karl Pribram.) *Psychology Today*, February 1979, p. 71.

Goleman, Daniel. "Split-Brain Psychology: Fad of the Year." *Psychology Today*, October 1977, p. 89.

Goleman, Daniel. *The Varieties of Meditative Experience*. New York: Dutton, 1977.

Goodspeed, Bennett. "The World's-Smartest-Man Syndrome." *Journal of Portfolio Management*, Summer 1978, pp. 41–44.

Gordon, William. *Synectics*. New York: Harper & Row, 1961.

Gowan, John Curtis. "Some New Thoughts on the Development of Creativity." *Journal of Creative Behavior*, 1977, *11*, pp. 77–90.

Goy, Robert W., and McEwen, Bruce S. *Sexual Differentiation of the Brain*. Cambridge: MIT Press, 1980.

Gurumurti, D. "Intuition in Indian Philosophy." *Aryan Path*, 1957, *28*, pp. 213–217.

Hadamard, Jacques. *An Essay on the Psychology of Invention in the Mathematical Field*. Princeton: Princeton University Press, 1945.

Hamilton, Lee V. "Intuitive Psychologist or Intuitive Lawyer? Alternative Models of the Attribution Process." *Journal of Personality and Social Psychology*, November 1980, pp. 767–772.

Hampden-Turner, Charles. *Maps of the Mind*. New York: Macmillan, 1981.

Hathaway, S. "Clinical Intuition and Inferential Accuracy." *Journal of Personality*, 1955, *24*, pp. 223–250.

Hayes, John R. *The Complete Problem Solver*. Philadelphia: Franklin Institute Press, 1981.

Hofstadter, Douglas. *Godel, Escher, Bach: An Eternal Golden Braid*. New York: Basic Books, 1979.

Hudson, William Donald. *Ethical Intuitionism*. New York: St. Martin's, 1967.

Hunt, Morton. *The Universe Within*. New York: Simon and Shuster, 1982.

Hutcheson, Joseph C. "The Judgment Intuitive: The Function of the 'Hunch' in Judicial Decision." *The Cornell Law Quarterly*, 1929, *14*, pp. 274–288.

Huxley, Aldous. *The Perennial Philosophy*. New York: Harper & Row, 1944.

Judson, Horace Freeland. *The Search for Solutions*. New York: Holt, Rinehart & Winston, 1980.

Jung, Carl Gustav. *Man and His Symbols*. Garden City, N.Y.: Doubleday, 1964.

Jung, Carl Gustav. *Psychological Types*. Princeton: Princeton University Press, 1971.

Kaplan, Harold A. "Intuitive Preference, Conditions of Arousal, and Their Effects on Intuitive Problem Solving." Unpublished doctoral dissertation, University of Kansas, 1974.

Kline, Morris. *Mathematics: The Loss of Certainty*. New York: Oxford University Press, 1980.

Koestler, Arthur. *The Act of Creation*. New York: Macmillan, 1964.

Konner, Melvin. *The Tangled Wing*. New York: Holt, Rinehart & Winston, 1982.

Krippner, Stanley, et al. "The Creative Person and Non-Ordinary Reality." *Gifted Child Quarterly*, 1972, *16*, pp. 203–228.

Kuhn, Thomas. *The Structure of Scientific Revolutions.* Chicago: University of Chicago Press, 1962.

La Berge, Stephen. "Lucid Dreaming: Directing the Action as It Happens." *Psychology Today*, January 1981, p. 48.

Landau, Barbara, et al. "Spatial Knowledge and Geometric Representation in a Child Blind from Birth." *Science*, September 11, 1981, pp. 1275–1277.

Larkin, Jill, et al. "Expert and Novice Performance in Solving Physics Problems." *Science*, June 1980, pp. 1335–1342.

Loye, David. "Forecasting for Everyone: An Examination of the True Powers of the Mind." *Planning Review*, January 1980, pp. 15–19.

Luft, Joseph. "Implicit Hypotheses and Clinical Predictions." *Journal of Abnormal and Social Psychology*, 1950, *45*, pp. 756–759.

Maharishi Mahesh Yogi. *On the Bhaghavad Gita: A New Translation and Commentary.* New York: Penguin, 1967.

Maritain, Jacques. *Creative Intuition in Art and Poetry.* New York: New American Library, 1953.

Maslow, Abraham. *The Psychology of Science.* New York: Harper & Row, 1966.

Maslow, Abraham. *Toward a Psychology of Being.* New York: Van Nostrand Reinhold, 1968.

May, Rollo. *The Courage to Create.* New York: Norton, 1975.

McKenney, James L., and Keen, Peter G. W. "How Managers' Minds Work." *Harvard Business Review*, May/June 1974, pp. 79–90.

Mintzberg, Henry. *The Nature of Managerial Work.* New York: Harper & Row, 1973.

Mintzberg, Henry. "Planning on the Left Side and Managing on the Right." *Harvard Business Review*, July/August 1976, pp. 49–58.

Mitroff, Ian I. "The Myth of Objectivity, or Why Science Needs a New Psychology of Science." *Management Science*, June 1972, pp. B613–B618.

Morowitz, Harold. "The Beauty of Mathematics." *Science 82*, October 1982, p. 26.

Moss, Thelma. *The Probability of the Impossible*. Los Angeles: Tarcher, 1974.

Myers, Isabel Briggs. *The Myers-Briggs Type Indicator*. Palo Alto, Calif.: Consulting Psychologists Press, 1962.

Neisser, Ulric. *Cognitive Psychology*. Englewood Cliffs, N.J.: Prentice-Hall, 1967.

Nietzsche, Friedrich. *Philosophy in the Tragic Age of the Greeks*. Chicago: Regnery Gateway, 1962.

Nisbett, Richard, and Ross, Lee. *Human Inference: Strategies and Shortcomings*. Englewood Cliffs, N.J.: Prentice-Hall, 1980.

Olton, Robert M., and Johnson, David M. "Mechanisms of Incubation in Creative Problem Solving." *American Journal of Psychology*, December 1976, pp. 617–630.

Ornstein, Robert. *The Psychology of Consciousness*. San Francisco: W. H. Freeman, 1972.

Osborn, Alex. *Applied Imagination*. New York: Scribners, 1953.

Pelletier, Kenneth R., and Garfield, Charles. *Consciousness East and West*. New York: Harper & Row, 1976.

Perkins, D. N. *The Mind's Best Work*. Cambridge: Harvard University Press, 1981.

Peters, Joan T., and Hammond, Kenneth R. "A Note on Intuitive vs. Analytic Thinking." *Organizational Behavior and Human Performance*, 1974, *12*, pp. 125–131.

Pirsig, Robert M. *Zen and the Art of Motorcycle Maintenance*. New York: Bantam, 1975.

Polanyi, Michael. *The Tacit Dimension*. Garden City, N.Y.: Doubleday, 1966.

Poole, Roger. *Toward Deep Subjectivity*. New York: Harper & Row, 1972.

Prabhavananda, Swami, and Isherwood, Christopher. *How to Know God: The Yoga Aphorisms of Patanjali*. New York: New American Library, 1969.

Radhakrishnan, Sarvepalli, and Moore, Charles A. *A Source Book in Indian Philosophy*. Princeton: Princeton University Press, 1957.

Rao, Nagaraja P. "Logic and Intuition in Indian Philosophy." *Aryan Path*, 1950, *21*, pp. 511–514.

Rico, Gabriele Lusser. *Writing the Natural Way*. Los Angeles: Tarcher, 1983.

Rothenberg, Albert. "Creative Contradictions." *Psychology Today*, June 1979, pp. 55–62.

Rouse, W. H. D. (trans.). *Great Dialogues of Plato*. New York: New American Library, 1956.

Rowan, Roy. "Those Business Hunches Are More Than Blind Faith." *Fortune*, April 23, 1979, pp. 111–114.

Royce, Joseph R., et al. "Psychological Epistemology: A Critical Review of the Empirical Literature and the Theoretical Issues." *Genetic Psychology Monographs*, 1978, *97*, pp. 265–353.

Rucker, Rudy. "Master of the Incomplete." *Science 82*, October 1982, p. 56.

Russell, Peter. *The Brain Book*. New York: Dutton, 1979.

Schilpp, P. (ed.). *Albert Einstein: Philosopher-Scientist*. La Salle, Ill.: Open Court, 1973.

Schubert, Daniel S. P. "Is Incubation a Silent Rehearsal of Mundane Responses?" *Journal of Creative Behavior*, 1979, *13*, pp. 36–38.

Schustack, Miriam W., and Sternberg, Robert J. "Evaluation of Evidence in Causal Inference." *Journal of Experimental Psychology*, 1981, *110*, pp. 101–120.

Shear, Jonathan. "Maharishi, Plato, and the TM-Sidhi Program on Innate Structures of Consciousness." *Metaphilosophy*, January 1981, pp. 72–84.

Sheldrake, Rupert. *A New Science of Life*. Los Angeles: Tarcher, 1981.

Simonton, Dean K. "Creativity, Task Complexity, and Intuitive Versus Analytical Problem Solving." *Psychological Reports*, 1975, pp. 351–354.

Simonton, Dean K. "Intuition and Analysis: A Predictive and Explanatory Model." *Genetic Psychology Monographs*. August 1980, pp. 3–60.

Somers, Roni. "A Phenomenological Approach to the Intuitive Experience." Unpublished doctoral dissertation, California School of Professional Psychology, 1977.

Springer, Sally, and Deutsch, George. *Left Brain, Right Brain*. San Francisco: W. H. Freeman, 1981.

Sternberg, Robert J., and Schustack, Miriam W. "Components of Causal Inference." *NR Reviews*, Fall/Winter 1980/1981, pp. 49–61.

Suzuki, D. T. *Zen Buddhism*. Garden City, N.Y.: Doubleday/Anchor, 1956.

"System Dynamics Aids Intuition." *Leading Edge Bulletin*, April 26, 1982, pp. 1–2.

Taft, R. "The Ability to Judge People." *Psychological Bulletin*, 1955, *52*, pp. 1–28.

Targ, Russell, and Puthoff, Harold. *Mind-Reach*. New York: Dell, 1978.

Taylor, Donald W., et al. "Education for Research in Psychology." *The American Psychologist*, 1959, *14*, pp. 167–179.

Toben, Bob. *Space-Time and Beyond*. New York: Dutton, 1975.

Tobias, Sheila. "Sexist Equations." *Psychology Today*, January 1982, p. 14.

Torrance, E. Paul. "An Instructional Model for Enhancing Incubation." *Journal of Creative Behavior*, 1979, *13*, pp. 23–34.

Valentine, C. "The Relative Reliability of Men and Women in Intuitive Judgments of Character." *British Journal of Psychology*, 1929, XIX, Part 3, pp. 213–238.

VanGundy, Arthur B. *Training Your Creative Mind*. Englewood Cliffs, N.J.: Prentice-Hall, 1982.

Vaughan, Frances E. *Awakening Intuition*. Garden City, N.Y.: Doubleday/Anchor, 1979.

Villoldo, Alberto, and Dychtwald, Ken. *Millennium*. Los Angeles: Tarcher, 1981.

Wallas, Graham. *The Art of Thought*. New York: Harcourt Brace, 1926.

Watson, Lyall. *Lifetide*. New York: Bantam, 1980.

Weber, Renee. "The Physicist and the Mystic—Is a Dialogue Between Them Possible?" (A conversation with David Bohm.) *ReVision*, Spring 1981, *4*, pp. 22–35.

Weintraub, Pamela. "The Brain: His and Hers." *Discover*, April 1981, pp. 15–20.

Westcott, Malcolm. "On the Measurement of Intuitive Leaps." *Psychological Reports*, 1961, *9*, pp. 267–274.

Westcott, Malcolm. *Toward a Contemporary Psychology of Intuition*. New York: Holt, Rinehart & Winston, 1968.

Westcott, Malcolm, and Ranzoni, Jane. "Correlates of Intuitive Thinking." *Psychological Reports*, 1963, *12*, pp. 595–613.

Whitehead, Alfred North. *Science and the Modern World*. New York: Macmillan, 1925.

Wilber, Ken. *The Atman Project*. Wheaton, Ill.: Theosophical Publishing House, 1980.

Wilber, Ken (ed.). *The Holographic Paradigm and Other Paradoxes: Exploring the Leading Edge of Science*. Berkeley, Calif.: Shambhala, 1982.

Wilber, Ken. *The Spectrum of Consciousness*. Wheaton, Ill.: Theosophical Publishing House, 1977.

Wittrock, M. C. (ed.). *The Human Brain*. Englewood Cliffs, N.J.: Prentice-Hall, 1977.

Yankelovich, Daniel. "Managing in an Age of Anxiety." *Industry Week*, October 24, 1977, pp. 52–58.

Yogananda, Paramahansa. *The Autobiography of a Yogi*. Los Angeles: Self-Realization Fellowship, 1969.

Yu-Lan, Fung. *A Short History of Chinese Philosophy*. New York: Macmillan, 1960.

Zukav, Gary. *The Dancing Wu Li Masters*. New York: Morrow, 1979.

Index

978-0-595-41665-3
0-595-41665-9

CPSIA information can be obtained
at www.ICGtesting.com
Printed in the USA
LVOW03s1510180418
573963LV00002B/442/P